W. Peters. R.A. Pinxt.

The Works of
HENRY FIELDING ESQ.
comprising his
NOVELS, PLAYS, POEMS AND
MISCELLANEOUS WRITINGS
Complete and Unabridged.

Illustrated

NEW YORK
GROSCUP & STERLING CO.

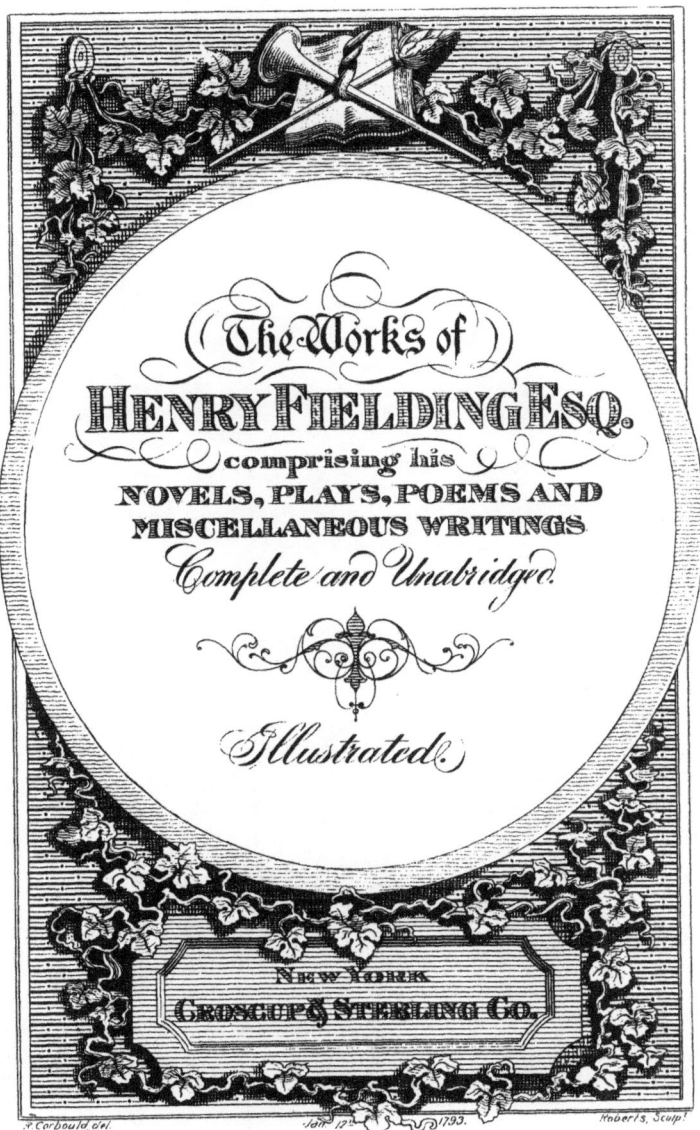

R. Corbould, del.   Jan 17   1793.   Roberts, Sculp!

The Complete Works of
HENRY FIELDING, ESQ.
With an Essay on the Life, Genius and Achievement of the Author,
by
WILLIAM ERNEST HENLEY, LL.D.

LEGAL WRITINGS

Illustrated with
Reproductions of Rare Contemporary Drawings
and Portraits

PRINTED FOR SUBSCRIBERS ONLY BY
CROSCUP & STERLING COMPANY
NEW YORK

CONTENTS

LEGAL WRITINGS

CONTENTS

LIST OF ILLUSTRATIONS

LEGAL WRITINGS.

AN

ENQUIRY

Into the CAUSES of the late

Increaſe of Robbers, &c.

WITH SOME

PROPOSALS for Remedying this GROWING EVIL.

IN WHICH

The Preſent Reigning VICES are impartially
expoſed; and the Laws that relate to the
Proviſion for the POOR, and to the Puniſh-
ment of FELONS are largely and freely examined.

*Non jam ſunt mediotres hominum libidines, non humanæ auda-
ciæ ac tolerandæ. Nibil cogitant niſi cædem, niſi incendia,
niſi rapinas.* CIC. in Catil. 2ᵈᵃ.

By HENRY FIELDING, Eſq;

Barriſter at Law, and One of His Majeſty's Juſtices
of the Peace for the County of *Middleſex*, and for
the City and Liberty of *Weſtminſter*.

LONDON:

Printed for A. MILLAR, oppoſite to *Katharine-Street*,
in the *Strand*. M. DCC. LI.

[Price 2 *s.* 6 *d.*]

DEDICATION

TO THE RIGHT HONOURABLE

PHILIP LORD HARDWICKE

LORD HIGH CHANCELLOR OF GREAT BRITAIN

MY LORD,—As the reformation of any part of our civil polity requires as much the knowledge of the statesman as of the lawyer, the following sheets are, with the strictest propriety, addressed to a person of the highest eminence in both these capacities.

The subject of this treatise cannot be thought unworthy of such a protection, because it touches only those evils which have arisen in the lower branches of our constitution. This consideration will account for their having hitherto escaped your lordship's notice; and that alone will account for their having so long prevailed; but your lordship will not, for this reason, think it below your regard; since, however ignoble the parts may be in which the disease is first engendered, it will in time be sure to affect the whole body.

The subject, indeed, is of such importance, that we may truly apply to it those words of Cicero, in his first book of laws: *Ad Reipublicœ formandas et stabiliendas vires, et ad sanandos Populos omnis pergit Oratio.* How far I have been able to succed in the execution must be submitted to your lordship's candour. I hope I have no immodest opinion of my own abilities; but, in truth, I have much less confidence in my authority. Indeed, the highest authority is necessary to any degree of success in an attempt of this kind. Permit me, therefore, my lord, to fly to the protection of the highest which doth not exist, or which perhaps ever did exist, in this kingdom.

This great sanction is, I am convinced, always ready to support what really tends to the public utility; if I fail, therefore, of obtaining the honour of it, I shall be fully satisfied that I do not deserve it, and shall sit down contented with the merit of a good intent; for surely there is some praise due to the bare design of doing a service to the public. Nor can my enemies, I think deny that I am entirely disinterested in my endeavour, unless they should discover the gratification which my ambition finds in the opportunity of this address. I am, with the most profound respect,

My Lord,

Your Lordship's most obedient,

Most devoted humble servant,

HENRY FIELDING.

PREFACE

THERE is nothing so much talked of, and so little understood in this country as the Constitution. It is a word in the mouth of every man; and yet when we come to discourse of the matter there is no subject on which our ideas are more confused and perplexed. Some, when they speak of the Constitution, confine their notions to the law; others to the legislature; others, again, to the governing or executive part; and many there are, who jumble all these together in one idea. One error, however, is common to them all; for all seem to have the conception of something uniform and permanent, as if the constitution of England partook rather of the nature of the soil than of the climate, and was as fixed and constant as the former, not as changing and variable as the latter.

Now in this word, the Constitution, are included the original and fundamental laws of the kingdom, from whence all powers are derived, and by which they are circumscribed; all legislative and executive authority; all those municipal provisions which are commonly called the Laws; and, lastly, the customs, manners, and habits of the people. These, joined together, do, I apprehend, form the political, as the several members of the body, the animal economy, with the humours and habit, compose that which is called the natural constitution.

The Greek philosophy will, perhaps, help us to a better idea; for neither will the several constituent parts, nor the contexture of the whole, give an adequate notion of the word. By the Constitution is, indeed, rather meant something which results from the order and disposition of the whole; something resembling that harmony for which the Theban in Plato's Phædo contends; which he calls ἀόρατόν τι καὶ ἀσώματον *something invisible and incorporeal.* For many of the Greeks imagined the soul to result from κρᾶσις, or composition of the parts of the body, when these were properly tempered together; as harmony doth from the proper composition of the several parts in a well-tuned musical instrument: In the same manner, from the disposition of the several parts in a state, arises that which we call the Constitution.

In this disposition the laws have so considerable a share, that, as no man can perfectly understand the whole, without knowing the parts of which it is composed, it follows, that, to have a just notion of our constitution without a competent knowledge of the laws, is impossible. Without this, the reading over our historians may afford amusement, but will very little instruct us in the true essentials of our constitution. Nor will this knowledge alone serve our purpose. The mere lawyer, however skilful in his profession, who is not versed in the genius, manners, and habits of the people, makes but a wretched politician. Hence the historian, who is ignorant of our law, and the lawyer, who is ignorant of our history, have agreed in that common error, remarked above, of considering our constitution as something fixed and permanent; for the exterior form of government (however the people are changed) still, in a great degree, remains what it was; and the same, notwithstanding all its alterations, may be said of the law.

To explain this a little farther: From the original of the lower house of parliament to this day, the supreme power hath been vested in the king and the two houses of parliament. These two houses have, each at different times, carried very different weights in the balance, and yet the form of government remained still one and the same; so hath it happened to the law; the same courts of justice, the same form of trials, &c., have preserved the notion of identity, though, in real truth, the present governing powers, and the present legal provisions, bear so little resemblance to those of our ancestors in the reign of King John, or indeed in later times, that could any lawyer or statesman of those days be recalled to life, he would make, I believe, a very indifferent figure in Westminster Hall, or in any of the parts there adjacent.

To perceive the alterations in our constitution, doth, in fact, require a pretty just knowledge both of the people and of the laws; for either of these may be greatly changed, without producing any immediate effect on the other. The alterations in the great wheels of state above mentioned, which are so visible in our historians, are not noticed in our laws, as very few of the great changes in the law have fallen under the eye of our historians.

Many of both kinds have appeared in our constitution; but I shall at present confine myself to one only, as being that which principally relates to the subject of the following treatise.

If the constitution, as I have above asserted, be the result of the disposition of the several parts before mentioned, it follows, that this disposition can never be altered, without producing a proportional change to the constitution. "If the soul," says Simmias in Plato, "be a harmony resulting from the disposition of the corporeal parts, it follows, that when this disposition is confounded, and the body is torn by diseases or other evils, the soul immediately (whatever be her divinity) must perish." This will be apparent, if we cast our eyes a moment towards the animal economy; and it is no less true in the political.

The customs, manners, and habits of the people, do, as I have said, form one part of the political constitution; if these are altered, therefore, this must be changed likewise; and here, as in the natural body, the disorder of any part will, in its consequence, affect the whole.

One known division of the people in this nation is into the nobility, the gentry, and the commonalty. What alterations have happened among the two former of these, I shall not at present inquire; but that the last, in their customs, manners, and habits, are greatly changed from what they were, I think to make appear.

If we look into the earliest ages, we shall find the condition of this third part to have been very low and mean. The highest order of this rank, before the conquest, were those tenants in socage, who held their lands by the service of the plough; who, as Lyttelton tells us, " were to come with their plough for certain days in the year, to plough and sow the demesne of the lords; " as the villains, saith the same author, " were to carry and recarry the dung of his lord, spread it upon his land, and to perform such like services."

This latter was rightly accounted a slavish tenure. The villains were indeed considered in law as a kind of chattel belonging to their masters; for though these had not the power of life and death over them, nor even of maiming them with impunity, yet these villains had not even the capacity of purchasing lands or goods; but the lord on such purchase, might enter into the one, and seize the other for his own use. And as for the land which they held in villanage, though Lord Coke says it was not only held at the will of the lord, but according to the custom of the manor; yet, in ancient times, if the lord ejected them, they were manifestly without remedy.

And as to the former, though they were accounted freemen, yet were they obliged to swear fealty to their lord; and though Mr. Rapine be mistaken, when he says they could not alienate the land (for before the statute of Magna Charta, chap. 32, they could have given or sold the whole, but without any alteration of the tenure,) yet was the estate of these but very mean. "Though they are called freemen," says Lord Coke, " yet they ploughed, harrowed, reaped, and mowed, &c., for the lord; " and Bracton, *Dicuntur Socmanni eo quod deputat sunt tantummodo ad culturam.*

Besides such as were bound by their tenures to the service of agriculture, the number of freemen below the degree of gentry, and who got their livelihood in the mercantile or mechanical way, was very inconsiderable. As to the servants, they were chiefly bound by tenure, and those of the lower sort differed very little from slaves.

That this estate of the commonalty is greatly changed, is

apparent; and to this alteration many causes in subsequent ages have contributed.

First, the oath of fealty, or fidelity, which of old time was administered with great ceremony, became afterwards to be omitted; and though this fealty still remained incident to every socage tenure, yet the omission of the form was not without its consequences; for, as Lord Coke says, speaking of homage, *Prudent antiquity did, for the more solemnity and better memory and observation of that which is to be done, express substances under ceremonies.*

Secondly, Whereas in the ancient tenures the principal reservation was of personal services from the inferior tenants, the rent being generally trifling, such as hens, capons, roses, spurs, hawks, &c., afterwards the avarice or necessity of the lords incited them to convert these for the most part into money, which tended gravely to weaken the power of the lord, and to raise the freedom and independency of the tenant.

Thirdly, The dismembering manors by leases for years, as it flowed from the same sources, so it produced the same effects. These were probably very rare before the reign of Edward I., at which time the statute of Gloucester secured the estate of the tenant.

Fourthly, The estate of the villain or copyhold seems clearly, as I have said, to have originally been holden only at the will of the lord; but the law was afterwards altered, and in the reign of Edward IV. some of the best judges were of opinion, that if the copyholder was unlawfully ejected by his lord, he should have an action of trespass against him at the common law.

From this time the estate of the copyholder (which, as Britton tells us, was formerly a base tenure) began to grow into repute, and, though still distinguished in some privileges from a freehold, became the possession of many opulent and powerful persons.

By these and such like means the commonalty, by degrees, shook off their vassalage, and became more and more independent on their superiors. Even servants, in process of time, acquired a state of freedom and independency, unknown to this rank in any other nation, and which, as the law now stands, is inconsistent with a servile condition.

But nothing hath wrought such an alteration in this order of people, as the introduction of trade. This hath indeed given a new face to the whole nation, hath in a great measure subverted the former state of affairs, and hath almost totally changed the manners, customs, and habits of the people, more especially of the lower sort. The narrowness of their fortune is changed into wealth; the simplicity of their manners into craft; their frugality into luxury; their humility into pride, and their subjection into equality.

The philosopher, perhaps, will think this a bad exchange, and may be inclined to cry out with the poet,

> ————" *Sævior armis*
> *Luxuria incubuit.*——
> *Nullum crimen abest, facinusque libidinis, ex quo*
> *Paupertas Romana perit.*"

Again,

> " *Prima peregrinos obscæna pecunia mores*
> *Intulit, et turpi fregerunt sæcula luxu*
> *Divitiæ molles*——."

But the politician finds many emoluments to compensate all the moral evils introduced by trade, by which the grandeur and power of the nation is carried to a pitch that it could never otherwise have reached; arts and sciences are improved, and human life is embellished with every ornament, and furnished with every comfort, which it is capable of tasting.

In all these assertions he is right; but surely he forgets himself a little, when he joins the philosopher in lamenting the introduction of luxury as a casual evil; for as riches are the *certain* consequence of trade, so is luxury the no less *certain* consequence of riches; nay, trade and luxury do indeed support each other; and this latter, in its turn, becomes as useful to trade, as trade had been before to the support of luxury.

To prevent this consequence therefore of a flourishing commerce is totally to change the nature of things, and to separate the effect from the cause. A matter as impossible in the political body as in the natural. Vices and diseases, with like physical necessity, arise from certain habits in both; and to restrain and palliate the evil consequence is all that lies within the reach of art. How far it is the business of the politician to interfere in the case of luxury, we have attempted to show in the following treatise.

Now, to conceive that so great a change as this in the people should produce no change in the constitution, is to discover, I think, as great ignorance as would appear in the physician, who should assert, that the whole state of the blood may be entirely altered from poor to rich, from cool to inflamed, without producing any alteration in the constitution of the man.

To put this in the clearest light; there appear to me to be four sorts of political power; that of bodily strength, that of the mind, the power of the purse, and the power of the sword. Under the second of these divisions may be ranged all the art of the legislator and politician, all the power of laws and government. These do constitute the civil power; and a state may then be said to be in good order, when all the other powers are subservient to this; when they own its superior excellence and energy, pay it a ready obedience, and all unite in support of its rule.

But so far are these powers from paying such voluntary submission, that they are all extremely apt to rebel, and to assert their own superiority; but none is more rebellious in its nature, or more difficult to be governed, than that of the purse or money. Self-opinion, arrogance, insolence, and impatience of rule, are its almost inseparable companions.

Now if these assertions are true, what an immense accession of this power hath accrued to the commonalty by the increase of trade; for though the other orders have acquired an addition by the same means, yet this is not in the same proportion, as every reader, who will revolve the proposition but a moment in his own mind, must be satisfied.

And what may we hence conclude? Is that civil power, which was adapted to the government of this order of people in that state in which they were at the conquest, capable of ruling them in their present situation? Hath this civil power kept equal pace with them in the increase of its force, or hath it not rather, by the remissness of the magistrate, lost much of its ancient energy? Where is now that power of the sheriff, which could formerly awaken and arm a whole county in an instant? where is that *posse comitatus,* which attended at his beck? What is become of the Constitutions of Alfred, which the reader will find set forth at large in the following treatise? what of the ancient conservators of the peace? Have the justices, on whom this whole power devolves, an authority sufficient for the purpose? In some counties, perhaps, you may find an overgrown tyrant, who lords it over his neighbours and tenants with despotic sway, and who is as regardless of the law as he is ignorant of it; but as to the magistrate of a less fortune, and more knowledge, every riotous independent butcher or baker, with two or three thousand pounds in his pocket, laughs at his power, and every pettifogger makes him tremble.

It is a common and popular complaint, that the justices of peace have already too much power. Indeed, a very little is too much, if it be abused; but, in truth, this complaint proceeds from a mistake of business for power: The business of the justice is indeed multiplied by a great number of statutes; but I know not of any (the Riot Act perhaps excepted) which hath at all enlarged his power. And what the force of that act is, and how able the magistrate is, by means of the civil power alone, to execute it in any popular commotion, I have myself experienced. But when a mob of chairmen or servants, or a gang of thieves and sharpers, are almost too big for the civil authority to suppress, what must be the case in a seditious tumult, or general riot of the people?

From what hath been said, I may, I think, conclude, that the constitution of this country is altered from its ancient state.

Secondly, That the power of the commonalty hath received an immense addition: and that the civil power having not increased, but decreased, in the same proportion, is not able to govern them.

What may and must be the consequences of this, as well as what remedy can be applied to it, I leave to the consideration of others: I have proceeded far enough already on the subject, to draw sufficient ill-will on myself, from unmeaning or ill-meaning people, who either do not foresee the mischievous tendency of a total relaxation of government, or who have some private wicked purpose to effect from public confusion.

In plain truth, the principal design of this whole work is to rouse the civil power from its present lethargic state. A design, which alike opposes those wild notions of liberty that are inconsistent with all government, and those pernicious schemes of government which are destructive of true liberty. However contrary indeed these principles may seem to each other, they have both the same common interest; or, rather, the former are the wretched tools of the latter; for anarchy is almost sure to end in some kind of tyranny.

Dr. Middleton, in his Life of Cicero, hath a fine observation to my present purpose, with which I will conclude this Preface:—

" From the railleries of the Romans (says he) on the *barbarity and misery of our island,* one cannot help reflecting on the surprising fate and revolutions of kingdoms; how Rome, once the mistress of the world, the seat of arts, empire, and glory, now lies sunk in sloth, ignorance, and poverty; enslaved to the most cruel, as well as to the most contemptible of tyrants, *superstition,* and *religious imposture:* while this remote country, anciently the jest and contempt of *the polite Romans,* is become the happy seat of liberty, plenty, and letters; flourishing in all the arts and refinements of civil life; yet running perhaps, the same course, which Rome itself had run before it; from virtuous industry to wealth; from wealth to luxury; from luxury to an impatience of discipline and corruption of morals; till, by a total degeneracy and loss of virtue, being grown ripe for destruction, it falls a prey at last to some hardy oppressor, and, with the loss of liberty, losing every thing else that is valuable, sinks gradually again into its original barbarism."

AN INQUIRY INTO THE CAUSES

OF THE LATE

INCREASE OF ROBBERS, &c.

INTRODUCTION

THE great increase of robberies within these few years is an evil which to me appears to deserve some attention; and the rather as it seems (though already become so flagrant) not yet to have arrived to that height of which it is capable, and which it is likely to attain; for diseases in the political, as in the natural body, seldom fail going on to their crisis, especially when nourished and encouraged by faults in the constitution. In fact, I make no doubt, but that the streets of this town, and the roads leading to it, will shortly be impassable without the utmost hazard; nor are we threatened with seeing less dangerous gangs of rogues among us, than those which the Italians call the Banditti.

Should this ever happen to be the case, we shall have sufficient reason to lament that remissness by which this evil was suffered to grow to so great a height. All distempers, if I may once more resume the allusion, the sooner they are opposed, admit of the easier and the safer cure. The great difficulty of extirpating desperate gangs of robbers, when once collected into a body, appears from our own history in former times. France hath given us a later example in the long reign of Cartouche, and his banditti; and this under an absolute monarchy, which affords much more speedy and efficacious remedies against these political disorders, than can be administered in a free state, whose forms of correction are extremely slow and uncertain, and whose punishments are the mildest and the most void of terror of any other in the known world.

For my own part, I cannot help regarding these depredations in a most serious light; nor can I help wondering that a nation so jealous of her liberties, that from the slightest cause, and often without any cause at all, we are always murmuring at our superiors, should tamely and quietly support the invasion of her properties by a few of the lowest and vilest among us: doth not this situation in reality level us with the most enslaved countries? If I am to be assaulted, and pillaged, and plundered; if I can neither sleep in my own house nor walk the streets, nor travel in safety; is not my condition almost equally bad whether a licensed or unlicensed rogue, a dragoon or a robber, be the person who assaults and plunders me? The only difference which I can perceive is, that the latter evil appears to be more easy to remove.

If this be as I clearly think it is, the case, surely there are few matters of more general concern than to put an immediate end to these outrages, which are already become so notorious, and which, as I have observed, seem to threaten us with such a dangerous increase. What indeed may not the public apprehend, when they are informed as an unquestionable fact, that there are at this time a great gang of rogues, whose number falls little short of a hundred, who are incorporated in one body, have officers and a treasury, and have reduced theft and robbery into a regular system. There are of this society men who appear in all disguises, and mix in most companies. Nor are they better versed in every art of cheating, thieving, and robbing, than they are armed with every method of evading the law, if they should ever be discovered and an attempt made to bring them to justice. Here, if they fail in rescuing the prisoner, or (which seldom happens) in bribing or deterring the prosecutor, they have for their last resource some rotten members of the law to forge

a defence for them, and a great number of false witnesses
ready to support it.

Having seen the most convincing proofs of all this, I
cannot help thinking it high time to put some stop to the
farther progress of such impudent and audacious insults, not
only on the properties of the subject, but on the national
justice, and on the laws themselves. The means of accomplishing this (the best which suggest themselves to me) I
shall submit to the public consideration, after having first
inquired into the causes of the present growth of this evil,
and whence we have great reason to apprehend its farther
increase. Some of these, I am too well versed in the affairs
of this world to expect to see removed; but there are others,
which, without being over sanguine, we may hope to remedy;
and thus perhaps one ill consequence, at least, of the more
stubborn political diseases may cease.

SECTION I.

OF TOO FREQUENT AND EXPENSIVE DIVERSIONS AMONG THE LOWER KIND OF PEOPLE.

FIRST then, I think, that the vast torrent of luxury, which
of late years hath poured itself into this nation, hath greatly
contributed to produce, among many others, the mischief I
here complain of. I am not here to satirise the great, among
whom luxury is probably rather a moral than a political evil.
But vices no more than diseases will stop with them; for bad
habits are as infectious by example, as the plague itself by
contact. In free countries, at least, it is a branch of liberty
claimed by the people to be as wicked and as profligate as
their superiors. Thus while the nobleman will emulate the
grandeur of a prince, and the gentleman will aspire to the
proper state of the nobleman, the tradesman steps from behind his counter into the vacant place of the gentleman.

Nor doth the confusion end here; it reaches the very dregs of the people, who aspiring still to a degree beyond that which belongs to them, and not being able by the fruits of honest labour to support the state which they affect, they disdain the wages to which their industry would entitle them; and abandoning themselves to idleness, the more simple and poor-spirited betake themselves to a state of starving and beggary, while those of more art and courage become thieves, sharpers, and robbers.

Could luxury be confined to the palaces of the great, the society would not, perhaps, be much affected with it; at least, the mischiefs, which I am now intending to obviate, can never be the consequence. For though, perhaps, there is not more of real virtue in the higher state, yet the sense of honour is there more general and prevalent. But there is a much stronger reason. The means bear no probable proportion to the end; for the loss of thousands, or of a great estate, is not to be relieved or supplied by any means of common theft or robbery.—With regard to such evils, therefore, the legislature might be justified in leaving the punishment as well as the pernicious consequence, to end in the misery, distress, and sometimes utter ruin of a private family. But when this vice descends downward to the tradesman, the mechanic, and the labourer, it is certain to engender many political mis-chiefs, and among the rest it is most evidently the parent of theft and robbery, to which not only the motive of want but of shame conduces; for there is no greater degree of shame than the tradesman generally feels at the first inability to make his regular payments; nor is there any difficulty which he would not undergo to avoid it. Here then the highway promises, and hath, I doubt not, often given relief. Nay, I remember very lately a highwayman who confessed several robberies before me, his motive to which, he assured me (and so it appeared), was to pay a bill that was shortly to become due. In this case, therefore, the public becomes interested, and consequently the legislature is obliged to interpose.

To give a final blow to luxury by any general prohibition, if it would be advisable, is by no means possible. To say the truth, bad habits in the body politic, especially if of any duration, are seldom to be wholly eradicated. Palliatives alone are to be applied; and these too in a free constitution must be of the gentlest kind, and as much as possible adapted to the taste and genius of the people.

The gentlest method which I know, and at the same time perhaps one of the most effectual, of stopping the progress of vice, is by removing the temptation. Now the two great motives to luxury, in the mind of men, are vanity and voluptuousness. The former of these operates but little in this regard with the lower order of people. I do not mean that they have less of this passion than their betters; but the apparent impossibility of gratifying it this way deters them, and diverts at least this passion into another channel; for we find it puts them rather on vying with each other in the reputation of wealth, than in the outward appearance of show and grandeur. Voluptuousness, or the love of pleasure, is that alone which leads them into luxury. Here then the temptation is with all possible care to be withdrawn from them.

Now what greater temptation can there be to voluptuousness, than a place where every sense and appetite of which it is compounded are fed and delighted; where the eyes are feasted with show, and the ears with music, and where gluttony and drunkenness are allured by every kind of dainty; nay, where the finest women are exposed to view, and where the meanest person who can dress himself clean, may in some degree mix with his betters, and thus perhaps satisfy his vanity as well as his love of pleasure?

It may possibly be said that these diversions are cheap: I answer, that is one objection I have to them; was the price as high as that of a ridotto, or an opera, it would, like these diversions, be confined to the higher people only; besides, the cheapness is really a delusion. Unthinking men are often deceived into expense, as I once knew an honest gentleman, who carried his wife and two daughters to a masquerade, being told that he could have four tickets for four guineas; but found afterwards, that in dresses, masques, chairs, &c., the night's entertainment cost him almost twelve. I am convinced that many thousands of honest tradesmen have found their expenses exceed their computation in a much greater proportion. And the sum of seven or eight shillings (which is a very moderate allowance for the entertainment of the smallest family) repeated once or twice a week through a summer, will make too large a deduction from the reasonable profits of any low mechanic.

Besides the actual expense in attending these places of pleasure, the loss of time, and neglect of business, are consequences which the inferior tradesman can by no means support. To be born for no other purpose than to consume the fruits of the earth is the privilege (if it may be really called a privilege) of very few. The greater part of mankind must sweat hard to produce them, or society will no longer answer the purposes for which it was ordained. *Six days shalt thou labour,* was the positive command of God in His own republic. A severity, however, which the divine wisdom was pleased somewhat to relax; and appointed certain times of rest and recreation for His people. Such were the feasts of the unleavened bread, the feast of the weeks, and the feast of the tabernacles. On which occasions it is written, " Thou shalt rejoice before the Lord thy God, thou, and thy son, and thy daughter, and thy servant, and thy maid, and the Levite that is within thy gates, and the stranger, and the fatherless, and the widow." [1]

All other nations have imitated this divine institution. It is true, among the Greeks, arising from the nature of their superstition, there were many festivals; yet scarce any of these were universal, and few attended with any other than religious ceremonies.[2] The Roman calendar is thinner strewed with these seasons of idleness. Indeed there seems

---

[1] Exod. chap. xxxiv. Deut. chap. xvi.

[2] The gods, says Plato, pitying the laborious condition to which men were born, appointed holy rites to themselves, as seasons of rest to men; and gave them the Muses, with Apollo their leader, and Bacchus, to assist in the celebrations, &c. De Leg. l. ii. p. 787, edit. Ficini.

to have been one kind only of universal sport and revelling
amongst them, which they called the *Saturnalia,* when much
too great indulgence was given to all kinds of licentiousness.
Public scenes of rendezvous they had none.   As to the
Grecian women, it is well known they were almost entirely
confined to their own houses; where the very entertainment
of their finest ladies was only work of the finer sorts.   And
the Romans by the Orchian law, which was made among
many others for the suppression of luxury, and was published in the third year from Cato's censorship, thought
proper to limit the number of persons who were to assemble
even at any private feast.[1]   Nay, the exhibitions of the
theatre were suffered only at particular seasons, and on
holidays.

Nor are our own laws silent on this head, with regard
at least to the lowest sort of people, whose diversions have
been confined to certain stated times.   Mr. Pulton,[2] speaking
of those games and assemblies of the people which are lawful, says, that they are lawful at certain places and seasons
of the year, allowed by old and ancient customs.   The statute
of Henry VIII.[3] goes farther, and expressly enacts, that no
manner of artificer or craftsman, of any handicraft or occupation, husbandman, apprentice, &c., shall play at the tables,
tennis, dice, cards, bowls, &c., out of Christmas, under the
penalty of 20s.

Thus we find that by divine as well as human institution,
as well by our own laws as those of other countries, the
diversions of the people have been limited and restrained to
certain seasons; under which limitations, Seneca calls these
diversions the necessary temperament of labour.   " Some
remission," says he, " must be given to our minds, which will
spring up the better and more brisk from rest.   It is with
the mind as with a fruitful field, whose fertility will be
exhausted if we give it no intermission.   The same will

---

[1] Macrob. Saturnal. lib. ii. c. xiii. Note, This RIOT ACT passed in
one of the freest ages of the Roman republic.

[2] De Pace, fol. 25.

[3] 33 Hen. VIII. c. ix.

accrue to the mind by incessant labours, whereas both from gentle remission will acquire strength.   From constant labour arises a certain dulness and langour of the spirits; nor would men with such eagerness affect them, if sport or merriment had not a certain natural sweetness inherent in themselves; the frequent use of which however will destroy all gravity and force in our minds.   Sleep is necessary to our refreshment, but if this be continued night and day, it will become death.   There is a great difference between the remission of any thing and its dissolution.   Lawgivers, therefore, instituted certain holidays, that the people might be compelled by law to merriment, interposing this as a necessary temperament to their labours." [1]

Thus the Greek and Latin philosophers, though they derive the institution differently, the one alleging a divine and the other a human original, both agree that a necessary relaxation from labour was the only end for which diversion was invented and allowed to the people.   This institution, as the former of these great writers tells us, was grossly perverted even in his time; but surely neither then, nor in any age or nation, until now, was this perversion carried to so scandalous an excess as it is at present in this kingdom, and especially in and near the metropolis, where the places of pleasure are almost become numberless; for, besides those great scenes of rendezvous, where the nobleman and his tailor, the lady of quality and her tirewoman, meet together and form one common assembly, what an immense variety of places have this town and its neighbourhood set apart for the amusement of the lowest order of the people; and where the master of the house, or wells, or garden, may be said to angle only in the kennels, where, baiting with the vilest materials, he catches only the thoughtless and tasteless rabble; these are carried on, not on a single day, or in a single week; but all of them during half, and some during the whole year.

If the computation was made of the money expended in these temples of idleness by the artificer, the handicraftsman,

---

[1] Sen. De Tranquill. Animi, p. 167. edit. Lips.

the apprentice, and even the common labourer, the sum would appear excessive; but without putting myself to that trouble, I · believe the reader will permit me to conclude that it is much greater than such persons can or ought to afford; especially as idleness, its necessary attendant, adds greatly to the debtor's side in the account; and that the necessary consequence must be ruin to many, who, from being useful members of the society, will become a heavy burden or absolute nuisance to the public. It being indeed a certain method to fill the streets with beggars, and the gaols with debtors and thieves.

That this branch of luxury hath grown to its present height, is owing partly to a defect in the laws; and this defect may, with great decency and respect to the legislature, be very truly imputed to the recency of the evil; for as our ancestors knew it not, they may be well excused for not having foreseen and guarded against it. If therefore it should seem now necessary to be retrenched, a new law will, I apprehend, be necessary for that purpose; the powers of the magistrate being scarce extensive enough, under any provision extant, to destroy a hydra now become so pregnant and dangerous. And it would be too dangerous as well as too invidious a task to oppose the mad humours of the populace, by the force of any doubtful obsolete law; which, as I have hinted before, could not have been directly levelled at a vice which did not exist at the time when the law was made.

But while I am recommending some restraint of this branch of luxury, which surely appears to be necessary, I would be understood to aim at the retrenchment only, not at the extirpation of diversion; nay, and in this restraint, I confine myself entirely to the lower order of people. Pleasure always hath been, and always will be, the principal business of persons of fashion and fortune, and more especially of the ladies, for whom I have infinitely too great an honour and respect to rob them of any their least amusement. Let them have their plays, operas, and oratorios, their masquerades and ridottos; their assemblies, drums, routs, riots, and hurricanes; their Ranelagh and Vauxhall; their Bath, Tunbridge, Bristol,

Scarborough, and Cheltenham; and let them have their beaus and danglers to attend them at all these; it is the only use for which such beaus are fit; and I have seen, in the course of my life, that it is the only one to which, by sensible women, they are applied.

In diversions, as in many other particulars, the upper part of life is distinguished from the lower. Let the great therefore answer for the employment of their time to themselves, or to their spiritual governors. The society will receive some temporal advantage from their luxury. The more toys which children of all ages consume, the brisker will be the circulation of money, and the greater the increase of trade.

The business of the politician is only to prevent the contagion from spreading to the useful part of mankind, the ΕΠΙΠΟΝΟΝ ΠΕΦΥΚΟΣ ΓΕΝΟΣ; [1] and this is the business of persons of fashion and fortune too, in order that the labour and industry of the rest may administer to their pleasures, and furnish them with the means of luxury. To the upper part of mankind time is an enemy, and (as they themselves often confess) their chief labour is to kill it; whereas, with the others, time and money are almost synonymous; and as they have very little of each to spare, it becomes the legislature, as much as possible, to suppress all temptations whereby they may be induced too profusely to squander either the one or the other; since all such profusion must be repaired at the cost of the public.

Such places of pleasure, therefore, as are totally set apart for the use of the great world, I meddle not with. And though Ranelagh and Vauxhall, by reason of their price, are not entirely appropriated to the people of fashion, yet they are seldom frequented by any below the middle rank; and a strict regard to decency is preserved in them both. But surely two such places are sufficient to contain all those who have any title to spend their time in this idle, though otherwise innocent way. Nor should such a fashion be allowed to spread into every village in London, and by degrees

[1] Plato.

all over the kingdom; by which means, not only idleness, but all kinds of immorality, will be encouraged.

I cannot dismiss this head, without mentioning a notorious nuisance which hath lately arisen in this town; I mean, those balls where men and women of loose reputation meet in disguised habits. As to the masquerade in the Haymarket, I have nothing to say; I think really it is a silly rather than a vicious entertainment; but the case is very different with those inferior masquerades; for these are indeed no other than the temples of drunkenness, lewdness, and all kinds of debauchery.

SECTION II.

OF DRUNKENNESS, A SECOND CONSEQUENCE OF LUXURY AMONG THE VULGAR.

BUT the expense of money, and loss of time, with their certain consequences, are not the only evils which attend the luxury of the vulgar; drunkenness is almost inseparably annexed to the pleasures of such people. A vice by no means to be construed as a spiritual offence alone, since so many temporal mischiefs arise from it; amongst which are very frequently robbery, and murder itself.

I do not know a more excellent institution than that of Pittacus, mentioned by Aristotle in his Politics;[1] by which a blow given by a drunken man was more severely punished than if it had been given by one that was sober; "For Pittacus," says Aristotle, "considered the utility of the public (as drunken men are more apt to strike) and not the excuse which might otherwise be allowed to their drunkenness." And so far both the civil law and our own have followed this institution, that neither have admitted drunkenness to be an excuse for any crime.

This odious vice (indeed the parent of all others), as

[1] L. ii. c. x.

history informs us, was first introduced into this kingdom by the Danes, and with very mischievous effects. Wherefore that excellent Prince Edgar the Peaceable, when he set about reforming the manners of his people, applied himself very particularly to the remedy of this great evil, and ordered silver or gold pins to be fixed to the sides of their pots and cups, beyond which it was not lawful for any person to drink.[1]

What penalty was affixed to the breach of this institution I know not; nor do I find any punishment in our books for the crime of drunkenness, till the time of Jac. I. in the fourth year of whose reign it was enacted, " That every person lawfully convicted of drunkenness, shall, for every such offence, forfeit the sum of five shillings, to be paid within a week next after his, her, or their conviction, to the hands of the churchwardens of the parish where, &c., to the use of the poor. In default of payment, the sum to be levied by distress, and, in default of distress, the offender is to be committed to the stocks, there to remain for the space of six hours." [2]

For the second offence they are to be bound to their good behaviour, with two sureties, in a recognisance of ten pounds.[3]

Nor is only that degree of drunkenness forbidden, which Mr. Dalton describes, " so as to stagger and reel to and fro, and where the same legs which carry him into a house cannot carry him out again," [4] for, by the same act of parliament, all persons who continue drinking or tippling in any inn, victualling-house, or alehouse, in their own city, town or parish (unless such as, being invited by a traveller, shall accompany him during his necessary abode there; or except labouring and handicraftsmen in cities and corporate and market towns, upon a working-day, for an hour at dinner-time, in alehouses where they take their diet; and except labourers and workmen, who, during their continuance in any work, shall lodge or victual in any inn, &c., or except

[1] Eachard, p. 88.   [2] Jac. I. chap. v.
[3] Jac. I. chap. v. sect. 6.   [4] Dalt. chap. vii. sect. 5.

for some urgent and necessary occasion, to be allowed by two justices of the peace), shall forfeit the sum of three shillings and sixpence, for the use of the poor; to be levied as before, and, for want of distress, to be put in the stocks for four hours.[1]

This act hath been still farther enforced by another in the same reign.[2]   By the latter act, the tippler is liable, whether his habitation be within the same or any other parish.   Secondly, The proof by one witness is made sufficient; and thirdly, A very extraordinary clause is added, by which the oath of the party offending, after having confessed his own crime, is made evidence against any other offender, though at the same time.

Thus we see the legislature have taken the utmost care not only to punish, but even to prevent this vice of drunkenness, which the preamble of one of the foregoing statutes calls a *loathsome* and *odious sin,* and the root and foundation of many other enormous sins, as murder, &c.   Nor doth the wisdom of our law stop here.   Our cautious ancestors have endeavoured to remove the temptation, and, in a great measure, to take away from the people their very power of offending this way.   And this by going to the fountain-head, and endeavouring to regulate and restrain the scenes of these disorders, and to confine them to those uses for which they were at first designed; namely, for the rest, refreshment, and convenience of travellers.

A cursory view of the statutes on this head will demonstrate of what consequence to society the suppression of this vice was in the opinion of our ancestors.

By the common law, inns and alehouses might be kept *ad libitum;* but if any disorders were suffered in them, they were indictable as a common nuisance.

The first reform which I find to have been made by parliament was in the reign of Henry VII.,[3] when two justices were empowered to suppress an alehouse.

The statute of Edward VI.[4] is the first which requires a

---

[1] Jac. I. chap. iv. sect. 4, & 1 Jac. I. chap. ix.   [2] 21 Jac. I. chap. vii.   [3] 11 Hen. VII.   [4] 5 Edw. VI. c. xxv.

precedent licence. By this act no man can keep an alehouse, without being licensed by the sessions, or by two justices; but now, by a late statute, all licences granted by justices out of their sessions are void.[1]

By the statute of Charles I.,[2] which alters the penalties of that of Edward VI., the punishment for keeping an alehouse, or common selling ale, beer, cyder, and perry, without a licence, is to pay twenty shillings to the use of the poor, to be levied by distress; which, if satisfaction be not made within three days, is to be sold. And if there be no goods whereon to distrain, and the money be not paid within six days after conviction, the offender is to be delivered to the constable or some inferior officer, to be whipped. For the second offence, he is to be committed to the house of correction for a month; and for the third, he is to be committed to the said house, till, by order of the justices, at their general sessions, he be discharged.

The conviction is to be on the view of the justice, confession of the party, or by the oath of two witnesses.

And by this statute, if the constable or officer to whom the party is committed to be whipped, &c., do not execute his warrant, the justice shall commit him to prison, there to remain till he shall procure some one to execute the said warrant, or until he shall pay forty shillings to the use of the poor.

The justices, at the time of granting the licence, shall take a recognisance from the party not to suffer any unlawful games, nor other disorders, in his house; which is to be certified to the sessions, and the justices there have a power to proceed for the forfeiture.[3]

By the statute of Jac. I.,[4] alehouse-keepers, who suffer townsmen to sit tippling, unless in the cases above mentioned,[5] forfeit ten shillings to the poor; the distress to be sold within six days; and if no distress can be had, the party is to be committed till the forfeiture is paid.

---

[1] 2 Geo. II. c. xxviii. sect. 11.   [2] 3 Car. I. cap. iv.
[3] 5 E. VI. ubi sup.   [4] Cap. ix. ubi sup.
[5] Supra, p. 14, in the case of tipplers.

Vintners who keep inns or victualling-houses are within this act.[1]

And by two several statutes,[2] alehouse-keepers, convicted of this offence, are prohibited from keeping an alehouse for the space of three years.

Justices of peace likewise, for any disorders committed in alehouses contrary to the condition of the recognisance, may suppress such houses;[3] but then the proceeding must be on the recognisance and the breach of the condition proved.[4]

Now, on the concise view of these several laws, it appears, that the legislature have been abundantly careful on this head; and that the only blame lies on the remissness with which these wholesome provisions have been executed.

But though I will not undertake to defend the magistrates of former times, who have surely been guilty of some neglect of their duty; yet, on behalf of the present commissioners of the peace, I must observe, their case is very different. What physicians tell us of the animal functions will hold true when applied to laws; both by long disuse lose all their elasticity and force. Froward habits grow on men, as they do on children, by long indulgence: nor will either submit easily to correction in matters where they have been accustomed to act at their pleasure. They are very different offices to execute a new or a well known law and to revive one which is obsolete. In the case of a known law, custom brings men to submission; and in all new provisions the ill-will, if any, is levelled at the legislature, who are much more able to support it than a few or a single magistrate. If therefore it be thought proper to suppress this vice, the legislature must once more take the matter into their hands; and to this perhaps they will be the more inclined when it comes to their knowledge, that a new kind of drunkenness, unknown to our ancestors, is lately sprung up amongst us, and which, if not put a stop to, will infallibly destroy a great part of the inferior people.

[1] 1 Car. I. cap. iv.   [2] 7 Jac. I. cap. x., 21 Jac. I. cap. vii.
[3] 5 E. VI. ubi sup.   [4] Salk. 45.

The drunkenness I here intend is that acquired by the strongest intoxicating liquors, and particularly by that poison called *Gin;* which I have great reason to think is the principal sustenance (if it may be so called) of more than a hundred thousand people in this metropolis. Many of these wretches there are who swallow pints of this poison within the twenty-four hours; the dreadful effects of which I have the misfortune every day to see, and to smell too. But I have no need to insist on my own credit, or on that of my informers; the great revenue arising from the tax on this liquor (the consumption of which is almost wholly confined to the lowest order of people) will prove the quantity consumed better than any other evidence.

Now, besides the moral ill consequences occasioned by this drunkenness, with which, in this treatise, I profess not to deal; how greatly must this be supposed to contribute to those political mischiefs which this essay proposes to remedy? This will appear from considering, that however cheap this vile potion may be, the poorer sort will not easily be able to supply themselves with the quantities they desire; for the intoxicating draught itself disqualifies them from using any honest means to acquire it, at the same time that it removes all sense of fear and shame, and emboldens them to commit every wicked and desperate enterprise. Many instances of this I see daily; wretches are often brought before me, charged with theft and robbery, whom I am forced to confine before they are in a condition to be examined; and when they have afterwards become sober, I have plainly perceived, from the state of the case, that the *Gin* alone was the cause of the transgression, and have been sometimes sorry that I was obliged to commit them to prison.

But beyond all this there is a political ill consequence of this drunkenness, which, though it doth not strictly fall within my present purpose, I shall be excused for mentioning, it being indeed the greatest evil of all, and which must, I think, awaken our legislature to put a final period to so destructive a practice. And this is that dreadful consequence which must attend the poisonous quality of this pernicious liquor to the health, the strength, and the very being of numbers of his majesty's most useful subjects. I have not enough of physical knowledge to display the ill effects which such poisonous liquors produce in the constitution; for these I shall refer the reader to The Physical Account of the Nature of all Distilled Spirituous Liquors, and the Effect they have on Human Bodies.[1] And though, perhaps, the consequence of this poison, as it operates slowly, may not so visibly appear in the diminution of the strength, health, and lives, of the present generation; yet let a man cast his eyes but a moment towards our prosperity, and there the dreadful consequences must strike on the meanest capacity, and must alarm, I think, the most sluggish degree of public spirit. What must become of the infant who is conceived in Gin? with the poisonous distillations of which it is nourished both in the womb and at the breast. Are these wretched infants (if such can be supposed capable of arriving at the age of maturity) to become our future sailors, and our future grenadiers? Is it by the labour of such as these that all the emoluments of peace are to be procured us, and all the dangers of war averted from us? What could an Edward or a Henry, a Marlborough or a Cumberland, effect with an army of such wretches? Doth not this polluted source, instead of producing servants for the husbandman or artificer, instead of providing recruits for the sea or the field, promise only to fill almshouses and hospitals, and to infect the streets with stench and diseases?

In solemn truth, there is nothing of more serious consideration, nor which more loudly calls for a remedy, than the evil now complained against. For what can be more worthy the care of the legislature, than to preserve the morals, the innocence, the health, strength, and lives, of a great part (I will repeat, the most useful part) of the people? So far am I, in my own opinion, from representing this in too serious or too strong a light, that I can find no words,

---

[1] This was composed by a very learned divine, with the assistance of several physicians, and published in the year 1736. The title is, Distilled Spirituous Liquors the Bane of the Nation.

or metaphor, adequate to my ideas on this subject.   The
first inventor of this diabolical liquor may be compared to
the poisoner of a fountain, whence a large city was to derive
its waters, the highest crime, as it hath been thought, of
which human nature is capable.   A degree of villainy,
indeed, of which I cannot recollect any example; but surely
if such was ever practised, the governors of that city could
not be thought blameless, did they not endeavour, to the
utmost, to withhold the citizens from drinking the poisonous
draught; and, if such a general thirst after it prevailed as
we are told possessed the people of Athens at the time of
the plague,[1] what could justify the not effectually cutting off
all acqueducts by which the poison was dispersed among the
people?

Nor will any thing less than absolute deletion serve on
the present occasion.   It is not making men pay 50*l.* or
500*l.* for a licence to poison; nor enlarging the quantity
from two gallons to ten, which will extirpate so stubborn an
evil.   Here may, perhaps, be no little difficulty.   To lay the
axe to the still-head, and prohibit all distillery in general,
would destroy the chemist.   If distilling this or that spirit
was forbidden, we know how easily all partial prohibitions
are evaded; nay, the chemist (was the matter confined to
him) would soon probably become a common distiller, and
his shop no better than a gin-shop; since what is more
common than for men to adopt the morals of a thief at
a fire, and to work their own private emolument out of a
public mischief?   Suppose all spirituous liquors were together
with other poison, to be locked up in the chemists' or apothe-
caries' shops, thence never to be drawn, till some excellent
physicians call them forth for the cure of nervous distemper;
or suppose the price was to be raised so high, by a severe im-
post, that gin would be placed entirely beyond the reach of
the vulgar! or perhaps the wisdom of the legislature may devise a better and more effectual way.

---

[1] Ἔδρασαν ἐς φρέατα ἀπαύστῳ τῇ δίψῃ ξυνεχόμενοι. They ran
into the wells, being constantly possessed by an inexhausted thirst.
Thucydid. p. 112. edit. Hudsoni.

But if the difficulty be really insuperable, or if there be any political reason against the total demolition of this poison, so strong as to countervail the preservation of the morals, health, and beings, of such numbers of his majesty's subjects, let us, however, in some measure, palliate the evil, and lessen its immediate ill consequences, by a more effectual provision against drunkenness than any we have at present, in which the method of conviction is too tedious and dilatory. Some little care on this head is surely necessary; for, though the increase of thieves, and the destruction of morality, though the loss of our labourers, our sailors, and our soldiers, should not be sufficient reasons, there is one which seems to be unanswerable, and that is, the loss of our gin-drinkers; since, should the drinking this poison be continued in its present height during the next twenty years, there will, by that time, be very few of the common people left to drink it.

SECTION III.

OF GAMING AMONG THE VULGAR; A THIRD CONSEQUENCE OF THEIR LUXURY.

I COME now to the last great evil which arises from the luxury of the vulgar; and this is gaming; a school in which most highwaymen of great eminence have been bred. This vice is the more dangerous as it is deceitful, and, contrary to every other species of luxury, flatters its votaries with the hopes of increasing their wealth; so that avarice itself is so far from securing us against its temptations, that it often betrays the more thoughtless and giddy part of mankind into them; promising riches without bounds, and those to be acquired by the most sudden as well as easy and indeed pleasant means.

And here I must again remind the reader, that I have only the inferior part of mankind under my consideration.

I am not so ill-bred as to disturb the company at a polite assembly; nor so ignorant of our constitution as to imagine that there is a sufficient energy in the executive part to control the economy of the great, who are beyond the reach of any, unless capital laws. Fashion, under whose guidance they are, and which created the evil, can alone cure it. With patience therefore must we wait, till this notable mistress of the few shall, in her good time, accomplish so desirable a change; in fact, till great men become wiser or better; till the prevalence of some laudable taste shall teach them a worthier manner of employing their time; till they have sense enough to be reasoned, modesty enough to be laughed, or conscience enough to be frightened, out of a silly, a shameful, and a sinful profligacy, attended with horrid waste of time, and the cruel destruction of the families of others, or of their own.

In the meantime, we may, I think, reasonably desire of these great personages, that they would keep their favourite vice to themselves, and not suffer others, whose birth or fortune gives them no title to be above the terror of the laws, or the censure of their betters, to share with them in this privilege. Surely we may give great men the same advice which Archer, in the play, gives to the officers of the army; *To kick out all——in red but their own.* What temptations can gamesters of fashion have to admit *inferior* sharpers into their society; common-sense surely will not suffer a man to risk a fortune against one who hath none of his own to stake against .t.

I am well apprised that this is not much the case with persons of the first figure; but to gentlemen (and especially the younger sort) of the second degree these fellows have found much too easy an access. Particularly at the several public places (I might have said gaming places) in this kingdom, too little care is taken to prevent the promiscuous union of company; and sharpers of the lowest kind have frequently there found admission to their superiors, upon no other pretence or merit than that of a laced coat, and with no other stock than that of assurance.

Some few of these fellows, by luckily falling in with an egregious bubble, some thoughtless young heir, or more commonly heiress, have succeeded in a manner which, if it may give some encouragement to others to imitate them, should, at the same time, as strongly admonish all gentlemen and ladies to be cautious with whom they mix in public places, and to avoid the sharper as they would a pest. But much the greater part of such adventures have met with a more probable and more deserved fate; and having exhausted their little fund in their attempts, have been reduced to a dilemma, in which it required more judgment and resolution than are the property of many men, and more true sense of honour than belongs to any debauched mind, to extricate themselves by honest means. The only means, indeed, of this kind, are to quit their assumed station, and to return to that calling, however mean and laborious, to which they were born and bred.

But, besides that the way to this is often obstructed with almost insuperable difficulties; and false shame, at its very entrance, dashes them in the face, how easily are they dissuaded from such disagreeable thoughts by the temptations with which fortune allures them, of a possibility, at least, of still supporting their false appearances, and of retrieving all their former hopes! how greedily, may we imagine, this enchanting alternative will be embraced by every bold mind, in such circumstances! for what but the danger of the undertaking can deter one, who hath nothing of a gentleman but his dress, to attain which he hath already divested himself of all sense of honesty? how easy is the transition from fraud to force! from a gamester to a rogue! perhaps, indeed, it is civil to suppose it any transition at all.

From this source, therefore, several of our most notable highwaymen have proceeded; and this hath likewise been the source of many other depredations on the honest part of mankind. So mischievous have been this kind of sharpers in society, that they have fallen under the particular notice of the legislature; for a statute in the reign of Queen Anne, reciting, "That divers lewd and dissolute persons live at great expense, having no visible estate, profession, or calling, to maintain themselves, but support those expenses by gaming only;" enacts, "That any two justices of the peace may cause to be brought before them all persons within their respective limits, whom they shall have just cause to suspect to have no visible estate, profession, or calling, to maintain themselves by, but do, for the most part, support themselves by gaming; and if such persons shall not make the contrary appear to such justices, they are to be bound to their good behaviour for a twelvemonth; and, in default of sufficient security, to be committed till they can find such security; which security (in case they give it) is to be forfeited on their playing or betting at any one time for more than the value of 20s." [1]

As to gaming in the lower classes of life, so plainly tending to the ruin of tradesmen, the destruction of youth, and to the multiplication of every kind of fraud and violence, the legislature hath provided very wholesome laws. [2]

[1] 9 Annæ, chap. xiv. sect. 6, 7. It would be of great service to the public to extend this statute to idle persons and sharpers in general; for many support themselves by frauds, by cheating practices, even worse than gaming; and have the impudence to appear in the dress of gentlemen, and at public places, without having any pretensions of birth and fortune, or without any honest or visible means of livelihood whatever. Such a law would not be without a precedent; for such is the excellent institution mentioned by Herodotus, in his Euterpe,—"Amasis" (says that historian) "established a law in Egypt, that every Egyptian should annually declare before the governor of the province by what means he maintained himself; and all those who did not appear, or who could not prove that they had some lawful livelihood, were punished by death. This law Solon introduced into Athens, where it was long inviolably preserved as a most just and equitable provision." Herod. edit. Hudsoni, p. 158. This punishment is surely too severe; but the law under a milder penalty is well worthy to be adopted.

[2] By a statute made in the reign of Edward IV. now repealed, playing at several games therein mentioned was punished by two years' imprisonment and the forfeiture of 10l, and the master of the house was to be imprisoned for three years and to forfeit 20l. A great sum in those days.

By the 33rd of Henry VIII. " Every artificer, craftsman of any handicraft or occupation, husbandman, labourer, servant at husbandry, journeyman or servant of artificer, mariners, fishermen, watermen, or any serving men, are prohibited from playing at tables, dice, cards, &c., out of Christmas, and in Christmas are permitted to play only in their masters' houses, or in his presence, under the penalty of 20s. And all manner of persons are prohibited from playing at any bowl or bowls, in any open place out of their garden or orchard, under the penalty of 6s. 8d.

" The conviction to be by action, information, bill, or otherwise, in any of the king's courts; one half of the penalty to the informer.

" Provided that servants may play at any times with their masters, or by their licence; and all persons who have 100l. per annum, freehold, may give their servants, or others, resorting to their houses, a licence to play within the precinct of their houses, gardens, or orchard."

By this statute likewise, " No person whatever, by himself, factor, deputy, servant, or other person, shall, for gain, keep, &c., any common, house, alley, or place of bowling, coyting, clash-coyls, half-bowl, tennis, dicing-table, or carding, or any other manner of game, prohibited by any statute heretofore made, or any unlawful game invented or made, or any other new unlawful game hereafter to be invented or made; the penalty is 40s. per day, for keeping the house, &c., and 6s. 8d. for every person haunting and playing at such house. These penalties to be recovered, &c., as above.

" And all leases of gaming-houses, alleys, &c., are made void at the election of the lessee."

Farther, by the said statute, " Power is given to all justices of peace, mayors, or other head-officers, in every city, &c., to enter suspected houses and places, and to commit the keepers of the said houses, and the persons there haunting, resorting, and playing, to prison; and to keep them in prison, till the keepers have found sureties to enter into a recognisance to the king's use, no longer to keep such house, &c., and the persons there found to be bound by themselves, or with sureties, &c., at the discretion of the justice, &c., no more to haunt the said places, or play at any of the said games."

And now, by the statute of George II. this last clause is enforced, by giving the justice the same power on the information of two persons, as he had before on view; and, by a more explicit power, to take sureties or not of the party at his discretion.

Lastly, the statute of Henry VIII. enjoins the justices, &c., to make due search weekly, or once per month at the farthest, under the penalty of forfeiting 40s. for every month during their neglect.

Thus stands the law; by which it may appear, that the magistrate is armed with sufficient authority to destroy all gaming among the inferior people; and that, without his neglect or connivance, no such instance can possibly exist.

And yet, perhaps, the fault may not so totally lie at his door; for the recognisance is a mere bugbear, unless the party who breaks it should be sued thereon; which, as it is attended with great expense, is never done; so that, though many have forfeited it, not a single example of an estreat hath been made within my remembrance.

Again, it were to be wished, that the statute of George II. had required no more than one witness to the information; for even one witness, as I have found by experience, is very difficult to be procured.

However, as the law now is, seeing that the general bent of the people opposes itself to this vice, it is certainly in a great measure within the magistrate's power to suppress it, and so to harass such as propose to find their account in it, that these would soon be discouraged from the undertaking; nor can I conclude without observing, that this hath been lately executed with great vigour within the liberty of Westminster.

There are, besides, several other provisions in our statute books against this destructive vice. By the statute of Queen

Anne [1] whoever cheats at play forfeits five times the sum won by such cheating, shall be deemed infamous, and suffer such corporal punishment as in case of perjury. And whoever wins above 10*l.* at any one sitting shall likewise forfeit five times the sum won. Going shares with the winner, and betting on his side, are, in both instances, within the act.

By the same act all securities for money won at play are made void; and if a mortgage be made on such account, the mortgagee doth not only lose all benefit of it, but the mortgage immediately enures to the use of the next heir. [2]

By this law persons who have lost above 10*l.* and have actually paid it may recover the same by action within three months; and if they do not sue for it within that time, any other person may. [3] And the defendant shall be liable to answer a bill for discovering such sum lost, upon oath.

By 18 George II. [4] whoever wins or loses 10*l.* at play or by betting at any one time, or 20*l.* within twenty-four hours, is liable to be indicted, and shall be fined five times the value of the money lost.

By 12 George II. [5] the games of Pharaoh, the Ace of Hearts, Basset, and Hazard, are declared to be lotteries; and all persons who set up, maintain, and keep them, forfeit 200*l.*, and all who play at them forfeit 50*l.* The conviction to be before one justice of peace, by the oath of one witness, or confession of the party. And the justice neglecting his duty forfeits 10*l.* *Note.* The prosecution against the keeper, &c., may be for a lottery, on the 8 George I. where the penalty is 500*l.*

The act of 18 George II. includes the game of Roly Poly, or other prohibited game at cards or dice, within the penalties of the above mentioned.

I have given this short sketch of these several acts partly for the use and encouragement of informers, and partly to

---

[1] 9 Annæ, chap. xiv. by which the statute of 16 C. II. is enlarged, and made more severe.   [2] Ibid. sect. 1.

[3] Ibid. sect. 2.   [4] Chap. xxxiv.   [5] Chap. xxviii.

insinuate to certain persons with what decency they can openly offend against such plain, such solemn laws, the severest of which many of themselves have, perhaps, been the makers of.   How can they seriously answer, either to their honour or conscience, giving the pernicious example of a vice, from which, as the legislature justly says in the preamble to the 16th of Charles II., "Many mischiefs and inconveniences do arise, and are daily found, in the encouraging of sundry idle and disorderly persons in their dishonest, lewd, and dissolute course of life; and to the circumventing, deceiving, cozening, and debauching of many of the younger sort, both of the nobility and gentry and others, to the loss of their precious time, and the utter ruin of their estates and fortunes, and withdrawing them from noble and laudable employments and exercises!" Will a nobleman, I ask, confess that he can employ his time in no better amusement; or will he frankly own that he plays with any other view than that of amusement? Lastly, what can a man who sins in open defiance of the laws of his country answer to the *vir bonus est quis?* Can he say,

" Qui consulta patrum, qui leges juraque servat?"

Or can he apply that celebrated line,

" Oderunt peccare boni virtutis honore,"

to himself, who owes to his greatness, and not to his innocence, that he is not deterred from such vices— *Formidine Pœnæ?*

SECTION IV.

OF THE LAWS THAT RELATE TO THE PROVISION FOR THE POOR.

HAVING now run through the several immediate consequences of a general luxury among the lower people, all which, as they tend to promote their distresses, may be reasonably sup-

posed to put many of them, of the bolder kind, upon unlawful
and violent means of relieving the mischief which such vices
have brought upon them, I come now to a second cause of the
evil, in the improper regulation of what is called the poor
in this kingdom, arising, I think, partly from the abuse of
some laws, and partly from the total neglect of others; and
(if I may presume to say it) somewhat perhaps from a defect
in the laws themselves.

It must be matter of astonishment to any man to reflect,
that in a country where the poor are, beyond all comparison,
more liberally provided for than in any other part of the
habitable globe, there should be found more beggars, more
distressed and miserable objects, than are to be seen throughout all the states of Europe.

And yet, undoubted as this fact is, I am far from agreeing
with Mr. Shaw,[1] who says, " There are few, if any, nations
or countries where the poor are more neglected, or are in a
more scandalous nasty condition, than in England. Whether,"
says he, " this is owing to that natural inbred cruelty for
which Englishmen are so much noted among foreigners, or
to that medley of religions which are so plentifully sown, and
so carefully cherished among us; who think it enough to
take care of themselves, and take a secret pride and pleasure
in the poverty and distresses of those of another persuasion," &c.

That the poor are in a very nasty and scandalous condition
is, perhaps, too true; but sure the general charge against
the people of England, as well as the invidious aspersion on
particular bodies of them, is highly unjust and groundless.
Nor do I know that any nation hath ventured to fix this
character of cruelty on us. Indeed, our inhospitality to
foreigners hath been sometimes remarked; but that we are
cruel to one another is not, I believe, the common, I am
sure it is not the true opinion. Can a general neglect of
the poor be justly charged on a nation in which the poor
are provided for by a tax, frequently equal to what is called
the land-tax, and where there are such numerous instances

[1] Vol. II. p. 1.

of private donations, such numbers of hospitals, almshouses, and charitable provisions of all kinds?

Nor can any such neglect be charged on the legislature; under whose inspection this branch of polity hath been almost continually, from the days of Queen Elizabeth to the present time. Insomuch, that Mr. Shaw himself enumerates no less than thirteen acts of parliament relating to the indigent and helpless poor.

If therefore there be still any deficiency in this respect, it must, I think, arise from one of the three causes above mentioned; that is, from some defect in the laws themselves, or from the perversion of these laws; or, lastly, from the neglect in their execution.

I will consider all these with some attention.

The 43rd of Eliz.[1] enacts:

First, that the churchwardens of every parish, and two substantial householders, at least, shall be yearly appointed to be overseers of the poor.

Secondly, that these overseers shall, with the consent of two justices of the peace, put out apprentices the children of poor people. And all married or unmarried persons, who have no means or trade to maintain themselves, shall be put to work.

Thirdly, that they shall raise by a parochial tax a convenient stock of flax, hemp, wool, thread, iron, and other ware and stuff, to set the poor to work.

Fourthly, that they shall, from the same tax, provide towards the necessary relief of the lame, impotent, old, blind, and others, being poor and not able to work.

Fifthly, that they shall, out of the same tax, put the children of poor persons apprentices.

That these provisions may all be executed, that act vested the overseers with the following powers; and enforced the executing them by the following penalties.

I. The overseers are appointed to meet once at least every month in the church after divine service; there, says the act, to consider of some good course to be taken, and some meet

[1] Chap. iii.

order to be set down *in the premises.* And to do this they are enjoined by a penalty; for every one absenting himself from such meeting, without a just excuse to be allowed by two justices of the peace, or being negligent in his office, or in the execution of the orders aforesaid, forfeits 20*s.*

And after the end of their year, and after other overseers nominated, they are, within four days, to make and yield up to two justices of the peace, a true and perfect account of all sums of money by them received or assessed, and of such stores as shall be in their hands, or in the hands of the poor, to work, and of all other things concerning their office, &c. And if the churchwardens and overseers refuse to account, they are to be committed by two justices till they shall have made a true account.

II. The overseers and churchwardens, both present and subsequent, are empowered, by warrant from two justices, to levy all the moneys assessed, and all arrearages of those who refuse to pay, by distress and sale of the refuser's goods; and the subsequent overseers may, in the same manner, levy the money and stock in the hands of the precedent; and for want of distress the party is to be committed by two justices, without bail, till the same be paid.

III. They have a power to compel the poor to work; and such as refuse or neglect, the justice may commit to the house of correction or common gaol.

IV. The overseers may compel children to be apprentices, and may bind them where they shall see convenient; till the man-child shall attain the age of twenty-four, and the woman-child the age of twenty-one, or till the time of her marriage; the indenture to be as effectual to all purposes as the covenant of one of full age.

V. They have a power to contract with the lord of the manor,[1] and, on any parcel of ground on the waste, to erect, at the general charge of the parish, convenient houses of dwelling for the impotent poor; and to place several inmates in the same cottage, notwithstanding the statute [2] of cottages.

---

[1] This must be done by consent and order of sessions.

[2] These cottages are never after to be applied to any other use.

VI. They can compel the father and grandfather, mother and grandmother, and children of every poor, old, blind, and impotent person, or of any other person not being able to work (provided such father, &c., be of sufficient ability) at their own charges to relieve and maintain such poor person, in such manner, and after such rate, as shall be assessed by the sessions, under the penalty of 20s. for every month's omission.

VII. If no overseers be named, every justice within the division forfeits 5*l*.

So far this statute of Elizabeth, by which the legislature may seem very fully to have provided, First, For the absolute relief of such poor, as are by age or infirmity rendered unable to work; and, Secondly, For the employment of such as are able.

"The former of these," says Lord Hale in his discourse on this subject, "seems to be a charity of more immediate exigence; but the latter (viz. the employment of the poor) is a charity of greater extent, and of very great and important consequence to the public wealth and peace of the kingdom, as also to the benefit and advantage of the poor." And this, as Mr. Shaw observes, "would prevent the children of our poor being brought up in laziness and beggary, whereby beggary is entailed from generation to generation: This is certainly the greatest charity; for though he who gives to any in want does well, yet he who employs and educates the poor, so as to render them useful to the public, does better; for that would be many hundred thousand pounds per annum benefit to this kingdom."

Now the former of these provisions hath, perhaps, though in a very slovenly and inadequate manner, been partly carried into execution; but the latter, I am afraid I may too boldly assert, hath been utterly neglected and disregarded. Surely this is a most scandalous perversion of the design of the legislature, which through the whole statute seems to have had the employment of the able poor chiefly under their consideration; for to this purpose only almost every power in it is established, and every clause very manifestly directed.

To say the truth, as this law hath been perverted in the execution, it were, perhaps, to be wished it had never been made. Not because it is not our duty to relieve real objects of distress; but because it is so much the duty of every man, and I may add, so much the inclination of most Englishmen, that it might have been safely left to private charity; or a public provision might surely have been made for it in a much cheaper and more effectual manner.

To prove the abuse of this law, my Lord Hale appeals to all the populous parishes in England (he might, I believe, have included some which are not over populous). " Indeed," says he, " there are rates made for the relief of the impotent poor; and, it may be, the same relief is also given in a narrow measure unto some others that have great families, and upon this they live miserably and at best from hand to mouth; and if they cannot get work to make out their livelihood, they and their children set up a trade of begging at best; but it is rare to see any provision of a stock in any parish for the relief of the poor; and the reasons are principally these: 1. The generality of people that are able, are yet unwilling, to exceed the present necessary charge; they do choose to live for an hour rather than project for the future; and, although possibly trebling their exhibition in one gross sum at the beginning of the year, to raise a stock might in all probability render their future yearly payments, for seven years together, less by half, or two-thirds, than what must be without it; yet they had rather continue on their yearly payments, year after year, though it exhaust them in time, and make the poor nothing the better at the year's end. 2. Because those places, where there are most poor, consist for the most part of tradesmen, whose estates lie principally in their stocks, which they will not endure to be searched into, to make them contributory to raise any considerable stock for the poor, nor indeed so much as to the ordinary contributions; but they lay all the rates to the poor upon the rents of lands and houses, which alone, without the help of the stocks, are not able to raise a stock for the poor, although it is very plain that stocks are as well by law rateable as lands, both

to the relief and raising a stock for the poor.   3. Because
the churchwardens and overseers, to whom this power is given,
are inhabitants of the same parish, and are either unwilling
to charge themselves, or to displease their neighbours in charging more than they needs must towards the poor; and although it were to be wished and hoped that the justices of
the peace would be forward to enforce them if they might,
though it may concern them also in point of present profit;
yet, if they would do any thing herein, they are not empowered to compel the churchwardens and overseers to do it,
who, most certainly, will never go about it to burden, as they
think, themselves, and displease their neighbours, unless
some compulsory power were not only lodged by law, but
also executed by some that may have a power over them to
enforce it; or to do it, if they do it either partially or too
sparingly.   4. Because people do not consider the inconvenience that in time grows to themselves by this neglect, and the
benefit that would in a little time accrue to them by
putting it in practice, if they would have but a little patience."

To these I will add a fifth reason; because the churchwardens and overseers are too apt to consider their office as
a matter of private emolument.   To waste part of the money
raised for the use of the poor in feasting and riot, and too
often to pervert the power given them by the statute to foreign, and sometimes to the very worst of purposes.

The above considerations bring my Lord Hale to complain of several defects in the law itself; "in which," says
he, "there is no power from the justices of the peace, nor
any superintendent power, to compel the raising of a stock
where the churchwardens and overseers neglect it.

"The act chargeth every parish apart, where it may be
they are liable to do little towards it; neither would it be
so effectual as if three, four, five, or more contiguous parishes
did contribute towards the raising of a stock proportionably
to their poor respectively.

"There is no power for hiring or erecting a common house,
or place, for their common workhouse; which may be, in

some respects, and upon some occasions, useful and necessary."

As to the first of these, I do not find any alteration hath
been made, nor if there was, might it possibly produce any
desired effect. The consequence, as it appears, would be only
making churchwardens of the justices of peace, which many
of them are already, not highly to the satisfaction of their
parishes; too much power vested in one man being too apt
perhaps to beget envy.

The second and third do pretty near amount to one and
the same defect; and this, I think, is at present totally removed. Indeed, in my Lord Hale's own time, though probably after he had written this treatise, a workhouse was
erected in London under the powers given by the statute
made in the 13 and 14 of Charles II.,[1] and I believe with
very good success.

Since that time other corporations have followed the example, as the city of Bristol in the reign of King William,[2]
and that of Worcester in the reign of Queen Anne,[3] and in
other places.

And now by a late statute, made in the reign of King
George I.,[4] the power of erecting workhouses is made general over the kingdom.

Now either this method, proposed by Lord Hale, is inadequate to the purpose; or this act of parliament hath been
grossly perverted; for certain it is that the evil is not removed, if indeed it be lessened, by the erection of work-
houses. Perhaps, indeed, one objection which my Lord Hale
makes to the statute of Eliz. may here recur, seeing that
there is nothing compulsory, but all left to the will and
direction of the inhabitants.

But in truth the method itself will never produce the desired effect, as the excellent Sir Josiah Child well observes,[5]
—" It may be objected," says he, " that this work (the provision for the poor) may as well be done in distinct parishes,
if all parishes were obliged to build workhouses, and employ

---

[1] Chap. xii.   [2] 8 and 9 W. III. c. xxx.   [3] 2 Annæ, c. viii.
[4] 9 George I. c. i.   [5] Essay on Trade, c. ii.

their poor therein, as Dorchester and some others have done with good success." I answer, "That such attempts have been made in many places, to my knowledge, with very good intents and strenuous endeavours; but all that I ever heard of proved vain and ineffectual." For the truth of which, I believe, we may appeal to common experience.

And, perhaps, no less ineffectual would be the scheme proposed by this worthy gentleman, though it seems to promise fairer than that of the learned chief justice; yet neither of them seem to strike at the root of the evil. Before I deliver any sentiments of my own, I shall briefly take a view of the many subsequent provisions with which the legislature have, from time to time, enforced and strengthened the foregoing statute of Elizabeth.

The power of putting out children [1] apprentices is enforced by the third of Charles I.[2] which enacts, "That all persons to whom the overseers shall bind children by virtue of the statute of Eliz. may receive and keep them as apprentices." But there yet wanted, as Lord Hale says, a *sufficient compulsory for persons to take them;* wherefore it is enacted, by 8 and 9 Will. III.,[3] "That all persons to whom apprentices are appointed to be bound by the overseers, with the consent of the justices, shall receive them and execute the other part of the indenture, under the penalty of 10*l.* for refusing, to be recovered before two justices, on the oath of one of the churchwardens or overseers."

The power of setting the poor to work is enlarged by 3 Charles I.[4] This act gives the churchwardens and overseers of the poor a power, with the consent of two justices, or of one, if no more justices shall be within their limits, to set up and occupy any trade for the setting the poor to work.

The power of relieving the impotent poor (*i. e.,* of dis-

---

[1] See 7 Jac. I. c. iii. which directs the manner of putting out apprentices, in pursuance of any gifts made to corporations, &c., for that purpose.

[2] Chap. iv. sect. 22, p. 8; the same clause is in 21 Jac. c. xxviii. par. 33.

[3] Chap. xxx. sect. 6.   [4] Chap. iv. sect. 22, ubi supra.

tributing the public money), the only one which hath much exercised the mind of the parish officers, the legislature seems to think rather wanted restraining than enlarging; accordingly, in the reign of King William [1] they made an act to limit the power of the officers in this respect. As the act contains the sense of parliament of the horrid abuse of the statute of Elizabeth, I will transcribe part of a paragraph from it *verbatim.*

" And whereas many inconveniences do daily arise in cities, towns corporate, and parishes, where the inhabitants are very numerous, by reason of the unlimited power of the churchwardens and overseers of the poor, who do frequently, upon frivolous pretences (but chiefly for their own private ends), give relief to what persons and number they think fit, and such persons being entered into the collection bill, do become after that a great charge to the parish, notwithstanding the occasion or pretence of their collection oftentimes ceases, by which means the rates for the poor are daily increased, contrary to the true intent of a statute made in the 43rd year of the reign of her majesty Queen Elizabeth, intituled, *An Act for the relief of the poor;* for remedying of which, the statute enacts, that, for the future, a book shall be provided and kept in every parish (at the charge of the same parish) wherein the names of all persons receiving collection, &c., shall be registered, with the day and year of their first receiving it. This book to be yearly, or oftener, viewed by the parishioners, and the names of the persons who receive collection shall be called over, and the reason of the receiving it examined, and a new list made; and no other person is allowed to receive collection but by order of a justice of peace, &c., except in case of pestilential diseases or small-pox." [2]

The 8th and 9th of the same king, reciting the fear of the legislature, *That the money, raised only for the relief of such as are as well impotent as poor, should be misapplied*

[1] 3 & 4 W. & M. c. xi. sect. 11.

[2] The same statute in another part charges the overseers, &c., with applying the poor's money to their own use.

and consumed by the idle, sturdy, and disorderly beggars,
" Enacts, that every person, his wife, children, &c., who shall
receive relief from the parish, shall wear a badge marked
with the letter *P., &c.,* in default of which, a justice of peace
may order the relief of such persons to be abridged, suspended, or withdrawn, or may commit them for twenty-one
days to the house of correction, there to be kept to hard
labour.   And every churchwarden or overseer, who relieves
any one without a badge, being convicted before one justice,
forfeits 20*s.*

Whether the justices made an ill use of the power given
them by the statute of the 3rd and 4th of King William, I
will not determine; but the parliament thought proper afterwards to abridge it; for by the 9th of George I.[1] the justices
are forbidden, " To make any order for the relief of a poor
person, till oath is first made of a reasonable cause; and that
application hath been made to the parishioners at the vestry,
or to two officers, and that relief hath been refused.   Nor
can the justice then give his order, till he hath summoned
the overseer to show cause why relief should not be given."

By the same statute, " Those persons to whom the justices
order relief, are to be registered in the parish books, as long
only as the cause of the relief continues.   Nor shall any
parish officer be allowed any money given to the unregistered
poor, unless on the most urgent occasion.   The penalty for
charging such money to the parish account is 5*l.*   The conviction is to be before two justices."

Lastly, That the parish may in all possible cases be relieved from the burden of the poor, whereas the statute of
Elizabeth obliges the father, mother, &c., and children, if
able, to relieve their poor children and parents; so, by the
5th of George I.,[2] it is provided, " That where any wife or
child shall be left by the husband or parents a charge to any
parish, the churchwardens or overseers may, by the order of
two justices, seize so much of the goods and chattels, and
receive so much of the annual rents and profits of the lands
and tenements of such husband or parent, as the justices shall

[1] Chap. xxx. sect. 2.   [2] Chap. viii.

order towards the discharge of the parish; and the sessions may empower the churchwardens and overseers, to dispose thereof, for the providing for the wife, and bringing up the children, &c."

Such is the law that relates immediately to the maintenance of the impotent poor; a law so very ample in its provision, so strongly fortified with enforcing powers, and so cautiously limited with all proper restraints, that, at first sight, it appears sufficiently adequate to every purpose for which it was intended, but experience hath convinced us of the contrary.

And here I am well aware of the delicate dilemma to which I may seem reduced; since how shall I presume to suppose any defects in a law, which the legislature seems to have laboured with such incessant diligence? but I am not absolutely driven to this disagreeable necessity, as the fault may so fairly be imputed to the non-execution of the law; and, indeed, to the ill-execution of the statute of Elizabeth, my Lord Chief Justice Hale chiefly imputes the imperfect provision for the poor in his time.

Sir Josiah Child, it is true, speaks more boldly, and charges the defects on the laws themselves: one general position, however, which he lays down, *That there never was a good law made, that was not well executed,* is surely very questionable. So therefore must be his opinion, if founded on that maxim; and this opinion, perhaps, he would have changed, had he lived to see the latter constitutions on this head.

But whatever defects there may be in the laws, or in the execution of them, I much doubt whether either of these great men hath found the means of curing them. And this I am the more forward to say, as the legislature, by a total neglect of *both* their schemes, seems to give sufficient countenance to my assertion.

In a matter then of so much difficulty, as well as so great importance, how shall I venture to deliver my own opinion? Such, indeed, is the difficulty and importance of this question, that Sir Josiah Child thinks, "If a whole session of

parliament were employed on this single concern, it would
be time spent as much to the glory of God, and good of this
nation, as in any thing that noble and worthy patriots of
their country can be engaged in."

However, under the protection of the candid, and with
deference to the learned reader, I will enter on this subject,
in which, I think, I may with modesty say I have had some
experience; and in which I can with truth declare I have
employed no little time. If any gentleman who hath had
more experience, hath more duly considered the matter, or
whose superior abilities enable him to form a better judgment, shall think proper to improve my endeavours, he hath
my ready consent. Provided the end be effected, I shall be
contented with the honour of my share (however inconsiderable) in the means. Nay, should my labours be attended only
with neglect and contempt, I think I have learned (for I am
a pretty good historian) to bear such misfortunes without
much repining.

By THE POOR, then, I understand such persons as have no
estate of their own to support them, without industry; nor
any profession or trade, by which, with industry, they may
be capable of gaining a comfortable subsistence.

This class of people may be considered under these three
divisions:

First. Such poor as are unable to work.

Secondly, Such as are able and willing to work.

Thirdly, Such as are able to work, but not willing.

As to the first of these, they are but few. An utter incapacity to work must arise from some defect, occasioned
either by nature or accident. Natural incapacities are
greatly the most (perhaps the only) considerable ones; for
as to accidental maims, how very rarely do they happen, and,
I must add, how very nobly are they provided for, when they
do happen! Again, as to natural incapacities, they are but
few, unless those two general circumstances, one of which
must, and the other may befall all men; I mean the extremes
of youth and age; for, besides these, the number of persons
who really labour under an utter incapacity of work will, on

a just inspection, be found so trifling, that two of the London
hospitals might contain them all. The reader will be pleased
to observe, I say of those who *really labour, &c.,* for he is
much deceived who computes the number of objects in the
nation from the great number which he daily sees in the
streets of London. Among whom I myself have discovered
some notorious cheats, and my good friend, Mr. Welch, the
worthy high constable of Holborn division, many more.
Nothing, as I have been well informed, is more common
among these wretches, than for the lame, when provoked, to
use their crutches as weapons instead of supporters; and for
the blind, if they should hear the beadle at their heels, to
outrun the dogs which guided them before. As to diseases,
to which human nature is universally liable, they sometimes
(though very rarely, for health is the happy portion of poverty) befall the poor; and at all such times they are certainly
objects of charity, and entitled, by the law of God, to relief
from the rich.

Upon the whole, this first class of the poor is so truly inconsiderable in number, and to provide for them in the most
ample and liberal manner would be so very easy to the public;
to support and cherish them, and to relieve their wants, is
a duty so positively commanded by our Saviour, and is withal
so agreeable and delightful in itself, affording the most desirable object to the strong passion of pity; nay, and in the
opinion of some, to pride and vanity also; that I am firmly
persuaded it might be safely left to voluntary charity, unen-
forced by any compulsive law. And if any man will profess
so little knowledge of human nature, and so mean and unjust an opinion of the Christianity, I might say the humanity,
of his country, as to affect a contrary opinion, notwithstanding all I have said, let him answer the following instance,
which may be called an argument *à posteriori,* for the truth
of my assertion. Such, I think, is the present bounty to
beggars; for, at a time when every man knows the vast tax
which is raised for the support of the poor, and when all
men of property must feel their contributions to this tax,
mankind are so forward to relieve the appearance of distress

in their fellow-creatures, that every beggar, who can but moderately well personate misery, is sure to find relief and encouragement; and this, though the giver must have great reason to doubt the reality of the distress, and when he can scarce be ignorant that his bounty is illegal,[1] and that he is encouraging a nuisance. What then must be the case, when there should be no such tax, nor any such contribution; and when, by relieving a known and certain object of charity, every good man must be assured, that he is not only doing an act which the law allows, but which Christianity and humanity too exact of him.

However, if there be any person who is yet unwilling to trust the poor to voluntary charity, or if it should be objected, that there is no reason to lay the whole burden on the worthier part of mankind, and to excuse the covetous rich; and that a tax is therefore necessary to force open the purses of these latter; let there be a tax then, and a very inconsiderable one would effectually supply the purpose.[2]

I come now to consider the second class. These are in reason, though not in fact, equally objects of the regard of the compassionate man, and much more worthy the care of the politician; and yet, without his care, they will be in a much worse condition than the others; for they have none of those incitements of pity which fill the pockets of the artful beggar, and procure relief for the blind, the lame, and other visible objects of compassion; such therefore, without a law, and without an honest and sensible execution of that law, must languish under, and often perish with want. A melancholy and dreadful reflection! and the more so, as they are capable of being made not only happy in themselves, but highly useful to the service of the community.

[1] This was forbidden by many statutes, and by the act of 27 Henry VIII. every person giving any money in alms, but to the common boxes and common gatherings in every parish, forfeits twelve times as much as he gives.

[2] The reader is desired to consider the author here as speaking only of the impotent poor, and as hoping that some effectual means may be found out of procuring work, and consequently maintenance, for the able and industrious.

To provide for these seems, as I have said, to have been the chief design of the statute of Elizabeth, as well as of several laws enacted since; and that this design hath hitherto failed, may possibly have arisen from one single mistake, but a mistake which must be fatal, as it is an error in the first concoction. The mistake I point at is, that the legislature have left the whole work to the overseers. They have rather told them what they are to do (viz. to employ the industrious poor) than how they shall do it. It is true, the original act directs them, by a parochial tax, to raise a convenient stock of flax, hemp, wool, thread, iron, and other ware and stuff to set the poor to work. A direction so general and imperfect, that it can be no wonder, considering what sort of men the overseers of the poor have been, that it should never have been carried into execution.

To say the truth, this affair of finding an universal employment for the industrious poor, is of great difficulty, and requires talents not very bountifully scattered by Nature among the whole human species. And yet, difficult as it is, it is not, I hope, impracticable, seeing that it is of such infinite concern to the good of the community. Hands for the work are already supposed, and surely trade and manufactures are not come to so low an ebb, that we should not be able to find work for the hands. The method of adapting only seems to be wanting. And though this may not be easy to discover, it is a task surely not above the reach of the British Parliament, when they shall think proper to apply themselves to it.

Nor will it, I hope, be construed presumption in me to say, that I have myself thought of a plan for this purpose, which I am ready to produce, when I shall have any reason to see the least glimpse of hope that my labour in drawing it out at length would not be absolutely and certainly thrown away.

The last and much the most numerous class of poor, are those who are able to work and not willing. This likewise hath fallen under the eye of the legislature, and provisions have been made concerning it; which, if in themselves efficacious, have at least failed of producing any good effect, from a total neglect in the execution.

By the 43 Eliz. the churchwardens and overseers, or greater part of them, with the consent of two justices, shall take order for the setting to work the children of all such parents as they shall think not able to maintain them; as also, all such married or unmarried persons, as shall have no means to maintain themselves, nor any ordinary trade or calling whereby to get their living.

Besides this power of compelling the poor to work, the legislature hath likewise compelled them to become, 1. Apprentices; and, 2. Servants. We have already seen the power of the overseers, with the assistance of the justices, to put poor children apprentices; and likewise to oblige their masters to receive them. And long before, a compulsion was enacted [1] on poor persons to become apprentices; so that any householder, having and using half a plough-land in tillage, may compel any poor person under twenty-one, and unmarried, to serve as an apprentice in husbandry, or in any other kind of art, mystery, or science (before expressed in the act [2]) ; and if such person, being so required, refuse to become an apprentice, one justice of peace may compel him, or commit him to prison, there to remain till he will be bound.

Secondly, The poor are obliged to become servants.

By the 5th of Eliz. [3] it is enacted, " That every person being unmarried, and every other person under the age of thirty, who hath been brought up in any of the sciences, &c., of clothiers, woollen cloth weavers, tuckers, fullers, clothworkers, shearmen, dyers, hosiers, tailors, shoemakers, tanners, pewterers, bakers, brewers, glovers, cutlers, smiths, farriers, curriers, saddlers, spurriers, tanners, tappers, hatmakers or feltmakers, butchers, cooks, or millers, or who hath exercised any of these trades by the space of three years or more; and not having in lands, rents, &c., an estate of 40s. clear yearly value, freehold, nor being worth in goods 10l. and so allowed by two justices of the county, where he hath most

---

[1] 5 Eliz. c. iv. sect. 35.   [2] Viz. every trade then used.

[3] Chap. iv. sect. 4.

commonly inhabited, or by the mayor, &c., nor being retained with any person in husbandry, nor retained in any of the above sciences, or in any other art or science; nor lawfully retained in household, or in any office, with any nobleman, gentleman, or others; nor having a convenient farm, or other holding in tillage, whereupon he may lawfully employ his labour, during the time that he shall continue unmarried, or under the age of thirty, upon request made by any person using the art of mystery, wherein the person so required hath been exercised as aforesaid, shall be retained.

" And every person between the age of twelve and sixty not being lawfully retained in the several services mentioned in the statute,[1] nor being a gentleman born, or a scholar in either university, or in any school, nor having an estate or freehold of 40*s*. per annum value, nor being worth in goods 10*l*. nor being heir to 10*l*. per annum, or 40*l*. in goods; nor being a necessary or convenient servant lawfully retained; nor having a convenient farm, or holding, nor otherwise lawfully retained, shall be compelled to be retained to serve in husbandry, by the year, with any person using husbandry within the same shire.

" Every such person refusing to serve upon request, or covenanting to serve, and not serving; or departing from his service before the end of his term, unless for some reasonable cause to be allowed before a justice of the peace, mayor, &c., or departing at the end of his term without a quarter's warning given before two witnesses, may be committed by two justices of the peace to prison, there to remain without bail or mainprize, till he shall become bound to his master, &c., to serve, &c.[2]

" Nor shall any master in any of the arts and sciences aforesaid, retain a servant for less than a year;[3] nor shall any master put away a servant retained by this act within his term, nor at the end of the term without a quarter's warning, under the penalty of 40*s*.[4]

" Artificers, &c., are compellable by a justice of the peace,

---

[1] Chap. iv. sect. 7.   [2] Chap. iv. sect. 5, 6, 9.
[3] Ib. sect. 3.   [4] Ib. sect. 5, 6, 8.

or the constable or other head officer of a township, to
serve in the time of hay or corn harvest. The penalty of
disobedience is imprisonment in the stocks by the space of
two days and one night.[1]

"Women between the ages of twelve and forty, may be
obliged, by two justices, to enter into service by the year,
week, or day; or may be committed *quousque*."[2]

The legislature having thus appointed what persons shall
serve, have gone farther, and have directed a method of
ascertaining how they shall serve; for which use principally
is that excellent constitution of 5 Elizabeth,[3] "That the
justices of the peace, wih the sheriff of the county, if he
conveniently may, the mayor, &c., in towns corporate, shall
yearly, within six weeks of Easter, assemble together, and
with the assistance of such discreet persons as they shall
think proper to call to them, and respecting the plenty or
scarcity of the time, and other circumstances, shall within
the limits of their commission, rate and appoint the wages
of artificers, labourers, &c., by the year, month, week, or
day, with or without meat and drink." Then the statute
enumerates several particulars, in the most explicit manner,
and concludes with these general words: "And for any other
kind of reasonable labour and service."

"These rates are appointed to be engrossed in parchment,
and are certified into chancery, before the 12th day of July;
and before the first day of September, several printed
proclamations, containing the rates, and a command to all
persons to observe them, are to be sent to the sheriff and
justices, and to the mayor, &c. These proclamations are to
be entered on record with the clerk of the peace, to be fixed
up in the market-towns, and to be publicly proclaimed in all
the markets till Michaelmas.[4]

"And if any person, after the said proclamations shall be
so sent down and published, shall, by any secret ways or
means, directly or indirectly retain or keep any servant,
workman, or labourer, or shall give any greater wages, or

[1] Ib. sect. 28.   [2] Ib. sect. 24.
[3] Ib. sect. 15.   [4] Chap. iv. sect. 16.

other commodity, contrary to the true intent of the statute, or contrary to the rates assessed, he shall forfeit 5*l*. and be imprisoned by the space of ten days.[1]

" And every person who is retained, or takes any wages contrary to the statute, shall be imprisoned twenty-one days.[2] And every such retainer, promise, gift and payment, or writing and bond for that purpose, are made absolutely void.

" Every justice of peace, or chief officer, who shall be absent at the rating of wages, unless the justices shall allow the reasonable cause of his absence, forfeits 10*l*." [3]

That this statute may, from time to time, be carefully and diligently put in execution, " The justices are appointed to meet twice a year, to make a special and diligent inquiry of the branches and articles of this statute, and of the good execution of the same, and severely to correct and punish any defaults; for which service they are allowed five shillings per day." [4] No inconsiderable allowance at that time.

But all this care of the legislature proved, it seems, ineffectual; for forty years after the making of this statute we find the parliament complaining, " That the said act had not, according to the true meaning thereof, been duly put in execution; and that the rates of wages for poor artificers, labourers, and other persons, had not been rated and proportioned according to the politic intention of the said act." [5] A neglect which seems to have been occasioned by some doubts raised in Westminster Hall, concerning the persons who were the subjects of this law. For the clearing therefore any such doubt, this subsequent statute gives the justice an express power "to rate the wages of any labourers, weavers, spinsters, and workmen or workwomen whatsoever, either working by the day, week, month, year, or taking any work at any person's hands whatsoever, to be done by the great or otherwise." [6]

---

[1] Ib. sect. 18.
[2] Ib. sect. 19, 20.
[3] Ib. sect. 17.
[4] Chap. iv. sect. 37, 38.
[5] Preamble to 1 Jac. c. vi.
[6] Ib. sect. 3.

And to render the execution of this law the more easy, the statute of James I. enacts, 1. " That in all counties where general sessions are kept in several divisions, the rating wages at such respective general sessions shall be as effectual within the division, as if they had been rated at the grand general session." [1]

2. The method of certifying the rates in chancery, appearing, I apprehend, too troublesome and tedious, " such certificate is made no longer necessary, but the rates being assessed and engrossed in parchment, under the hands and seals of the justices, the sheriff, or chief officer, of towns corporate, may immediately proclaim the same." [2]

And whereas wool is the great staple commodity of this kingdom, and the woollen trade its principal manufacture, the parliament have given particular attention to the wages of artificers in this trade.

For, 1. By the statute of James I, [3] " No clothier, being a justice of the peace in any precinct or liberty, shall be a rater of wages for any artisan depending upon the making of cloth."

2. " Clothiers not paying so much wages to their workmen or workwomen, as are rated by the justices, forfeit 10*s.* for every offence." [4]

By a late statute, [5] " All persons anywise concerned in employing any labourers in the woollen manufactory are required to pay the full wages or price agreed on, in money, . and not in goods, truck, or otherwise; nor shall they make any deduction from such wages or price, on account of any goods sold or delivered previous to such agreement. And all such wages are to be levied, on conviction, before two justices, by distress; and for want of distress, the party is to be committed for six months, or until full satisfaction is made to the party complaining. Besides which the clothier forfeits the sum of 100*l.*" [6]

4. By the same statute, " All contracts, byelaws, &c., made

[1] Ib. sect. 5.   [2] Ib. c. vi. sect. 6.
[3] Preamble to 1 Jac. sect. 7.   [4] Ib. sect. 7.
[5] 12 Geo. I. c. xxxiv. sect. 3.   [6] Ib. sect. 4.

in unlawful clubs, by persons brought up in, or exercising the art of, a wool-comber or weaver, for regulating the said trade, settling the prices of goods, advancing wages, or lessening the hours of work, are declared to be illegal and void; and any person concerned in the woollen manufactures, who shall knowingly be concerned in such contract, bye-law, &c., or shall attempt to put it in execution, shall, upon conviction before two justices, suffer three months imprisonment." [1]

But long before this act, a general law was made,[2] to punish all conspiracies for raising wages, limiting hours of work, &c., among artificers, workmen, and labourers; and if such conspiracy was to extend to a general advance of wages all over the kingdom, any insurrection of a number of persons in consequence of it, would be an overt act of high treason.

From this cursory view it appears, I think, that no blame lies at the door of the legislature, which hath not only given the magistrate, but even private persons, with his assistance, a power of compelling the poor to work; and, secondly, hath allotted the fullest powers, and prescribed the most effectual means for ascertaining and limiting the price of their labour.

But so very faulty and remiss hath been the execution of these laws, that an incredulous reader may almost doubt whether there are really any such existing. Particularly as to that which relates to the rating the wages of la-bourers; a law which at first, it seems, was too carelessly executed, and which hath since grown into utter neglect and disuse.

Hath this total disuse arisen, in common with the neglect of other wholesome provisions, for want of due attention to the public good? or is the execution of this law attended with any extraordinary difficulty? or, lastly, are we really grown, as Sir Josiah Child says, wiser than our forefathers, and have discovered any fault in the constitution itself;

---

[1] Ib. sect. 1. [2] 2 & 3 E. VI. c. xv.

and that to retrench the price of labour by a law is an error in policy?

This last seems to me, I own, to be very strange doctrine, and somewhat of a paradox in politics; however, as it is the sentiment of a truly wise and great man, it deserves a fair discussion. Such I will endeavour to give it; since no man is more inclined to respect the opinions of such persons, and as the revival of the law which he opposes, is, I think, absolutely necessary to the purpose I am contending for.

I will give the passage from Sir Josiah at length. It is in answer to this position, *That the dearness of wages spoils the English trade.* " Here," says he, " the author propounds the making a law to retrench the hire of poor men's labour (an honest charitable project, and well becoming an usurer!) the answer to this is easy. First, I affirm and can prove, he is mistaken in fact; for the Dutch, with whom we principally contend in trade, give generally more wages to all their manufacturers, by at least twopence in the shilling, than the English. Secondly, Wherever wages are high, universally throughout the whole world, it is an infallible evidence of the riches of that country; and wherever wages for labour run low, it is a proof of the poverty of that place. Thirdly, It is multitudes of people, and good laws, such as cause an increase of people, which principally enrich any country; and if we retrench by law the labour of our people, we drive them from us to other countries that give better rates; and so the Dutch have drained us of our seamen and woollen manufacturers, and we the French of their artificers and silk manufacturers; and many more we should, if our laws otherwise gave them fitting encouragement; of which more in due place. Fourthly, If any particular trades exact more here than in Holland, they are only such as do it by virtue of incorporations, privileges, and charters, of which the cure is easy, by an act of naturalization, and without compulsory laws. It is true our great-grandfathers did exercise such policy, of endeavouring to retrench the price of labour by a law (although they could never effect it); but that was before trade was introduced into this kingdom; we are since, with the rest of the trading world, grown wiser in this matter, and I hope shall so continue." [1]

To this I reply, 1. That the making such a law is not only an honest, but a charitable project; as it proposes, by retrenching the price of poor men's labour, to provide labour, and consequently hire for all the poor who are capable of labour. In all manufactures whatever, the lower the price of labour is, the cheaper will be the price to the consumer; and the cheaper this price is, the greater will be the consumption, and consequently the more hands employed. This is likewise a very charitable law to the poor farmer, and never more necessary than at this day, when the rents of lands are rated to the highest degree. The great hopes which the farmer hath (indeed his common relief from ruin) is of an exportation of corn. This exportation cannot be by law, unless where the corn is under such a particular price. How necessary then is it to him that the price of labour should be confined within moderate bounds, that the exportation of corn, which is of such general advantage to the kingdom, should turn, in any considerable manner, to his private profit? and what reason is there to imagine that his power of limiting wages should be executed in any dishonest or uncharitable manner? Is it not a power entrusted to all the justices of the county or division, and to the sheriff, with the assistance of grave, sober, and substantial persons, who must be sufficient judges of the matter, and who are directed to have regard to the plenty and scarcity of the times? Is it to be suspected that many persons of this kind should unite in a cruel and flagitious act, by which they would be liable to the condemnation of their own consciences, to the curses of the poor, and to be reproached by the example of all their neighbouring counties? Are not much grosser exorbitances to be feared on the other side, when the lowest artificers, husbandmen, and labourers, are made judges in their own cause; and when it is left to

[1] Preface to his Discourse on Trade.

their own discretion to exact what price they please for their labour of the poor farmer or clothier; of whom if they cannot exact an extravagant price they will fly to that alternative, which idleness often prefers, of begging or stealing? Lastly, such a restraint is very wholesome to the poor labourers themselves; of whom Sir Josiah observes,[1] " That they live better in the dearest countries for provisions than in the cheapest, and better in a dear year than in a cheap, especially in relation to the public good; for in a cheap year they will not work above two days in a week; their humour being such that they will not provide for a hard time, but just work so much and no more, as may maintain them in that mean condition to which they have been accustomed." Is it not therefore, upon this concession, demonstrable, that the poor man himself will live much better (his family certainly will) by these means? Again, many of the poor, and those the more honest and industrious, will probably gain by such a law; for, at the same time that the impudent and idle, if left to themselves, will certainly exact on their masters; the modest, the humble, and truly laborious, may often (and so I doubt not but the case is) be oppressed by them, and forced to accept a lower price for their labour than the liberality of gentlemen would allow them.

Secondly, The two assertions contained in the next paragraph both seem to me suspicious. First, that the Dutch and other nations have done all that in them lies to draw from us our seamen, and some of our manufacturers, is certainly true; and this they would do at any price; but that the Dutch do in general give more wages to their manufacturers than the English, is, I believe, not the fact. Of the manufacturers of Holland, the only considerable article which we ourselves take of them, except linen, are toys; and to this we are induced, not because the Dutch are superior to our workmen in genius and dexterity (points in which they are not greatly celebrated), but because they work much cheaper. Nor is, secondly, the immediate transition from

[1] Discourse on Trade.

trade to manufacture altogether so fair. The Dutch, it is true, are principally our rivals in trade in general, and chiefly as carriers; but not so in manufacture, particularly in the woollen manufacture. Here our chief rivals are the French, amongst whom the price of labour is known to be considerably lower than with us. To this, among other causes (for I know there are others, and some very scandalous ones,) they owe their success over us in the Levant. It is, indeed, a truth which needs no comment nor proof, that where goods are of equal value, the man who sells cheapest will have the most custom; and it is as certainly true, that he who makes up his goods in the cheapest manner can sell them so.

Thirdly, Sir Josiah asserts, " That wherever wages are high, universally throughout the world, 'tis an infallible evidence of the riches of that country: and wherever wages for labour run low, it is a proof of the poverty of that place."—If this be true, the concession will do him no service; for it will not prove, that to give high wages is the way to grow rich; since it is much more probable that riches would cause the advance of wages than that high wages should produce riches. This latter, I am sure, would appear a high solecism in private life, and I believe it is no less so in public.

Fourthly, his next assertion, *That to retrench by law the labour of our people is to drive them from us,* hath partly received an answer already. To give this argument any force, our wages must be reduced at least below the standard of other countries; which is, I think, very little to be apprehended; but, on the contrary, if the labourer should carry his demands ever so little higher, as may be reasonably expected, the consumption of many manufactures will not only be confined to our own people, but to a very few of those people.

Thus, I hope, I have given a full answer to this great man, whom I cannot dismiss without observing a manifest mistake of the question which runs through all his arguments; all that he advances concluding, indeed, only to the *quantum* of wages which shall be given for labour. He seems rather to argue against giving too little than against regulating what is to be given; so that his arguments are more proper for the consideration of the justices at their meeting for settling the rates of wages than for the consideration of the legislature in a debate concerning the expediency of the above law. To evince the expediency of which I appeal to the concurrent sense of parliament in so many different ages; for this is not only testified expressly in the above statute of Elizabeth and James, but may be fairly implied from those of Edward VI. and George I. above recited.

I have moreover, I think, demonstrated, 1. The equity of this law; and that it is as much for the service of the labourer as of his master. 2. The utility of it to trade: I shall only add the necessity of it, in order to execute the intention of the legislature, in compelling the idle to work; for is it not the same thing to have the liberty of working or not at your own pleasure, and to have the absolute nomination of the price at which you will work? the idleness of the common people in this town is, indeed, greatly to be attributed to this liberty; most of these, if they cannot exact an exorbitant price for their labour, will remain idle.   The habit of exacting on their superiors is grown universal, and the very porters expect to receive more for their work than the salaries of above half the officers of the army amount to.

I conclude then that this law is necessary to be revived (perhaps with some enlargements), and that still upon one account more; which is, to enable the magistrate clearly to distinguish the corrigible from the incorrigible in idleness; for when the price of labour is once established, all those poor who shall refuse to labour at that price, even at the command of a magistrate, may properly be deemed incorrigibly idle.

For these the legislature have, by several acts of parliament, provided a punishment, by commitment to Bridewell, either for more or less time; and a very severe punishment this is, if being confirmed in habits of idleness, and in every other vicious habit, may be esteemed so.

These houses are commonly called houses of correction, and the legislature intended them certainly for places of correction of idleness at least; for in many acts, where persons are ordered to be committed to Bridewell, it is added, *there to be kept to hard labour;* nay, in the statute of Jac. I.[1] these houses of correction are directed "to be built with a convenient backside adjoining, together with mills, turns, cards, and such like necessary implements, to set rogues and other idle people on work." Again, in the same statute, authority is given to the master or governor "To set to work such rogues, vagabonds, idle and disorderly persons, as shall be brought or sent unto the said house (being able) while they shall continue in the said house, and to punish them, by putting fetters on them, and by whipping; nor are the said rogues, &c., to have any other provision than what they shall earn by their labour."

The erection of these houses, as is usual with new institutions, did at first greatly answer the good purposes for which they were designed, insomuch that my Lord Coke observes, "That upon the making of the statute 39 Eliz. for the erection of houses of correction, and a good space after, whilst justices of peace and other officers were diligent and industrious, there was not a rogue to be seen in any part of England." And again he prophesies, that "from the erection of these houses we shall have neither beggar nor idle person in the commonwealth." [2]

But this great man was a much better lawyer than he was a prophet; for whatever these houses were designed to be, or whatever they at first were, the fact is, that they are at present, in general, no other than schools of vice, seminaries of idleness, and common sewers of nastiness and disease. As to the power of whipping, which the act of James I. vests in the governor, that, I believe, is very seldom used; and

---

[1] Chap. iv. These houses were first begun to be erected ann. 13 Eliz., the prison for idleness being, before that time, the stocks. In the 11th year of Henry VII. vagabonds, beggars, &c., are ordered to be set three days and three nights in the stocks.

[2] 2 Inst. 729.

perhaps when it is, not properly applied. And the justice in very few instances (in none of idleness) hath any power of ordering such punishment.[1]

And with regard to work, the intention of the law is, I apprehend, as totally frustrated. Insomuch, that they must be very lazy persons indeed who can esteem the labour imposed in any of these houses as a punishment. In some, I am told, there is not any provision made for work. In that of Middlesex in particular the governor hath confessed to me, that he hath had no work to employ his prisoners, and hath urged as a reason, that having generally great numbers of most desperate felons under his charge, who, notwithstanding his utmost care, will sometimes get access to his other prisoners, he dares not trust those who are committed to hard labour with any heavy or sharp instruments of work, lest they should be converted into weapons by the felons.

What good consequence then can arise from sending idle and disorderly persons to a place where they are neither to be corrected nor employed; and where, with the conversation of many as bad, and sometimes worse than themselves, they are sure to be improved in the knowledge, and confirmed in the practice, of iniquity? Can it be conceived that such persons will not come out of these houses much more idle and disorderly than they went in? The truth of this I have often experienced in the behaviour of the wretches brought before me; the most impudent and flagitious of whom have always been such as have been before acquainted with the discipline of Bridewell; a commitment to which place, though it often causes great horror and lamentation in the novice, is usually treated with ridicule and contempt by those who have already been there.

For this reason, I believe, many of the worthiest magistrates have, to the utmost of their power, declined a rigorous execution of the laws for the punishment of idleness, thinking that a severe reprimand might more probably work the conversion of such persons than the committing

---

[1] By the last vagabond act, which repeals all the former, rogues and vagabonds are to be whipt, or sent to the house of correction.

them to Bridewell.   This I am sure may with great certainty
be concluded, that the milder method is less liable to render
what is bad worse, and to complete the destruction of the
offender.

But this is a way of acting, however worthy be the motive,
which is sometimes more justifiable to a man's own conscience
than it would be in the court of King's Bench, which requires
the magistrate to execute the laws entrusted to his care, and
in the manner which those laws prescribe.   And besides the
indecency of showing a disregard to the laws in being, nothing
surely can be more improper than to suffer the idleness of
the poor, the cause of so much evil to society, to go entirely unpunished.

And yet should the magistrate do his duty as he is required,
will the intent and purpose of the legislature be answered?
The parliament was, indeed, too wise to punish idleness barely
by confinement.   Labour is the true and proper punishment
of idleness, for the same reason which the excellent Dr. Swift
gives why death is the proper punishment of cowardice.
Where then is the remedy?   Is it to enforce the execution of
the law as it now stands, and to reform the present conduct
of the several Bridewells?   This would, I believe, be as
difficult a work as the cleansing the Augean stables of old;
and would require as extraordinary a degree of political as
that did of natural strength to accomplish it.   In truth, the
case here is the same as with the overseers before; the trust
is too great for the person on whom it devolves; and though
these houses are in some measure under the inspection of the
justices of peace, yet this in the statute is recommended in
too general a manner to their care, to expect any good fruits
from it.   As " to the true and faithful account which they are
to yield to the justices, at the sessions, of the persons in
their custody," this is at present little more than matter of
form; nor can it be expected to be any other in the hurry
of a public sessions, and when the stench arising from the
prisoners is so intolerable that it is difficult to get any
gentleman to attend the court at that time.   In the last
vagrant act indeed two justices are appointed twice, or oftener,

every year to examine into the state and nature of houses of correction, &c., yet, as it gives them no power but of reporting to the sessions, I believe it hath not produced any good effect; for the business of the sessions is so complicated and various that it happens, as in all cases where men have too much to do, that they do little or nothing effectually.   Perhaps, indeed, if two or more justices of the peace were appointed to meet once every month at some convenient place, as near as possible to the Bridewell, there to summon the governor before them, to examine the accounts of his stock and implements for work, and to make such orders (under what restrictions the parliament shall think proper) as to such justices as shall seem requisite; this might afford a palliative at least. In short, the great cure for idleness is labour; and this is its only proper punishment; nor should it ever be in the power of the idle person to commute this punishment for any other.

In the reign of Edward VI.[1] a most severe law indeed was made for the punishment of idleness.—" If any person," says the statute, " shall bring to two justices of peace any runagate servant, or any other which liveth idly and loiteringly by the space of three days, the said justices shall cause the said idle and loitering servant or vagabond to be marked with a hot iron on the breast with the letter V, and adjudge him to be slave to the same person that brought and presented him, to have to him, his executors and assigns, for two years, who shall take the said slave, and give him bread, water, or small drink, and refuse meat, and cause him to work by beating, chaining, or otherwise, in such work and labour as he shall put him, be it never so vile.   And if such slave absent himself from his master within the term, by the space of fourteen days, he shall be adjudged by two justices of peace to be marked on the forehead, or the ball of the cheek, with a hot iron, with the sign of an S, and shall be adjudged to be slave to his said master for ever; and, if the said slave shall run away a second time, he shall be adjudged a felon."

This statute lived no longer than two years, indeed it deserved no longer a date; for it was cruel, unconstitu-

[1] 1 Edward VI. 13 Rep.

tional, and rather resembling the cruel temper of a Draco than the mild spirit of the English law. But, *est modus;* there is a difference between making men slaves and felons, and compelling them to be subjects; in short, between throwing the reigns on the neck of idleness, and riding it with spurs of iron.

Thus have I endeavoured to give the reader a general idea of the laws which relate to this single point of employing the poor; and, as well as I am able to discern, of their defects, and the reasons of those defects. I have likewise given some hints for the cure, and have presumed to offer a plan, which, in my humble opinion, would effectually answer every purpose desired.

But till this plan shall be produced; or (which is more to be expected) till some man of greater abilities, as well as of greater authority, shall offer some new regulation for this purpose; something at least ought to be done to strengthen the laws already made, and to enforce their execution. The matter is of the highest concern, and imports us not only as we are good men and good Christians, but as we are good Englishmen; since not only preserving the poor from the highest degrees of wretchedness, but the making them useful subjects, is the thing proposed: " A work," says Sir Josiah Child,[1] " which would redound some hundred of thousands per annum to the public advantage." Lastly, it is of the utmost importance to that point which is the subject matter of this treatise, for which reason I have thought myself obliged to give it a full consideration. " The want of a due provision," says Lord Hale,[2] for education and relief of the poor in a way of industry, is that which fills the gaols with malefactors, and fills the kingdom with idle and unprofitable persons, that consume the stock of the kingdom without improving it, and that will daily increase, even to a desolation, in time. And this error in the first concoction is never remediable but by gibbets and whipping."

[1] Page 88.
[2] At the end of his discourse touching the relief of the poor.

In serious truth, if proper care should be taken to provide for the present poor, and to prevent their increase by laying some effectual restraints on the extravagance of the lower sort of people, the remaining part of this treatise would be rendered of little consequence; since few persons, I believe, have made their exits at Tyburn who have not owed their fate to some of the causes before mentioned. But as I am not too sanguine in my expectations on this head, I shall now proceed to consider of some methods to obviate the frequency of robberies, which, if less efficacious, are, perhaps, much easier than those already proposed. And if we will not remove the temptation, at least we ought to take away all encouragement to robbery.

SECTION V.

OF THE PUNISHMENT OF RECEIVERS OF STOLEN GOODS.

Now one great encouragement to theft of all kinds is the ease and safety with which stolen goods may be disposed of. It is a very old and vulgar, but a very true saying, " That if there were no receivers there would be no thieves." Indeed could not the thief find a market for his goods, there would be an absolute end of several kinds of thefts; such as shoplifting, burglary, &c., the objects of which are generally goods and not money. Nay, robberies on the highway would so seldom answer the purpose of the adventurer, that very few would think it worth their while to risk so much with such small expectations.

But at present, instead of meeting with any such discouragement, the thief disposes of his goods with almost as much safety as the honestest tradesman: for first, if he hath made a booty of any value, he is almost sure of seeing it advertised within a day or two, directing him *to bring the goods to a certain place where he is to receive a reward* (sometimes the full value of the booty) *and no questions asked.* This method of recovering stolen goods by the owner a very learned judge formerly declared to have been, in his opinion, a composition of felony. And surely if this be proved to be carried into execution, I think it must amount to a full conviction of that crime. But, indeed, such advertisements are in themselves so very scandalous, and of such pernicious consequence, that if men are not ashamed to own they prefer an old watch or a diamond ring to the good of society, it is pity some effectual law was not contrived to prevent their giving this public countenance to robbery for the future.

But if the person robbed should prove either too honest, or too obstinate, to take this method of recovering his goods, the thief is under no difficulty in turning them into money. Among the great number of brokers and pawnbrokers several are to be found, who are always ready to receive a gold watch at an easy rate, and where no questions are asked, or at least, where no answer is expected but such as the thief can very readily make.

Besides the clandestine dealers this way, who satisfy their consciences with telling a ragged fellow, or wench, that *they hope* they came honestly by silver, and gold, and diamonds; there are others who scorn such pitiful subterfuges, who engage openly with the thieves, and who have warehouses filled with stolen goods only. Among the Jews, who live in a certain place in the city, there have been, and perhaps still are, some notable dealers this way, who, in an almost public manner, have carried on a trade for many years with Rotterdam, where they have their warehouses and factors, and whither they export their goods with prodigious profit, and as prodigious impunity. And all this appeared very plainly last winter in the examination of one Cadosa, a Jew, in the presence of the last excellent Duke of Richmond, and many other noblemen and magistrates.

What then shall we say? Is not this mischief worthy of some remedy, or is it not capable of it? The noble duke (one of the worthiest of magistrates, as well as of the best of men) thought otherwise, as would have appeared, had his valuable life, for the good of mankind, been prolonged.

Certain it is, that the law, as it now stands, is ineffectual to cure the evil. Let us see therefore, if possible, where the defect lies.

At the common law, any one might lawfully (says Lord Hale) have received his own goods from the felon who stole them.[1]   But, if he had received them upon agreement not to prosecute, or to prosecute faintly, this would have been theftbote, punishable by imprisonment and ransom.

But in neither of the foregoing cases would the receiver of the goods have become an accessory to the felon. So if one man had bought another's goods of the thief, though he had known them to be stolen, if he had given the just value for them, he would not have become an accessory.[2] But if he had bought them at an undervalue, this, Sir Richard Hyde held, would have made him an accessory. My Lord Hale differs from his opinion, and his reason to some readers may seem a pleasant one: *For if there be any odds* (says he), *he that gives more, benefits the felon more than he that gives less than value.*   However, this, his lordship thinks, may be a misdemeanour punishable by fine and imprisonment; but that the bare receiving of goods, knowing them to be stolen, makes not an accessory.

So says the great Lord Hale, and so indeed was the law; though the judges seem not to have been unanimous in their opinion. In the book of Assizes,[3] Scrope is said to have held otherwise; and though Shard there quashed an appeal of felony for receiving stolen goods only, yet I cannot help observing, that the reporter of the case hath left a note of astonishment at the judgment of the court. This, says he, was wonderful! and wonderful surely it is, if he who receives, relieves, comforts, or assists a felon, shall be an accessory, that he shall not be so, who knowingly

[1] Hist. P. C. vol. i. p. 546, 619, ib.   [2] Hist. P. C. ubi supra.
[3] 27 Assiz. 69.

buys the goods of the felon; which is generally, I believe, the strongest relief, comfort, and assistance which can be given him, and without the hope and expectation of which, he would never have committed the theft or robbery.

It is unnecessary, however, to enter farther into this controversy; since it is now expressly declared by statute,[1] " That the receivers of stolen goods, knowing them to be stolen, shall be deemed accessories after the fact."

But this statute, though it removed the former absurdity of the law, was not sufficient to remedy the evil; there yet remaining many difficulties in bringing these pernicious miscreants to justice, consistent with legal rules.   For,

1. As the offence of the accessory is dependent on that of the principal, he could not be tried or outlawed, till after the conviction of attainder of the principal; so that however strong evidence there might be against the receiver, he was still safe, unless the thief could be apprehended.

2. If the thief on his trial should be acquitted, as often happens through some defect of evidence in the most notorious cases, the receiver, being only an accessory, though he hath confessed his crime, or though the most undeniable evidence could be brought against him, must be acquitted likewise.

3. In petty larceny there can be no such accessory:[2] for though the statute says, that a receiver of stolen goods, knowing, &c., shall be an accessory after the fact, that is legally understood to mean only in cases where such accessory may be by law; and that is confined to such felonies as are to receive judgment of death, or to have the benefit of clergy.   Now, for petty larceny which is the stealing goods of less value than a shilling, the punishment at common law is whipping; and this was properly enough considered as too trifling an offence to extend the guilt to criminals in a second degree.   But since juries have taken upon them to consider the value of goods as immaterial, and

---

[1] 3 and 4 W. and M. c. ix.
[2] Cro. Eliz. 750.   Hale's Hist. vol. i. p. 530, 618.

to find upon their oaths, that what is proved to be worth several shillings, and sometimes several pounds, is of the value of tenpence, this is become a matter of more consequence.   For instance, if a pickpocket steal several handkerchiefs, or other things, to the value of twenty shillings, and the receiver of these, knowing them to be stolen, is discovered, and both are indicted, the one as principal, the other as accessory, as they must be; if the jury convict the principal, and find the goods to be of as high value as a shilling, he must receive judgment of death; whereas, by finding the goods (which they do upon their oaths) to be of the value of tenpence, the thief is ordinarily sentenced to be whipped, and returns immediately to his trade of picking pockets, and the accessory is of course discharged, and of course returns to his trade of receiving the booty.   Thus the jury are perjured, the public highly injured, and two excellent acts of parliament defeated, that two miscreants may laugh at their prosecutors, and at the law.

The two former of these defects are indeed remedied by a later statute,[1] which enacts, " That the buyers and receivers of stolen goods, knowing them to be stolen, may be prosecuted for a misdemeanour, and punished by fine and imprisonment, though the principal felon be not before convicted of felony."

This last statute is again repeated in the 5th of Queen Anne;[2] and there the power of the court to punish in the case of the misdemeanor, is farther increased to any other corporal punishment, which the court shall think fit to inflict, instead of fine and imprisonment; and, in the case of the felony, the accessory is to receive judgment of death; but the benefit of clergy is not taken away.   Lastly, by the statute of George II.[3] the receivers of stolen goods, knowing, &c., are to be transported for fourteen years.   And by the same statute, every person taking money or reward, directly or indirectly, under pretence or upon account of helping any to stolen goods, unless such person apprehend and bring

[1] 3 and 4 W. and M. c. ix.   [2] Chap. xxxi.

[3] Chap. xi.

to his trial the felon, and give evidence against him, is made guilty of felony without benefit of clergy.

And thus stands the law at this day: which, notwithstanding the repeated endeavours of the legislature, experience shows us, is incapable of removing this deplorable evil from society.

The principal defect seems, to me, to lie in the extreme difficulty of convicting the offender; for,

1. Where the thief can be taken, you are not at liberty to prosecute for the misdemeanour.

2. The thief himself, who must be convicted before the accessory is to be tried, cannot be a witness.

3. Without such evidence it is very difficult to convict of the knowledge that the goods were stolen: which, in this case, can appear from circumstances only. Such are principally, first, Buying goods of value, of persons very unlikely to be the lawful proprietors. Secondly, Buying them for much less than their real value. Thirdly, Buying them, or selling them again, in a clandestine manner, concealing them, &c. None of these are commonly liable to be proved; and I have known a man acquitted, where most of these circumstances have appeared against him.

What then is to be done, to extirpate this stubborn mischief? To prove the pernicious consequence of which, I need, I think, only appeal to the sense of parliament, testified in so many repeated acts, and very strongly expressed in their preambles.

First, Might it not be proper to put an effectual stop to the present scandalous method of compounding felony by public advertisements in the newspapers? Might not the inserting such advertisements be rendered highly criminal in the authors of them, and in the printers themselves, unless they discover such authors?

Secondly, Is it impossible to find any means of regulating brokers and pawnbrokers? if so, what arguments are there against extirpating entirely a set of miscreants, which, like other vermin, harbour only about the poor, and grow fat by sucking their blood?

Thirdly, Why should not the receiving stolen goods, knowing them to be stolen, be made an original offence? by which means the thief, who is often a paltry offender in comparison of the receiver, and sometimes his pupil, might, in little felonies, be made a witness against him; for thus the trial of the receiver would in no case depend on the trial or conviction of the thief.

Fourthly, Why may not the bare buying or taking to pawn stolen goods, above a certain value, be made evidence of receiving with knowledge, &c., unless the goods were bought in market overt (no broker's or pawnbroker's shop to be reputed such market overt), or unless the defendant could prove, by a credible witness to the transaction, that he had good cause to regard the seller or pawner of the goods to be the real owner. If twenty shillings was the value limited, it would answer all the purposes contended for; and would in nowise interfere with the honest trade (if indeed it ever be so) between the pawnbroker and the poor.

If none of these methods be thought possible or proper, I hope better will be found out. Something ought to be done, to put an end to the present practice, of which I daily see the most pernicious consequences; many of the younger thieves appearing plainly to be taught, encouraged, and employed by the receivers.

SECTION VI.

OF LAWS RELATING TO VAGABONDS.

THE other great encouragement to robbery, besides the certain means of finding a market for the booty, is the probability of escaping punishment.

First, then, the robber hath great hopes of being undiscovered; and this is one principal reason why robberies are more frequent in this town, and in its neighbourhood, than in the remoter parts of the kingdom.

Whoever indeed considers the cities of London and Westminster, with the late vast addition of their suburbs, the great irregularity of their buildings, the immense number of lanes, alleys, courts, and bye-places; must think, that, had they been intended for the very purpose of concealment, they could scarce have been better contrived. Upon such a view the whole appears as a vast wood or forest, in which a thief may harbour with as great security as wild beasts do in the deserts of Africa or Arabia; for, by *wandering* from one part to another, and often shifting his quarters, he may almost avoid the possibility of being discovered.

Here, according to the method I have hitherto pursued, I will consider, what remedy our laws have applied to this evil, namely, the *wandering* of the poor, and whether and wherein these remedies appear defective.

There is no part of our ancient constitution more admirable than that which has calculated to prevent the concealment of thieves and robbers. The original of this institution is given to Alfred, at the end of his wars with the Danes, when the English were very much debauched by the example of those barbarians, and betook themselves to all manner of licentiousness and rapine. These evils were encouraged, as the historians say, by the vagabond state of the offenders, who, having no settled place of abode, upon committing any offence, shifted their quarters, and went where it was difficult to discover them. To remedy this mischief, therefore, Alfred having limited the shires or counties in a better manner than before, divided them into hundreds, and these again into tithings, decennaries, or ten families.[1]

[1] " By these ten families (says the annotator to Rapin) we are not to understand ten housekeepers, but ten lords of manors, with all their vassals, tenants, labourers and slaves; who, though they did not all live under their lord's roof, were all counted part of his family. As there were no little freeholders in those times, nor for long after, ten such families must occupy a large space of ground,

Over every one of these tithings or decennaries, there was a chief, called a tithingman or burgh-holder, who had a power to call a court, and to try small offences; the greater being referred to that court, which was in like manner established over every hundred.

Every one of these heads of families were pledges to each other for the behaviour of all their family; and were likewise reciprocally pledges for each other to the hundred.

If any person was suspected of a crime, he was obliged to find security for his good behaviour out of the same hundred and tithing.   This if he could not find, he had reason to apprehend being treated with great severity; and if any accused person, either before or after his finding bail, had fled from justice, the whole tithing and hundred should pay a fine to the king.

In case of the default of appearance in a decenner, his nine pledges had one-and-thirty days to bring the delinquent forth to justice.   If this failed, then the chief of those decenners, by the vote of that and the neighbour decennaries, was to purge himself both of the guilt of the fact, and of being party to the flight of the delinquent.   And if they could not do this, then they were, by their own oaths, to acquit themselves, and to bind themselves to bring the delinquent to justice as soon as they could; and, in the meantime, to pay the damage out of the estate of the delinquent; and, if that were not sufficient, then out of their own estate.[1]

Every subject in the kingdom was registered in some tithing; only persons of the first rank had the privilege (says Mr. Rapin [2]) that their single family should make a tithing, for which they were responsible.   " All archbishops, bishops, earls, barons, and all (says Bracton) who have sok and sac,

and might well constitute a rural tithing."   But this rural tithing would be larger than the hundred itself; and the very name and office of a tithingman, continued in parishes to this day, shows that lords of manors could not be here meant.

[1] Bacon's Histor. Disc. p. 43.

[2] Dissertation on the Government of the Anglo-Saxons.

tol and team, and these kinds of liberties, ought to have
under their FRIDBURGH, all their knights, servants, esquires;
and, if any of them prove delinquent, the lord shall bring
him to justice, or pay his fine." [1]

The master of the family was answerable for all who
fed at his board, and were of his livery, and for all his
servants of every kind, even for those who served him for
their food only, without wages. These were said to be of
his manupast; so were his guests; and if a man abode at
any house but two nights, the master of that house was
answerable for him. [2]

In a word, says Bracton, every man, as well freeman as
others, ought to belong to some frankpledge (*i. e.* to some
decenna) unless he be a traveller, or belong to the manupast
of some other; or unless he give some countervailing security
to the public, as dignity (viz. nobility) order (knighthood, or
of the clergy) or estate (viz. either freehold in land, or
personal effects, *res immobiles*) if he be a citizen.

By the laws of Edward the Confessor, every person, of
the age of twelve years, ought to be sworn in a view of
frankpledge, *That he will neither become a thief himself, nor
be anywise accessory to theft.*

This court, Britton [3] tells us, was to be holden twice a
year, which was afterwards reduced to once a year by
Magna Charta; and no man, says the Mirror, was, by an
ancient ordinance, suffered to remain in the kingdom, who
was not enrolled *in decenna,* and had freemen for his
pledges. [4]

Such was this excellent constitution, which even in
Alfred's time, when it was in its infancy, wrought so
admirable an effect, that Ingulphus says, a traveller might
have openly left a sum of money safely in the fields and
highways, and have found it safe and untouched a month
afterwards. [5] Nay, William of Malmesbury tells us, the king

---

[1] Bract. l. iii. De Corona, cap. x.
[2] Bract. ubi sup. Brit. 19. b.   [3] Brit. 36. b.
[4] Mirr. chap. i. sect. 17, and chap. v. sect. 1.
[5] Script. post Bedam, p. 87*v*.

ordered bracelets of gold to be hung up in the cross ways, as a proof of the honesty of his people, none ever offering to meddle with them.[1]

But this constitution would have been deficient, if it had only provided for the incorporating the subjects, unless it had confined them to the places where they were thus incorporated.

And therefore by the laws of Alured, or Canute, it was rendered unlawful for any of the decenners to depart from their dwelling, without the consent of their fellow-pledges; nor were they at liberty to leave the country, without the licence of the sheriff or governor of the same.[2]

And if a person, who fled from one tithing, was received in another, the tithing receiving him should answer for his deed (*i. e.* by amercement) if he was there found.[3]

"Before this order was established," says Rapine, "the meaner sort of people might shift their quarters, by reason of their obscurity, which prevented them from being taken notice of. But it was impossible for them to change their habitation, after they were obliged to bring a testimonial from their tithing, to enable them to settle and be registered in another."[4]

"Whilst this ancient constitution remained entire, such peace," says Lord Coke, "was preserved within the realm, as no injuries, homicides, robberies, thefts, riots, tumults, or other offences, were committed; so as a man, with a white wand, might safely have ridden, before the conquest, with much money about him, without any weapon, through England."[5] Nay, even in the tumultuous times of William the Conqueror, the historians tell us, there was scarce a robber to be found in the kingdom.

This view of frankpledge remained long after the conquest: for we find it twice repeated in one chapter of Magna Charta;[6] and there particularly it is said, *Fiat autem visus de frankpleg' sic videlicet* QUOD PAX NOSTRA TENEATUR.

---

[1] Ib. p. 44.
[3] Brit. ubi supra.
[5] 2 Instit. 73.

[2] Bacon, p. 44.
[4] Rapin, ubi sup.
[6] Chap. xxxiii.

Nay Bracton, who wrote after that time, and Fleta after him, speak of frankpledge as then subsisting.

The statute of Marlborough likewise, which was made the 52nd of Henry III. mentions the same court; as doth Britton, who wrote still later, in many places. And in the 17th of Edward II. an act was made called *The statute for the view of Frankpledge.*[1]

Nay, in the reign of Henry IV. we find an amercement for not coming to a view of frankpledge; and there the whole court of king's bench were of opinion, that every man, as well masters as servants, were obliged to repair to this court;[2] and though then possibly it was degenerated, and become little more than form.

But in process of time, this institution dwindled to nothing; so that Lord Coke might truly say, *Quod vera institutio illius curiæ evanuit, et velut umbra ejusdem adhuc remanet*; and a little after, speaking of the frankpledge, the *Decennarii,* and the *Decenna,* he says, " They are names continued only as shadows of antiquity."[3] Nay, this great man himself (if, after a most careful and painful perusal of all he hath writ, as well here as in his 4th Institute, and other places on the subject, I may be allowed to say so) seems to have no very clear idea concerning them; and might have fairly owned, of the original of the leet of frankpledge, what one of the sages doth of a hundred, in the book of Henry VII: " That a hundred had existed above a hundred years; and therefore, as to the true definition of a hundred, and whether it was composed of a hundred towns, or a hundred lordships, and whether it had anciently more or less jurisdiction, he frankly owned that he knew nothing of the matter."[4]

The statute of Marlborough[5] had perhaps given a fatal

---

[1] But this matter was before that transferred from the decennary court to the leets and sheriff's tourn.

[2] Hill. 3 H. IV. Pl. 19.

[3] 2 Inst. 71, 73.   [4] 8 H. VII. 3 b.

[5] Chap. xxiv. By which justices in eyre are forbidden to amerce townships, because all of twelve years old were not sworn.

blow to the true and ancient use of the view of frankpledge; of which, as Lord Coke says,[1] the sheriffs had made an ill use; for, in the 3rd year of the succeeding king,[2] we find the legislature providing against notorious felons, and such as be openly of evil fame, that they shall not be admitted to bail; and, in the 13th, the statute of Winchester entirely altered the law, and gave us a new constitution on this head.

1. By this act the whole hundred is made answerable in case of robberies.

2. In order to prevent the concealment of robbers in towns, it is enacted, 1. That the gates of all walled towns shall be shut from sun-setting to sun-rising. 2. A watch is appointed, who are to arrest all strangers. 3. No person is to lodge in the suburbs, nor in any place out of the town, unless his host will answer for him. 4. The bailiffs of towns shall make inquiry once within fifteen days at the farthest, of all persons lodged in the suburbs, &c., and of those who have received any suspicious persons.

3. To prevent the concealment of robbers without the towns, it is enacted, that the highways leading from one market-town to another shall be enlarged, and no bushes, woods, or dykes, in which felons may be concealed, shall be suffered therein.

4. Felons are to be pursued by hue and cry.

This statute, says Lord Coke, was made against a gang of rogues then called Roberdsmen, that took their denomination of one Robin Hood, who lived in Yorkshire in the reign of Richard I., and who, with his companions, harbouring in woods and deserts, committed a great number of robberies and other outrages on the subject. From this arch-thief a great number of idle and dissolute fellows, who were called Drawlatches, Ribauds, and Roberdsmen, took their rise, and infested this kingdom for above a century, notwithstanding the many endeavours of the legislature from time to time to suppress them.

In all these laws, the principal aim visibly was, to prevent

[1] 2 Instit. 147.   [2] Westminster, 1 chap. xv.

idle persons wandering from place to place, which, as we have before seen, was one great point of the decennary constitution.

Thus by a law made in the 34th year of Edward III. a labourer departing from his service into another county was to be burned in the forehead with the letter F. And, by the same statute, if a labourer or servant do fly into a city or borough, the chief officer, on request, was to deliver him up.

Again, in the 7th year of Richard II. the justices of peace are ordered to examine vagabonds; and, if they have no sureties for their good behaviour, to commit them to prison.

In the 11th year of Henry VII. it was enacted, that vagabonds and idle persons shall be set on the stocks three days and three nights, and have no other sustenance but bread and water, and then shall be put out of the town, and whosoever gave such idle persons relief forfeited 12*d.*

By 22 Henry VIII. persons calling themselves Egyptians shall not come into the realm, under penalty of forfeiting their goods; and, if they do not depart within fifteen days after they are commanded, shall be imprisoned.

By the 1 and 2 Philip and Mary,[1] Egyptians coming into the kingdom, and remaining here a month, are made guilty of felony without benefit of clergy.

And those who bring them into the realm forfeit 40*l.*

By the 5 Elizabeth the crime of felony without clergy is extended to all who are found in the company of Egyptians, or who shall counterfeit, transform, or disguise themselves as such.

By 22 Henry VIII. a vagabond taken begging shall be whipped, and then sworn to return to the place of his birth, or last abode for three years, there to put himself to labour.

By 27 Henry VIII. a valiant beggar or sturdy vagabond shall be whipped for the first offence, and sent to the place of his birth, &c., for the second, the upper part of the gristle

---

[1] Chap. iv.

of his right ear cut off; and if after that he be taken wandering in idleness, &c., he shall be adjudged and executed as a felon.

I shall mention no more acts (for several were made) between this and the 39th Elizabeth, when the former acts concerning vagabonds were all repealed, and the several provisions against them were reduced to one law.

This act, which contained many wholesome provisions, remained in force a long time, but at length was totally repealed by the 12th of Queen Anne; as this was again by the 13th George II. which last-mentioned statute stands now repealed by another, made about six years ago.[1]

I have taken this short view of these repealed laws, in order to enforce two considerations. First, that the removal of an evil which the legislature have so often endeavoured to redress is of great importance to society. Secondly, That an evil which so many subsequent laws have failed of removing is of a very stubborn nature, and extremely difficult to be cured.

Here I hope to be forgiven when I suggest, that the law hath probably failed in this instance from want of sufficient direction to a single point. As on a former head the disease seems to be no other than *idleness,* so here *wandering* is the cause of the mischief, and that alone to which the remedy should be applied. This, one would imagine, should be the chief, if not sole intent, of all laws against vagabonds, which might, in a synonymous phrase, be called laws against wanderers. But as the word itself hath obtained by vulgar use a more complex signification, so have the laws on this head had a more general view than to extirpate this mischief; and by that means, perhaps, have failed of producing such an effect.

I will therefore confine myself, as I have hitherto done on this head, to the single point of preventing the poor from wandering, one principal cause of the increase of robbers; as it is the chief means of preserving them from the pursuit of justice. It being impossible for any thief to carry on

[1] 17 George II. c. 5.

his trade long with impunity among his neighbours, and where not only his person, but his way of life, must be well known.

Now to obviate this evil the law, as it now stands, hath provided in a twofold manner. 1. By way of prevention; and, 2. By way of remedy.

As to the first, the statute of Elizabeth declares,[1] that no person retained in husbandry, or in any art or science in the act mentioned,[2] after the time of his retainer is expired, shall depart out of any city, parish, &c., nor out of the county, &c., to serve in any other, unless he have a testimonial under the seal of the city or town corporate, or of the constable or other head officer, and two other honest householders of the city, town, or parish, where he last served, declaring his lawful departure, and the name of the shire and place where he served last. This certificate is to be delivered to the servant, and registered by the parson, for 2*d.*, and the form of it is given in the act.

And no person is to be retained in any other service, without showing such testimonial to the chief officer of the town corporate, and in every other place to the constable, curate, &c., on pain of imprisonment, till he procure a testimonial; and, if he cannot procure such testimonial within twenty-one days he shall be whipped, and treated like a vagabond; so shall he be if found with a forged testimonial. And those who receive him without showing such testimonial as aforesaid forfeit 5*l.*

As to the second, the law hath been extremely liberal in its provisions. These are of two sorts, 1. Simply compulsory; and, 2. Compulsory with punishment. Under the former head may be ranged the several acts of parliament relating to the settlement, or rather removal of the poor.

As these statutes, though very imperfectly executed, are pretty generally known (the nation having paid some millions to Westminster Hall for the knowledge of them), I shall mention them very slightly in this place.

---

[1] 5 Eliz. c. iv. sect. 10, in force, though not in use.

[2] *i. e.* in almost every trade.

The statute of Elizabeth, together with the wise execution of it, having made the poor an intolerable burden to the public, disputes began to arise between parishes, to whose lot it fell to provide for certain individuals; for the laws for confining the poor to their own homes being totally disregarded, these used to ramble wherever whim or conveniency invited them. The overseers in one parish were perhaps more liberal of the parochial fund than those in another; or, sometimes, probably, the overseer of the parish A was a friend or a relation of a poor person of the parish B, who did not choose to work. From some such reason the poor of one parish began to bring a charge on another.

To remedy such inconveniences, immediately after the restoration,[1] a statute was made by which if any poor man likely to be chargeable came to inhabit in a foreign parish, unless in a tenement of 10*l.* a year, the overseers might complain to one justice within forty days, and then two justices were to remove the poor person to the place of his last legal settlement.

By a second act,[2] the forty days are to be reckoned after notice given in writing to the churchwarden or overseer by the poor person, containing the place of his abode, number of his family, &c.

But by the same statute the executing a public annual office during a year, or being charged with and paying to the public taxes, &c., or (if unmarried and not having a child) being lawfully hired into any parish, and serving for one year, or being bound apprentice by indenture, and inhabiting, &c., are all made good settlements without notice.

By a third statute,[3] persons bringing a certificate signed by the overseers, &c., and allowed by two justices, cannot be removed till they become chargeable.

By a fourth,[4] no such certificate person shall gain a settlement by any other act than by *bona fide* taking a lease of a

[1] 13 and 14 Car. II. c. xii.
[2] 3 and 4 W. & M. c. xi. See 1 Jac. II. c. xvii.
[3] 8 and 9 W. III. c. xxx.
[4] 9 and 10 W. III. c. xi.

tenement of 10*l.* per annum, or by executing an annual office.

By a fifth,[1] no apprentice or hired servant of certificate person shall, by such service or apprenticeship, gain any settlement.

By a sixth,[2] no person by any purchase of which the consideration doth not *bona fide* amount to 30*l.* shall gain any settlement longer than while he dwells on such purchase.

So much for these laws of removal, concerning which there are several other acts of parliament, and law cases innumerable.

And yet the law itself is, as I have said, very imperfectly executed at this day, and that for several reasons.

1. It is attended with great trouble; for as the act of Charles II. *very wisely* requires two justices, and the Court of King's Bench requires them both to be present together (though they seldom are so), the order of removal is sometimes difficult to be obtained, and more difficult to be executed; for the parish to which the party is to be removed (perhaps with a family) is often in a distant county; nay, sometimes they are to be carried from one end of the kingdom to another.

2. It is often attended with great expense, as well for the reason aforesaid as because the parish removing is liable to an appeal from the parish to which the poor is removed. This appeal is sometimes brought by a wealthy and litigious parish against a poor one, without any colour of right whatever.

3. The removal is often ineffectual; for, as the appeal is almost certain to be brought if an attorney lives in the neighbourhood; so is it almost as sure to succeed if a justice lives in the parish. And as for relief in the King's Bench, if the justices of peace will allow you to go thither (for that they will not always do) the delay, as well as the cost, is such, that the remedy is often worse than the disease.

For these reasons it can be no wonder that parishes are not very forward to put this law in execution. Indeed, in all cases of removal, the good of the parish, and not of the

---

[1] 12 Anne, c. xviii.   [2] Geo. I. c. vii.

public, is consulted; nay, sometimes, the good of an individual only; and therefore the poor man who is capable of getting his livelihood by his dexterity at any handicraft, and likely to do it by his industry, is sure to be removed with his family; especially if the overseer, or any of his relations, should be of the same occupation; but the idle poor, who threaten to rival no man in his business, are never taken any notice of, till they become actually chargeable; and if, by begging or robbing, they avoid this, as it is no man's interest, so no man thinks it his duty to apprehend them.

It cannot therefore be expected, that any good of the kind I am contending for should be effected by this branch of the law; let us therefore, in the second place, take a view of that which is expressly levelled at vagrants, and calculated, as it appears, for the very purpose of suppressing wanderers.

To survey this branch will be easy, as all the laws concerning vagrants are now reduced into one act of parliament; and it is the easier still, as this act is very clearly penned, and (which is not always the case) reduced to a regular and intelligible method.

By this act then three degrees of offences are constituted.

First, persons become idle and disorderly within the act, by, 1. Threatening to run away and to leave their wives or children to the parish. 2. Unlawfully returning to the place from whence they have been legally removed by the order of two justices, without bringing a certificate, &c. 3. Living idle without employment, and refusing to work for usual and common wages. 4. By begging in their own parishes.

Secondly, persons by, 1. Going about as patent-gatherers, or gatherers of alms under pretence of loss by fire, or other casualty; or, 2. Going about as collectors for prisons, gaols, or hospitals. 3. Being fencers and bearwards. 4. Or common players of interludes, &c. 5. Or minstrels, jugglers. 6. Pretending to be gipsies, or wandering in such habit. 7. Pretending to physiognomy, or like crafty science, &c. 8. Using any subtle craft to deceive and impose on any of his Majesty's subjects. 9. Playing or sitting at unlawful games. 10. Running away, and leaving wives or children, whereby they become chargeable to any parish. 11. Wandering abroad as petty chapmen or pedlars, not authorized by law. 12. Wandering abroad and lodging in alehouses, barns, out-houses, or in the open air, not giving a good account of themselves. 13. Wandering abroad and begging, pretending to be soldiers, mariners, seafaring men, or pretending to go to work at harvest. 14. Wandering abroad and begging—are to be deemed rogues and vagabonds.

Thirdly, 1. End-gatherers offending against the 13 George I. entituled, *An Act for the better Regulation of the Woollen Manufacturers,* &c., being convicted of such offence; 2. Persons apprehended as rogues and vagabonds escaping; or, 3, refusing to go before a justice; or, 4, refusing to be examined on oath; or, 5, refusing to be conveyed by a pass; or, 6, on examination giving a false account of themselves, after warning of the punishment. 7. Rogues and vagabonds escaping out of the house of correction, &c.; or, 8, those who have been punished as rogues and vagabonds, shall offend again as such, are made incorrigible rogues.

Now as to the first of these three divisions, it were to be wished, that persons who are found in alehouses, nighthouses, &c., after a certain hour at night, had been included; for many such, though of very suspicious characters, taken up at privy searches, fall not under any of the above descriptions. Some of these I have known discharged against whom capital complaints have appeared when it hath been too late. Why might not the justice be entrusted with a power of detaining any suspicious person who could produce no known housekeeper, or one of credit, to his character, for three days, within which time he might, by means of an advertisement, be viewed by numbers who have been lately robbed? some such have been, I know, confined upon an old statute as persons of evil fame, with great emolument to the public.

But I come to the second head, namely, of vagabonds; and here I must observe, that *wandering* is of itself made no offence: so that unless such wanderer be either a petty chapman, or a beggar or lodger in alehouses, &c., he is not within the act of parliament.

Now, however useful this excellent law may be in the country, it will by no means serve the purpose in this town; for, though most of the rogues who infest the public roads and streets, indeed almost all the thieves in general are vagabonds in the true sense of the word, being wanderers from their lawful place of abode, very few of them will be proved vagabonds within the words of this act of parliament. These vagabonds do, indeed, get their livelihood by thieving, and not as petty beggars or petty chapmen; and have their lodging not in alehouses, &c., but in private houses, where many of them resort together, and unite in gangs, paying each 2*d.* per night for their beds.

The following account I have had from Mr. Welch, the high-constable of Holborn; and none who know that gentleman, will want any confirmation of the truth of it.

"That in the parish of St. Giles's there are great numbers of houses set apart for the reception of idle persons and vagabonds, who have their lodgings there for twopence a night; that in the above parish, and in St. George, Bloomsbury, one woman alone occupies seven of these houses, all properly accommodated with miserable beds from the cellar to the garret, for such twopenny lodgers: that in these beds, several of which are in the same room, men and women, often strangers to each other, lie promiscuously; the price of a double bed being no more than threepence, as an encouragement to them to lie together; but as these places are thus adapted to whoredom, so are they no less provided for drunkenness, gin being sold in them all at a penny a quartern; so that the smallest sum of money serves for intoxication; that in the execution of search-warrants Mr. Welch rarely finds less than twenty of these houses open for the receipt of all comers at the latest hours; that in one of these houses, and that not a large one, he hath numbered fifty-eight persons of both sexes, the stench of whom was so intolerable that it compelled him in a short time to quit the place." Nay, I can add, what I myself once saw in the parish of Shoreditch, where two little houses were emptied of near seventy men and women; amongst whom was one of the prettiest girls I had ever seen, who had been carried off by an Irishman, to consummate her marriage on her wedding-night in a room where several others were in bed at the same time.

If one considers the destruction of all morality, decency, and modesty; the swearing, whoredom, and drunkenness, which is eternally carrying on in these houses, on the one hand, and the excessive poverty and misery of most of the inhabitants on the other, it seems doubtful whether they are more the objects of detestation or compassion; for such is the poverty of these wretches, that, upon searching all the above number, the money found upon all of them (except the bride, who, as I afterwards heard, had robbed her mistress) did not amount to one shilling; and I have been credibly informed, that a single loaf hath supplied a whole family with their provisions for a week. Lastly, if any of these miserable creatures fall sick (and it is almost a miracle that stench, vermin, and want, should ever suffer them to be well) they are turned out in the streets by their merciless host or hostess, where, unless some parish officer of extraordinary charity relieves them, they are sure miserably to perish, with the addition of hunger and cold to their disease.

This picture, which is taken from the life, will appear strange to many; for the evil here described is, I am confident, very little known, especially to those of the better sort. Indeed this is the only excuse, and I believe the only reason, that it hath been so long tolerated; for when we consider the number of these wretches, which, in the outskirts of the town, amounts to a great many thousands,[1] it is a nuisance which will appear to be big with every moral and political mischief. Of these the excessive misery of the wretches themselves, oppressed with want, and sunk in every species of debauchery, and the loss of so many lives to the public, are obvious and immediate consequences. There are

---

[1] Most of these are Irish, against the importation of whom a severe law was made in the reign of Henry VI., and many of the repealed vagrant acts contained a clause for the same purpose.

LEGAL WRITINGS—7

some more remote, which, however, need not be mentioned to the discerning.

Among other mischiefs attending this wretched nuisance, the great increase of thieves must necessarily be one. The wonder in fact is that we have not a thousand more robbers than we have; indeed, that all these wretches are not thieves must give us either a very high idea of their honesty, or a very mean one of their capacity and courage.

Where then is the redress? Is it not *to hinder the poor from wandering,* and this by compelling the parish and peace officers to apprehend such wanderers or vagabonds, and by empowering the magistrate effectually to punish and send them to their habitations? Thus if we cannot discover, or will not encourage any cure for idleness, we shall at least compel the poor to starve or beg at home; for there it will be impossible for them to steal or rob without being presently hanged or transported out of the way.

SECTION VII.

OF APPREHENDING THE PERSONS OF FELONS.

I COME now to a third encouragement which the thief flatters himself with; viz. In his hopes of escaping from being apprehended.

Nor is this hope without foundation: How long have we known highwaymen reign in this kingdom after they have been publicly known for such? Have not some of these committed robberies in open daylight, in the sight of many people, and have afterward rode solemnly and triumphantly through the neighbouring towns without any danger or molestation? This happens to every rogue who is become eminent for his audaciousness, and is thought to be desperate; and is, in a more particular manner, the case of great and numerous gangs, many of which have, for a long time, com-

mitted the most open outrages in defiance of the law. Officers of justice have owned to me, that they have passed by
such with warrants in their pockets against them without
daring to apprehend them; and, indeed, they could not be
blamed for not exposing themselves to sure destruction; for
it is a melancholy truth, that, at this very day, a rogue no
sooner gives the alarm, within certain purlieus, than twenty
or thirty armed villains are found ready to come to his
assistance.

On this head the law may seem not to have been very defective in its cautions; First, by vesting not only the officers
of justice, but every private man, with authority for securing
these miscreants, of which authority it may be of service to
the officers, as well as to the public in general, to be more
particularly informed.

First, By Westminster I.[1] Persons of evil fame are to be
imprisoned without bail. By the statute of Winchester [2]
suspicious night-walkers are to be arrested and detained by
the watch. A statute made in 5 Edw. III.[3] reciting that
many manslaughters, felonies, and robberies, had been done
in times past, enacts, that if any person have an evil suspicion of such offenders, they shall be incontinently arrested
by the constable, and shall be delivered to the bailiff of the
franchise, or to the sheriff, to be kept in prison till the coming of the justices. The 34 Edw. III.[4] gives power to the
justices of peace, *inter alia,* to inquire of wanderers, and such
as will not labour, and to arrest and imprison suspicious persons, and to take sureties of the good behaviour of persons
of evil fame, " to the intent," says the statute, " that the
people be not by such rioters, &c., troubled nor endamaged,
nor the peace blemished, nor merchants nor others passing
by the highways of the realm disturbed, nor put in peril by
such offenders."

Secondly, By the common law every person who hath committed a felony may be arrested and secured by any private
man present at the said fact, though he hath no general nor

---

[1] Westm. I. chap. xv.   [2] Winton. chap. iv.
[3] 5 Edw. III. chap. xiv.   [4] 34 Edw. III. c.

particular authority, *i. e.* though he be no officer of justice, nor have any writ or warrant for so doing; and such private man may either deliver the felon to the constable, secure him in a gaol, or carry him before a magistrate.[1] And if he refuses to yield, those who arrest may justify beating [2] him; or, in case of absolute necessity, killing him.[3]

Nor is this arrest merely allowed; it is enjoined by law, and the omission, without some good excuse, is a misdemeanour punishable by amercement or fine and imprisonment.[4]

Again, every private man may arrest another on suspicion of felony, though he was not present at the fact.[5] But then, if the party arrested should prove innocent, two circumstances are necessary to justify the arrest. First, A felony must be actually committed; and, Secondly, There must be a reasonable cause of suspicion;[6] and common fame hath been adjudged to be such cause.[7]

But in this latter case my Lord Hale advises the private person, if possible, to have recourse to the magistrate and obtain his warrant and the assistance of the constable;[8] for this arrest is not required by law, nor is the party punishable for neglecting it; and should the person arrested, or endeavoured to be arrested, prove innocent, the party arresting him, &c., will, in a great measure, be answerable for the ill consequence; which, if it be the death of the innocent person occasioned by force or resistance, this will, at least, be manslaughter; and if the other should be killed in the attempt, this likewise will amount to manslaughter only.[9]

[1] Hale's Hist. P. C. vol. i. 587, vol. ii. 77.
[2] Pult. 10, a.
[3] Hale's Hist. vol. i. 588.
[4] Hale, vol. i. 588, vol. ii. 76, 77.
[5] Lamb. l. ii. c. 3. Dalt. 403. Hale's Hist. vol. i. 588, 3 Hen. VII. c. i.
[6] Hale's Hist. vol. ii. 80.
[7] Dalt. 407, 5 H. VII. 4, 5.
[8] Hale's Hist. vol. ii. 76.
[9] Ib. vol. ii. 82—3—4.

Again, any private person may justify arresting a felon pursued by hue and cry. This, as the word imports, is a public alarm raised all over the country, in which the constable is first to search his own vill or division, and then to raise all the neighbouring vills about, who are to pursue the felon with horse and foot.[1] And this hue and cry may either be after a person certain, or on a robbery committed where the person is not known; and in the latter case those who pursue it may take such persons as they have probable cause to suspect,[2] vagrants, &c.

This method of pursuit lies at the common law, and is mentioned by Bracton;[3] and it is enforced by many statutes, as by Westm. I.,[4] "All are to be ready at the summons of the sheriff, and at the cry of the county, to arrest felons as well within franchises as without." By 4 Edw. I. "Hue and cry is ordered to be levied for all murders, burglaries, men slain, or in peril to be slain, and all are to follow it." And, lastly, the statute of Winton enacts as we have seen before.

And this pursuit may be raised, 1. By a private person. 2. By the country without an officer. 3. By an officer without a warrant. 4. By the warrant of a magistrate. And this last, if it can be obtained, is the safest way; for then all who assist are enabled by the statutes 7 and 21 Jac. to plead the general issue.[5]

The common law so strictly enjoined this pursuit, that if any defect in raising it lay in the lord of the franchise, the franchise should be seized into the king's hands; and, if the neglect lay in the bailiff, he should have a heavy fine, and a year's imprisonment, or suffer two years' imprisonment without a fine.[6] And now, by a very late[7] statute, "If any

[1] Ib. vol. ii. 101.
[2] Ib. vol. ii. 102.
[3] Lib. iii. c. i.
[4] Cap. ix.
[5] Hale's Hist. vol. i. 405, vol. ii. 99, 100.
[6] Fleta, l. i. c. 24, ad Init.
[7] 8 Geo. II. c. 16.

constable, headborough, &c., of the hundred where any robberies shall happen, shall refuse or *neglect* to make hue and
cry after the felons with the utmost expedition, as soon as
he shall receive notice thereof, he shall, for every such refusal and neglect, forfeit 5*l.,* half to the king and half to the
informer."

Now hue and cry is of three different kinds: 1. Against
a person certain by name. 2. Against a person certain by
description. 3. On a robbery, burglary, &c., where the person is neither known nor capable of being described.

When a hue and cry is raised, every private man is not
only justified in pursuing, but may be obliged, by command
of the constable, to pursue the felon, and is punishable, if
he disobey, by fine and imprisonment.[1] And in this case,
whether a felony was committed or not, or whether the person arrested (provided he be the person named or described
by the hue and cry) be guilty or innocent, or of evil or good
fame, the arrest is lawful and justifiable, and he who raised
the hue and cry is alone to answer for the justice of it.[2]

In this pursuit likewise the constable may search suspected
houses, if the doors be open; but breaking the door will not
be justifiable, unless the felon be actually in the house: nor
even then, unless admittance hath been first demanded and
denied.[3] And what the constable may do himself will be
justifiable by any other in his assistance, at least, by his
command.[4] Indeed a private person may justify the arrest
of an offender by the command of a peace-officer; for he is
bound to be aiding and assisting to such officer, is punishable for his refusal, and is consequently under the protection
of the law.[5]

Lastly, a private person may arrest a felon by virtue of a
warrant directed to him; for though he is not bound to execute such warrant, yet if he doth, it is good and justifiable.[6]

---

[1] Hale's Hist. vol. i. 58, vol. ii. 104.
[2] 29 Ed. III. 39, 35 Hen. IV. Pl. 24, Hale's Hist. vol. ii. 101—2.
[3] Ib. 102, 103.   [4] Hale's Hist. vol. ii. 104.
[5] Pult. 6, 15, Hale's Hist. vol. ii. 86.
[6] Dalt. 408. Hale's Hist. vol. ii. 86.

Thirdly, Officers of public justice may justify the arrest of a felon by virtue of their office, without any warrant. Whatever therefore a private person may do as above will certainly be justifiable in them.

And, as the arresting felons, &c., is more particularly their duty, and their fine will be heavier for the neglect, so will their protection by the law be the greater; for if, in arresting those that are *probably suspected,* the constable should be killed, it is murder; on the other hand, if persons pursued by these officers for felony, or *justifiable suspicion* thereof, shall resist or fly from them; on being apprehended shall rescue themselves, resist, or fly; so that they cannot *otherwise* be apprehended or re-apprehended, and are of *necessity* slain, it is no felony in the officers, or in their assistants, though possibly the parties killed are innocent; for, by resisting the king's authority in his officers, they draw their own blood on themselves.[1]

Again, to take a felon or suspected felon, the constable without any warrant may break open the door. But to justify this he must show; 1. That the felon, &c., was in the house. 2. That his entry was denied. 3. That it was denied after demand and notice that he was constable.[2]

Lastly, a felon may be apprehended by virtue of a warrant issuing from a magistrate lawfully authorized; in the execution of which the officer hath the same power, and will, at least, have the same protection by law as in the arrest *virtute officii.* And this warrant, if it be specially directed to him, the constable may execute in any part within the jurisdiction of the magistrate; but he is only obliged to execute it within the division for which he is constable, &c.

In the execution of a warrant for felony the officer may break open the doors of the felon, or of any person where he is concealed; and the breaking the doors of the felon is lawful at all events, but in breaking those of a stranger the

[1] Dalt. 409.   13 Edw. IV. 4 & 9, 5 to 92.   Hale's Hist. vol. ii. 86, 90, 91.

[2] Ib. vol. i 581, vol. ii. 110.

officer acts at his peril; for he will be a trespasser if the felon should not be there.[1]

Such are the powers which the law gives for the apprehending felons (for as to the particular power of sheriffs and coroners, and the process of superior courts, they may well be passed by in this place.) Again, these powers we see are enforced with penalties; so that not only every officer of justice, but every private person, is obliged to arrest a known felon, and may be punished for the omission.

Nor does the law stop here. The apprehending such felons is not only authorized and enjoined, but even encouraged, with impunity to persons guilty themselves of felony, and with regard to others.

By 3 and 4 of William and Mary,[2] persons guilty of robbery in the highway, fields, &c., who, being out of prison, shall discover any two offenders to be convicted of such robbery, are entitled to his majesty's pardon of such robberies, &c., as they shall have then committed.

By 10 and 11 of William III.,[3] this is extended to burglary, and such felonies as are mentioned in the act.

By the same act all persons who shall apprehend a felon for privately stealing goods to the value of 5s. out of shop, warehouse, coach-house, or stable, by night or by day (provided the felon be convicted thereof) shall be entitled to a certificate, which may be assigned once, discharging such apprehender or his assignee from all parochial offices in the parish or ward where such felony was committed. This certificate is to be enrolled by the clerk of the peace, and cannot be assigned after it hath been used.

If any man be killed by such housebreaker, &c., in the attempt to apprehend him, his executors or administrators shall be entitled to such certificate.

By the 3 and 4 of W. and M.[4] whoever shall apprehend and prosecute to conviction any robber on the highway, shall

[1] Ib. vol. i. 582, vol. i. 117. 5 Co. 91, b.
[2] Chap. viii.
[3] Chap. xxiii.
[4] Chap. viii. ubi supra.

J. H. Brandon, Pinxt.

receive of the sheriff 40*l*. within a month after the conviction, for every offender; and in case of the death or removal
of the sheriff, the money to be paid by the succeeding sheriff
within a month after the demand and certificate brought.
The sheriff on default forfeits double his sum, to be recovered
of him by the party, his executors, &c.

And if the person be killed in this attempt by any such
robber, the executors of such person, &c., are entitled to the
reward, under the like penalty.

Again, by the same act, the horse, furniture, arms, money,
or other goods, taken with such highwayman, are given to
the apprehender who shall prosecute to conviction, notwithstanding the right or title of his majesty, any body politic
or lord of franchise, or of those who lent or let the same to
hire to such robber, with a saving only of the right of such
persons from whom such horses, &c., were feloniously taken.

By a statute of Queen Anne the 40*l*. reward is extended
to burglary and housebreaking.

But though the law seems to have been sufficiently provident on this head, there is still great difficulty in carrying its
purpose into execution, arising from the following causes:

First, With regard to private persons, there is no country,
I believe, in the world where that vulgar maxim so generally
prevails, that what is the business of every man is the business of no man; and for this plain reason, that there is no
country in which less honour is gained by serving the public.
He therefore who commits no crime against the public is
very well satisfied with his own virtue; far from thinking
himself obliged to undergo any labour, expend any money,
or encounter any danger, on such account.

Secondly, The people are not entirely without excuse from
their ignorance of the law; for so far is the power of apprehending felons, which I have above set forth, from being
universally known, that many of the peace-officers themselves
do not know that they have any such power, and often, from
ignorance, refuse to arrest a known felon till they are authorized by a warrant from a justice of peace. Much less
then can the compulsory part to the private persons carry

any terror of a penalty of which the generality of mankind are totally ignorant; and of inflicting which they see no example.

Thirdly, So far are men from being animated with the hopes of public praise to apprehend a felon, that they are even discouraged by the fear of shame. The person of the informer is in fact more odious than that of the felon himself; and the thief-catcher is in danger of worse treatment from the populace than the thief.

Lastly, As to the reward, I am afraid that the intention of the legislature is very little answered. For, not to mention that the prosecutor's title to it is too often defeated by the foolish lenity of juries, who, by acquitting the prisoner of the burglary, and finding him guilty of the simple felony only, or by finding the goods to be less than the value of 5s., both often directly contrary to evidence, take the case entirely out of the act of parliament; and sometimes even when the felon is properly convicted, I have been told that the money does not come so easily and fully to the pockets of those who are entitled to it as it ought.

With regard to the first and fourth of these objections, I choose to be silent: to prescribe any cure for the former I must enter into disquisitions very foreign to my present purpose; and for the cure of the latter, when I consider in whose power it is to remedy it, a bare hint will I doubt not suffice.

The second objection, namely, the excuse of ignorance, I have here endeavoured to remove, by setting forth the law at large.

The third therefore only remains, and to that I shall speak more fully, as the opinion on which it is founded is of the most pernicious consequence to society; for what avail the best of laws if it be a matter of infamy to contribute towards their execution? The force of this opinion may be seen in the following instance: We have a law by which every person who drives more than six horses in a waggon forfeits as many horses as are found to exceed that number. This law is broken every day, and generally with impunity; for, though many men yearly venture and lose their lives by stealing horses, yet there are very few who dare seize a horse where the law allows and encourages it, when by such a seizure he is to acquire the name of an informer, so much worse is this appellation in the opinion of the vulgar than that of thief; and so much more prevalent is the fear of popular shame than of death.

This absurd opinion seems to have first arisen from the statute of 18 Elizabeth,[1] entitled, *An Act to redress Disorders in Common Informers.* By this statute it appears, that very wicked uses had been made of penal statutes by these informers, who my Lord Coke calls *turbidum hominum genus;*[2] and says, "That they converted many penal laws which were obsolete, and in time grown impossible or inconvenient to be performed, into snares to vex and entangle the subject."

By the statute itself it appears, that it was usual at that time among these persons to extort money of ignorant and fearful people by the terror of some penal law; for the breach of which the informer either instituted a process, or pretended to institute a process, and then brought the timorous party to a composition.

This offence therefore was by this act made a high misdemeanor, and punished with the pillory.

Now who, that knows any thing of the nature or history of mankind, doth not easily perceive here a sufficient foundation for that odium to all informers which have since become so general; for what is more common than from the abuse of any thing to argue against the use of it, or to extend the obloquy from particulars to universals?

For this the common aptitude of men to scandal will sufficiently account; but there is still another and stronger motive in this case, and that is the interest of all those who have broken or who intend to break the laws. Thus the general cry being once raised against prosecutors on penal laws, the thieves themselves have had the art and impudence to join it, and have put their prosecutors on the footing of all others;

---

[1] Chap. v. [2] 3 Inst. c. lxxxvii.

nay, I must question whether, in the acceptation of the vulgar, a thief-catcher be not a more odious and contemptible name than even that of informer.

Nothing, I am sensible, is more vain than to encounter popular opinion with reason; nor more liable to ridicule than to oppose general contempt, and yet I will venture to say, that if to do good to society be laudable, so is the office of a thief-catcher; and if to do this good at the extreme hazard of your life be honourable, then is this office honourable. True, it may be said, but he doth this with a view to a reward. And doth not the soldier and the sailor venture his life with the same view? for who, as a great man lately said, serves the public for nothing?

I know what is to be my fate in this place, or what would happen to one who should endeavour to prove that the hangman was a great and an honourable employment. And yet I have read, in Tournefort, of an island in the Archipelago where the hangman is the first and highest officer in the state. Nay, in this kingdom the sheriff himself (who was one of the most considerable persons in his county) is in law the hangman, and Mr. Ketch is only his deputy.

If to bring thieves to justice be a scandalous office, what becomes of all those who are concerned in this business, some of whom are rightly thought to be among the most honourable officers in government? If on the contrary this be, as it surely is, very truly honourable, why should the post of danger in this warfare alone be excluded from all share of honour?

To conclude a matter in which, though serious, I will not be too tedious, what was the great Pompey in the piratic war? [1] what Hercules, Theseus, and the other heroes of old, *Deorum in templa recepti*—Were they not the most eminent of thief-catchers?

[1] Cicero, in his oration *Pro Lege Manilia*, calls this, if I remember rightly, *Bellum Turpe;* but speaks of the extirpation of these robbers as of the greatest of all Pompey's exploits.

SECTION VIII.

OF THE DIFFICULTIES WHICH ATTEND PROSECUTIONS.

I now come to a fourth encouragement which greatly holds up the spirit of robbers, and which they often find to afford no deceitful consolation; and this is drawn from the remissness of prosecutors, who are often,

1. Fearful, and to be intimidated by the threats of the gang; or,

2. Delicate, and cannot appear in a public court; or,

3. Indolent, and will not give themselves the trouble of a prosecution; or,

4. Avaricious, and will not undergo the expense of it; nay, perhaps, find their account in compounding the matter; or,

5. Tender-hearted, and cannot take away the life of a man; or,

Lastly, Necessitous, and cannot really afford the cost, however small, together with the loss of time which attends it.

The first and second of these are too absurd, and the third and fourth too infamous, to be reasoned with. But the two last deserve more particular notice, as the fifth is an error springing originally out of a good principle in the mind, and the sixth is a fault in the constitution very easily to be remedied.

With regard to the former of these, it is certain that a tender-hearted and compassionate disposition, which inclines men to pity and feel the misfortunes of others, and which is, even for its own sake, incapable of involving any man in ruin and misery, is of all tempers of mind the most amiable; and though it seldom receives much honour, is worthy of the highest. The natural energies of this temper are indeed the very virtues principally inculcated in our excellent religion; and those who, because they are natural, have denied them the name of virtues seem not, I think, to be aware of the direct and impious tendency of a doctrine that denies all merit to a mind which is naturally, I may say necessarily, good.

Indeed the passion of love or benevolence, whence this admirable disposition arises, seems to be the only human passion that is in itself simply and absolutely good; and in Plato's commonwealth, or (which is more) in a society acting up to the rules of Christianity, no danger could arise from the highest excess of this virtue; nay, the more liberally it was indulged, and the more extensively it was expanded, the more would it contribute to the honour of the individual, and to the happiness of the whole.

But, as it hath pleased God to permit human societies to be constituted in a different manner, and knaves to form a part (a very considerable one, I am afraid) of every community, who are ever lying in wait to destroy and ensnare the honest part of mankind, and to betray them by means of their own goodness, it becomes the good-natured and tender-hearted man to be watchful over his own temper; to restrain the impetuosity of his benevolence, carefully to select the objects of his passion, and not by too unbounded and indiscriminate an indulgence to give the reins to a courser which will infallibly carry him into the ambuscade of the enemy.

Our Saviour Himself inculcates this prudence among His disciples, telling them, that He " sent them forth like sheep among wolves; be ye therefore," says He, " wise as serpents, but innocent as doves."

For want of this wisdom a benevolent and tender-hearted temper very often betrays men into errors not only hurtful to themselves but highly prejudicial to the society. Hence men of invincible courage, and incorruptible integrity, have sometimes falsified their trust; and those whom no other temptation could sway have paid too little regard to the sanction of an oath from this inducement alone. Hence likewise the mischief which I here endeavour to obviate hath often arisen; and notorious robbers have lived to perpetrate future acts of violence, through the ill-judging tenderness and compassion of those who could and ought to have prosecuted them.

To such a person I would suggest these considerations:

First, As he is a good man, he should consider, that the

principal duty which every man owes is to his country, for the safety and good of which all laws are established, and therefore his country requires of him to contribute all that in him lies to the due execution of those laws. Robbery is an offence not only against the party robbed, but against the public, who are therefore entitled to prosecution, and he who prevents or stifles such prosecution is no longer an innocent man, but guilty of a high offence against the public good.

Secondly, As he is a good-natured man, he will behold all injuries done by one man to another with indignation. What Cicero says of a pirate is as true of a robber, that he is *hostis humani generis;* and if so, I am sure every good-natured man must be an enemy to him. To desire to save these wolves in society may arise from benevolence, but it must be the benevolence of a child or a fool, who, from want of sufficient reason, mistakes the true objects of his passion, as a child doth when a bugbear appears to him to be the object of fear. Such tender-heartedness is indeed barbarity, and resembles the meek spirit of him who would not assist in blowing up his neighbour's house to save a whole city from the flames. " It is true," said a learned chief justice,[1] in a trial for treason, " here is the life of a man in the case, but then you (speaking to the jury) must consider likewise the misery and desolation, the blood and confusion, that must have happened had this taken effect; and put one against the other, I believe that consideration which is on behalf of the king will be much the stronger." Here likewise is the life of a man concerned; but of what man? Why, of one who, being too lazy to get his bread by labour, or too voluptuous to content himself with the produce of that labour, declares war against the properties, and often against the persons, of his fellow-subjects; who deprives his countrymen of the pleasure of travelling with safety, and of the liberty of carrying their money or their ordinary conveniences with them; by whom the innocent are put in terror, affronted and alarmed with threats and execrations, endangered with loaded pistols, beat with bludgeons, and hacked with cutlasses, of which the loss of health, of

---

[1] Lord Chief Justice Pratt.

limbs, and often of life, is the consequence; and all this without any respect to age, or dignity, or sex. Let the good-natured man, who hath any understanding, place this picture before his eyes, and then see what figure in it will be the object of his compassion.

I come now to the last difficulty which obstructs the prosecution of offenders; namely, the extreme poverty of the prosecutor. This I have known to be so absolutely the case, that the poor wretch who hath been bound to prosecute was under more concern than the prisoner himself. It is true that the necessary cost on these occasions is extremely small; two shillings, which are appointed by act of parliament for drawing the indictment, being, I think, the whole which the law requires; but when the expense of attendance, generally with several witnesses, sometimes during several days together, and often at a great distance from the prosecutor's home; I say, when these articles are summed up, and the loss of time added to the account, the whole amounts to an expense which a very poor person, already plundered by the thief, must look on with such horror (if he should not be absolutely incapable of the expense) that he must be a miracle of public spirit if he doth not rather choose to conceal the felony, and sit down satisfied with his present loss; but what shall we say when (as is very common in this town) he may not only receive his own again, but be farther rewarded, if he will agree to compound it?

Now, how very inconsiderable would be the whole cost of this suit, either to the country or the nation, if the public to whom the justice of peace gives his whole labour on this head gratis, was to defray the cost of such trial (by a kind of *forma pauperis* admission); the sum would be so trivial that nothing would be felt but the good consequences arising from such a regulation.

I shall conclude this head with the words of my Lord Hale: "It is," says he, "a great defect in the law, to give courts of justice no power to allow witnesses against criminals their charges; whereby," says he, "many poor persons grow weary of their attendance, or bear their own charges therein to their great hindrance and loss."

Miller, del.

SECTION IX.

OF THE TRIAL AND CONVICTION OF FELONS.

BUT if, notwithstanding all the rubs which we have seen to lie in the way, the indictment is found, and the thief brought to his trial, still he hath sufficient hopes of escaping, either from the caution of the prosecutor's evidence or from the hardiness of his own.

In street-robberies the difficulty of convicting a criminal is extremely great. The method of discovering these is generally by means of one of the gang, who, being taken up perhaps for some other offence, and thinking himself in danger of punishment, chooses to make his peace at the expense of his companions.

But when, by means of this information, you are made acquainted with the whole gang, and have with great trouble and often with great danger, apprehended them, how are you to bring them to justice? for though the evidence of the accomplice be ever so positive and explicit, nay, ever so connected and probable, still, unless it be corroborated by some other evidence, it is not sufficient.

Now how is this corroborating evidence to be obtained in this case? Street-robberies are generally committed in the dark, the persons on whom they are committed are often in chairs and coaches, and if on foot the attack is usually begun by knocking the party down, and for the time depriving him of his senses. But if the thief should be less barbarous he is seldom so uncautious as to omit taking every method to prevent his being known, by flapping the party's hat over his face, and by every other method which he can invent to avoid discovery.

But indeed any such methods are hardly necessary; for when we consider the circumstance of darkness, mentioned before, the extreme hurry of the action, and the terror and consternation in which most persons are in at such a time,

LEGAL WRITINGS—8

how shall we imagine it possible that they should afterwards be able, with any (the least) degree of certainty, to swear to the identity of the thief, whose countenance is, perhaps, not a little altered by his subsequent situation, and who takes care as much as possible he can, by every alteration of dress, and otherwise, to disguise himself?

And if the evidence of the accomplice be so unlikely to be confirmed by the oath of the prosecutor, what other means of confirmation can be found? for as to his character, if he himself doth not call witnesses to support it (which in this instance is not incumbent on him to do), you are not at liberty to impeach it: the greatest and most known villain in England, standing at the bar equally *rectus in curia* with the man of highest estimation, if they should be both accused of the same crime.

Unless therefore the robbers should be so unfortunate as to be apprehended in the fact (a circumstance which their numbers, arms, &c., renders ordinarily impossible) no such corroboration can possibly be had; but the evidence of the accomplice standing alone and unsupported, the villain, contrary to the opinion and almost direct knowledge of all present, is triumphantly acquitted, laughs at the court, scorns the law, vows revenge against his prosecutors, and returns to his trade with a great increase of confidence, and commonly of cruelty.

In a matter therefore of so much concern to the public I shall be forgiven if I venture to offer my sentiments.

The words of my Lord Hale are these: " Though a *particeps criminis* be admissible as a witness in law, yet the credibility of his testimony is to be left to the jury; and truly it would be hard to take away the life of any person upon such a witness that swears to save his own, and yet confesseth himself guilty of so great a crime, unless there be also very considerable circumstances, which may give the greater credit to what he swears." [1]

Here I must observe, that this great man seems rather to complain of the hardship of the law, in taking away the life

[1] Hale's Hist. vol. i. 305.

of a criminal on the testimony of an accomplice, than to deny that the law was so. This indeed he could not well do; for not only the case of an approver, as he himself seems to acknowledge, but many later resolutions would have contradicted that opinion.

Secondly, He allows that the credibility of his testimony is to be left to the jury; and so is the credibility of all other testimonies. They are absolute judges of the fact; and God forbid that they should in all cases be tied down by positive evidence against a prisoner, though it was not delivered by an accomplice.

But surely, if the evidence of an accomplice be not sufficient to put the prisoner on his defence, but the jury are directed to acquit him, though he can produce no evidence on his behalf, either to prove an *alibi* or to his character, the credibility of such testimony cannot well be said to be left to a jury. This is virtually to reject the competency of the witness; for to say the law allows him to be sworn, and yet gives no weight to his evidence, is, I apprehend, a mere play of words, and conveys no idea.

In the third place, this great man asserts the hardship of such conviction.—Now if the evidence of a supposed accomplice should convict a man of fair and honest character; it would, I confess, be hard; and it is a hardship of which, I believe, no experience can produce any instance. But if, on the other hand, the testimony of an accomplice with every circumstance of probability attending it against a vagabond of the vilest character, and who can produce no single person to his reputation, is to be absolutely rejected, because there is no positive proof to support it; this, I think, is in the highest degree hard (I think I have proved how hard) to the society.

I shall not enter here into a disquisition concerning the nature of evidence in general; this being much too large a field; nor shall I examine the utility of those rules which our law prescribes on this head. Some of these rules might perhaps be opened a little wider than they are without either mischief or inconvenience; and I am the bolder in the assertion as I know a very learned judge who concurs with this opinion. There is no branch of the law more bulky, more full of confusion and contradiction, I had almost said of absurdity, than the law of evidence as it now stands.

One rule of this law is, that no man interested shall be sworn as a witness. By this is meant pecuniary interest; but are mankind governed by no other passion than avarice? Is not revenge the sweetest morsel, as a divine calls it, which the devil ever dropped into the mouth of a sinner? Are not pride, hatred, and the other passions, as powerful tyrants in the mind of man; and is not the interest which these passions propose to themselves by the enjoyment of their object, as prevalent a motive to evil as the hope of any pecuniary interest whatever?

But, to keep more closely to the point—Why shall not any credit be given to the evidence of an accomplice?—My Lord Hale tells us, that he hath been guilty of a great crime: and yet, if he had been convicted and burnt in the hand, all the authorities tell us that his credit had been restored: a more miraculous power of fire than any which the Royal Society can produce. The same happens if he be pardoned.

Again, says Lord Hale, he swears to save his own life. This is not altogether so; for when once a felon hath impeached his companions, and is admitted an evidence against them, whatever be the fate of his evidence, the impeacher always goes free. To this, it is true, he hath no positive title, no more hath he, if a single felon be convicted on his oath. But the practice is as I mention, and I do not remember any instance to the contrary.

But what inducement hath the accomplice to perjure himself; or what reason can be assigned why he should be suspected of it? That he himself was one of the robbers appears to a demonstration; and that he had accomplices in the robbery is as certain. Why then should he be induced to impeach A and B, who are innocent, and not C and D, who are guilty? Must he not think that he hath a better chance of convicting the guilty than the innocent? Is he not liable if he gives a false information to be detected in it? One of his companions may be discovered and give a true information, what will then become of him and his evidence? And why should he do this? From a motive of friendship? Do the worst of men carry this passion so much higher than is common with the best? But he must not only run the risk of his life, but of his soul too. The very mention of this latter risk may appear ridiculous when it is considered of what sort of persons I am talking. But even these persons can scarce be thought so very void of understanding as to lose their souls for nothing, and to commit the horrid sins of perjury and murder without any temptation, or prospect of interest, nay, even against their interest. Such characters are not to be found in history, nor do they exist any where but in distempered brains, and are always rejected as monsters when they are produced in works of fiction: for surely we spoil the verse rather than the sense by saying, *nemo* gratis *fuit turpissimus.* Under such circumstances, and under the caution of a good judge and the tenderness of an English jury, it will be the highest improbability that any man should be wrongly convicted; and utterly impossible to convict an honest man: for I intend no more than that such evidence shall put the prisoner on his defence, and oblige him either to controvert the fact by proving an *alibi,* or by some other circumstance; or to produce some reputable person to his character. And this brings me to consider the second fortress of the criminal, in the hardiness of his own evidence.

The usual defence of a thief, especially at the Old Bailey, is an *alibi;* [1] to prove this by perjury is a common act of Newgate friendship; and there seldom is any difficulty in procuring such witnesses. I remember a felon within this twelvemonth to have been proved to be in Ireland at the time when the robbery was sworn to have been done in London, and acquitted; but he was scarce gone from the bar, when the witness was himself arrested for a robbery committed in London, at that very time when he swore both he and his friend were in Dublin; for which robbery, I think, he was tried and executed. This kind of defence was in a great measure defeated by the late Baron Thompson, when he was

---

[1] *i. e.* That he was at another place at the time.

Recorder of London, whose memory deserves great honour for the services he did the public in that post. These witnesses should always be examined with the utmost care and strictness, by which means, the truth (especially if there be more witnesses than one to the pretended fact) will generally be found out. And as to character, though I allow it to have great weight, if opposed to the single evidence of an accomplice, it should surely have but little where there is good and strong proof of the fact; and none at all unless it comes from the mouths of persons who have themselves some reputation and credit.

SECTION X.

OF THE ENCOURAGEMENT GIVEN TO ROBBERS BY FREQUENT PARDONS.

I COME now to the sixth encouragement to felons, from the hopes of a pardon, at least with the condition of transportation.

This I am aware is too tender a subject to speak to. To pardon all crimes where the prosecution is in his name, is an undoubted prerogative of the king. I may add, it is his most amiable prerogative, and that which, as Livy observes,[1] renders kingly government most dear to the people; for in a republic there is no such power. I may add farther, that it seems to our excellent sovereign to be the most favourite part of his prerogative, as it is the only one which hath been carried to its utmost extent in the present reign.

Here therefore I beg to direct myself only to those persons who are within the reach of his Majesty's sacred ear. Such persons, will, I hope, weigh well what I have said already on the subject of false compassion, all which is applicable

[1] Dec. 1. l. ii. cap. 3. " Esse gratiæ locum, esse beneficio; et irasci et ignoscere posse (*Regem scilicet*); inter amicum atque inimicum discrimen nosse: leges, rem surdam, inexorabilem esse," &c.

on the present occasion: and since our king (as was with less truth said of another [1]) *is of all men the truest image of his Maker in mercy,* I hope too much good-nature will transport no nobleman so far as it did once a clergyman in Scotland, who in the fervour of his benevolence prayed to God that he would graciously be pleased to pardon the poor devil.

To speak out fairly and honestly,[2] though mercy may appear more amiable in a magistrate, severity is a more wholesome virtue; nay, severity to an individual may, perhaps, be in the end the greatest mercy, not only to the public in general, for the reason given above, but to many individuals for the reasons to be presently assigned.

To consider a human being in the dread of a sudden and violent death: to consider that his life or death depend on your will; to reject the arguments which a good mind will officiously advance to itself; that violent temptations, necessity, youth, inadvertency, have hurried him to the commission of a crime which hath been attended with no inhumanity; to resist the importunities, cries, and tears, of a tender wife and affectionate children, who, though innocent, are to be reduced to misery and ruin by a strict adherence to justice:—these altogether form an object which whoever can look upon without emotion must have a very bad mind; and whoever, by the force of reason, can conquer that emotion, must have a very strong one.

And what can reason suggest on this occasion? First, That by saving this individual I shall bring many others into the same dreadful situation. That the passions of the man are to give way to the principles of the magistrate. Those may lament the criminal, but these must condemn him. It was nobly said by Bias to one who admired at his shedding tears while he passed sentence of death, " Nature exacts my tenderness, but the law my rigour." The elder Brutus [3] is a worthy pattern of this maxim; an example,

---

[1] By Dryden of Charles II.

[2] Disc. l. iii. c. 3.

[3] He put his two sons to death for conspiring with Tarquin. Neither Livy or Dionysius give any character of cruelty to Brutus;

says Machiavel, most worthy of being transmitted to posterity. And Dionysius Halicarnassus [1] calls it a *great and wonderful action, of which the Romans were proud in the most extraordinary degree.* Whoever derives it, therefore from the want of humane and paternal affections is unjust; no instances of his inhumanity are recorded. "But the severity," says Machiavel, "was not only profitable but necessary," and why? Because a single pardon granted *ex mera gratiâ et favore,* is a link broken in the chain of justice, and takes away the concatenation and strength of the whole. The danger and certainty of destruction are very different objects, and strike the mind with different degrees of force. It is of the very nature of hope to be sanguine, and it will derive more encouragement from one pardon than diffidence from twenty executions.

It is finely observed by Thucydides,[2] "That though civil societies have allotted the punishment of death to many crimes, and to some of the inferior sort, yet hope inspires men to face the danger; and no man ever came to a dreadful end who had not a lively expectation of surviving his wicked machinations."—Nothing certainly can more contribute to the raising of this hope than repeated examples of ill-grounded clemency; for, as Seneca says, *ex clementiâ omnes idem sperant.*[3]

Now what is the principal end of all punishment? is it not, as Lord Hale [4] expresses it, "To deter men from the breach of laws, so that they may not offend, and so not suffer at all? And is not the inflicting of punishment more for example, and to prevent evil, than to punish?" And therefore, says he, presently afterwards, "Death itself is necessary to be annexed to laws in many cases by the prudence of lawgivers, though possibly beyond the single merit of the offence simply considered." No man indeed of common humanity or com-

indeed the latter tells us that he was superior to all those passions which disturb human reason. *Τῶν ἐπιτάραττοντων τοὺς λογισμοὺς παθῶν κάρτερος.*

[1] Page 272, edit. Hudson.   [2] Page 174, edit. Hudson.
[3] De Clementia, lib. i. c. i.   [4] Hale's Hist. vol. i. p. 13.

mon sense can think the life of a man and a few shillings
to be of an equal consideration, or that the law in punishing
theft with death proceeds (as perhaps a private person sometimes may) with any view to vengeance. The terror of the
example is the only thing proposed, and one man is sacrificed
to the preservation of thousands.

If therefore the terror of this example is removed (as it
certainly is by frequent pardons) the design of the law is
rendered totally ineffectual; the lives of the persons executed
are thrown away, and sacrificed rather to the vengeance than
to the good of the public, which receives no other advantage
than by getting rid of a thief, whose place will immediately
be supplied by another. Here then we may cry out with the
poet : [1]

> ——" *Sævior ense*
> *Parcendi rabies* ——"

This I am confident may be asserted, that pardons have
brought many more men to the gallows than they have saved
from it. So true is that sentiment of Machiavel, that examples of justice are more merciful than the unbounded exercise
of pity.[2]

SECTION XI.

OF THE MANNER OF EXECUTION.

BUT if every hope which I have mentioned fails the thief:
if he should be discovered, apprehended, prosecuted, convicted, and refused a pardon; what is his situation then?
Surely most gloomy and dreadful, without any hope and without any comfort. This is, perhaps, the case with the less
practised, less spirited, and less dangerous rogues; but with
those of a different constitution it is far otherwise. No

[1] Claudian.   [2] In his Prince.

hero sees death as the alternative which may attend his undertaking with less terror, nor meets it in the field with more imaginary glory. Pride, which is commonly the uppermost passion in both, is in both treated with equal satisfaction. The day appointed by law for the thief's shame is the day of glory in his own opinion. His procession to Tyburn, and his last moments there, all are triumphant; attended with the compassion of the meek and tender-hearted, and with the applause, admiration, and envy, of all the bold and hardened. His behaviour in his present condition, not the crimes, how atrocious, soever, which brought him to it, are the subject of contemplation. And if he hath sense enough to temper his boldness with any degree of decency, his death is spoken of by many with honour, by most with pity, and by all with approbation.

How far such an example is from being an object of terror, especially to those for whose use it is principally intended, I leave to the consideration of every rational man; whether such examples as I have described are proper to be exhibited must be submitted to our superiors.

The great cause of this evil is the frequency of executions: the knowledge of human nature will prove this from reason; and the different effects which executions produce in the minds of the spectators in the country, where they are rare, and in London, where they are common, will convince us by experience. The thief who is hanged to-day hath learned his intrepidity from the example of his hanged predecessors, as others are now taught to despise death, and to bear it hereafter with boldness, from what they see to-day.

One way of preventing the frequency of executions is by removing the evil I am complaining of: for this effect in time becomes a cause; and greatly increases that very evil from which it first arose. The design of those who first appointed executions to be public, was to add the punishment of shame to that of death; in order to make the example an object of greater terror. But experience has shown us that the event is directly contrary to this intention. Indeed, a competent knowledge of human nature might have foreseen the consequence. To unite the ideas of death and shame is not so easy as may be imagined; all ideas of the latter being absorbed by the former. To prove this, I will appeal to any man who hath seen an execution, or a procession to an execution; let him tell me, when he hath beheld a poor wretch, bound in a cart, just on the verge of eternity, all pale and trembling with his approaching fate, whether the idea of shame hath ever intruded on his mind? much less will the bold daring rogue, who glories in his present condition, inspire the beholder with any such sensation.

The difficulty here will be easily explained, if we have recourse to the poets (for the good poet and the good politician do not differ so much as some who know nothing of either art affirm, nor would Homer or Milton have made the worst legislators of their times) : the great business is to raise terror ; and the poet will tell you that admiration, or pity, or both, are very apt to attend whatever is the object of terror in the human mind. That is very useful to the poet, but very hurtful on the present occasion to the politician, whose art is to be here employed to raise an object of terror, and at the same time, as much as possible, to strip it of all pity and all admiration.

To effect this, it seems that the execution should be as soon as possible after the commission and conviction of the crime ; for if this be of an atrocious kind, the resentment of mankind being warm, would pursue the criminal to his last end, and all pity for the offender would be lost in detestation of the offence. Whereas, when executions are delayed so long as they sometimes are, the punishment and not the crime is considered ; and no good mind can avoid compassionating a set of wretches who are put to death we know not why, unless, as it almost appears, to make a holiday for, and to entertain, the mob.

Secondly. It should be in some degree private. And here the poets will again assist us. Foreigners have found fault with the cruelty of the English drama, in representing frequent murders upon the stage. In fact, this is not only cruel but highly injudicious: a murder behind the scenes, if the poet knows how to manage it, will affect the audience with greater terror than if it was acted before their eyes. Of this we have an instance in the murder of the king in Macbeth, at which, when Garrick acts the part, it is scarce an hyperbole to say I have seen the hair of an audience stand on end. Terror hath, I believe, been carried higher by this single instance than by all the blood which hath been spilt on the stage.—To the poets I may add the priests, whose politics have never been doubted. Those of Egypt in particular, where the sacred mysteries were first devised, well knew the use of hiding from the eyes of the vulgar what they intended should inspire them with the greatest awe and dread. The mind of man is so much more capable of magnifying than his eye, that I question whether every object is not lessened by being looked upon: and this more especially when the passions are concerned: for these are ever apt to fancy much more satisfaction in those objects which they affect, and much more of mischief in those which they abhor, than are really to be found in either.

If executions therefore were so contrived that few could be present at them, they would be much more shocking and terrible to the crowd without doors than at present, as well as much more dreadful to the criminals themselves, who would thus die in the presence only of their enemies; and where the boldest of them would find no cordial to keep up his spirits, nor any breath to flatter his ambition.

Thirdly. The execution should be in the highest degree solemn. It is not the essence of the thing itself, but the dress and apparatus of it which makes an impression on the mind, especially on the minds of the multitude, to whom beauty in rags is never a desirable, nor deformity in embroidery a disagreeable, object.

Montaigne, who of all men, except Aristotle, seems best to have understood human nature, inquiring into the causes why death appears more terrible to the better sort of people than to the meaner, expresses himself thus: " I do verily believe, that it is those terrible ceremonies and preparations wherewith we set it out that more terrify us than the thing itself; a new and contrary way of living, the cries of mothers, wives, and children, the visits of astonished and afflicted friends, the attendance of pale and blubbered servants, a dark room set round with burning tapers, our beds environed with physicians and divines, in fine, nothing but ghastliness and horror round about us, render it so formidable that a man almost fancies himself dead and buried already." [1]

"If the image of death," says the same author, "was to appear thus dreadful to an army they would be an army of whining milksops; and where is the difference but in the apparatus? Thus in the field (I may add at the gallows) what is encountered with gaiety and unconcern, in a sick bed becomes the most dreadful of all objects."

In Holland the executions (which are very rare) are incredibly solemn. They are performed in the area before the starthouse, and attended by all the magistrates. The effect of this solemnity is inconceivable to those who have not observed it in others or felt it in themselves; and to this perhaps, more than to any other cause, the rareness of executions in that country is owing.

Now the following method which I shall venture to prescribe, as it would include all the three particulars of celerity, privacy, and solemnity, so would it, I think, effectually remove all the evils complained of, and which at present attend the manner of inflicting capital punishment.

Suppose then that the court at the Old Bailey was, at the end of the trials, to be adjourned during four days; that against the adjournment day a gallows was erected in the area before the court; that the criminals were all brought down on that day to receive sentence; and that this was executed the very moment after it was pronounced, in the sight and presence of the judges.

Nothing can, I think, be imagined (not even torture, which I am an enemy to the very thought of admitting) more terrible than such an execution; and I leave it to any man to resolve himself upon reflection, whether such a day at the

[1] Montaigne, Essay 19.

Old Bailey or a holiday at Tyburn would make the strongest impression on the minds of every one.

Thus I have, as well as I am able, finished the task which I proposed: have endeavoured to trace the evil from the very fountain-head, and to show whence it originally springs, as well as all the supplies it receives, till it becomes a torrent, which at present threatens to bear down all before it.

And here I must again observe, that if the former part of this treatise should raise any attention in the legislature, so as effectually to put a stop to the luxury of the lower people, to force the poor to industry, and to provide for them when industrious, the latter part of my labour would be of very little use; and indeed all the pains which can be taken in this latter part, and all the remedies which can be devised, without applying a cure to the former, will be only of the palliative kind, which may patch up the disease, and lessen the bad effects, but never can totally remove it.

Nor, in plain truth, will the utmost severity to offenders be justifiable unless we take every possible method of preventing the offence. *Nemo ad supplicia exigenda provenit, nisi qui remedia consumpsit,* says Seneca,[1] where he represents the governors of kingdoms in the amiable light of parents. The subject as well as the child should be left without excuse before he is punished; for in that case alone the rod becomes the hand either of the parent or the magistrate.

All temptations therefore are to be carefully moved out of the way; much less is the plea of necessity to be left in the mouth of any. This plea of necessity is never admitted in our law; but the reason of that is, says Lord Hale, because it is so difficult to discover the truth. Indeed that it is not always certainly false is a sufficient scandal to our polity; for what can be more shocking than to see an industrious poor creature, who is able and willing to labour, forced by mere want into dishonesty, and that in a nation of such trade and opulence?

Upon the whole, something should be, nay, must be done, or much worse consequences than have hitherto happened are

---

[1] De Clementia, lib. ii. Fragm.

very soon to be apprehended. Nay, as the matter now stands, not only care for the public safety, but common humanity, exacts our concern on this occasion; for that many cart-loads of our fellow-creatures are once in six weeks carried to slaughter is a dreadful consideration; and this is greatly heightened by reflecting, that, with proper care and proper regulations, much the greater part of these wretches might have been made not only happy in themselves, but very useful members of society, which they now so greatly dishonour in the sight of all Christendom.

TO THE PUBLIC

THE rude behaviour and insolence of servants of all kinds is become a general complaint: for which insolence the law has given no other power of punishing than by turning them away; and this would be often punishment enough, if the servant could not easily provide himself with another place: But here they find no manner of difficulty; for many persons are weak enough to take servants without any character; and if this be insisted on, there is an ingenious method in this town of obtaining a false character from one who personates the former master or mistress: To obviate all this, an office is erected in the *Strand,* opposite *Cecil-Street,* where the best servants in every capacity are to be heard of; and where the public may be assured, that no servant shall ever be register'd, who cannot produce a real good character from the last place in which he or she actually lived; the method of ascertaining which may be seen at the said office; where estates, houses, lodgings, and every thing else that could be sold or left, are carefully register'd; and where consequently they may be heard of, by those who desire to hire or purchase the same.

Note, This office is established by a society of gentlemen on the principles recommended by *Montaigne* in his *Essays,* and must soon become of the highest utility to the public. Nay, that great author laments the want of such an office, as a great defect in the *French* Government. We have thought it therefore not improper to recommend this office at the end of a work, in which the public utility is sincerely intended, as it seems to deserve the encouragement of all, who think the public utility worthy of their regard.

NOTE: It is not certain that Fielding wrote the above Notice, appended to the first edition of his pamphlet entitled, " An Inquiry into the Causes of the Late increase of Robbers, &c.," published in 1751.

As it throws a curious light upon a practical difficulty in household management (more fully exploited by Daniel Defoe in his paper under the peculiar title,—" What's Every-bodies business is Nobodies business ") a difficulty possibly not unknown in the present day, it has been thought of sufficient interest to be included in the present edition of Fielding's Complete Works, in the connection in which it originally appeared.—G. E. C.

A PROPOSAL

FOR

Making an Effectual Provision

FOR THE

POOR,

FOR

Amending their MORALS,

AND FOR

Rendering them useful MEMBERS of the SOCIETY.

To which is added,

A PLAN of the BUILDINGS propofed, with proper Elevations.

Drawn by an Eminent Hand.

By HENRY FIELDING, Efq;

Barrifter at Law, and one of his Majefty's Juftices of the Peace for the County of Middlefex.

Ifta fententia maximè et fallit imperitos, et obeft fæpiffime Reipublicæ, cùm aliquid verum et rectum effe dicitur, fed obtineri, id eft obfifti poffe populo, negatur.
Cic. de Leg. lib 3.

LONDON:
Printed for A. MILLAR, in the Strand.
MDCCLIII.

EXPLANATION OF THE PLAN

A Men's courts, containing 3,000 persons.
B Women's courts, containing 2,000 persons.
C Chapel.
D Prison court, containing 1,000 persons.
E Justice hall.
F Governor's house.
G Deputy Governor's house.
H Chaplain's house.
I Treasurer's house.
K Receiver's house.
L Sutleries.
M Burying grounds.
N Women's airing ground.
O Men's airing ground.
P Sutlery ground.
Q Front grounds.
R Elevation of the Governor's house.
S Front of the Deputy Governor's house.
T Front of the Chaplain's house.

a Principal gate.
b Place of the steeple.
c Men's way to the chapel.
d Prisoner's chapel.
e Prisoners' way to their chapel.
g Gates.
h Prisons, or fasting rooms,
i Cells.
k Whipping post.
l Keepers' houses.
m Lodges for the assistants.
n Women's infirmary.
p Matron's house.
r Officers' houses.
s Stairs.
t Men's infirmary.
u, v Privies.
w Workrooms, above which are the lodging-wards, 160 in number.
x Lodges for the watchmen and assistants.
y Storehouses.

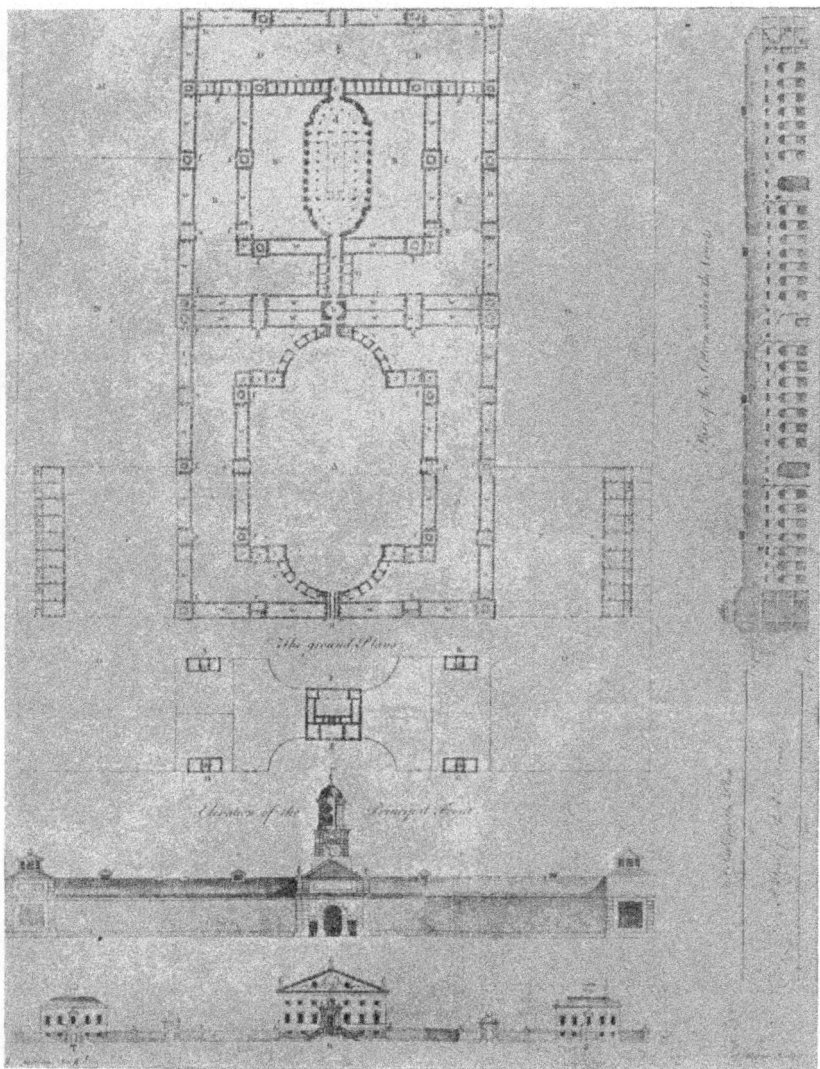

The grand Plan.

Elevation of the Principal Front.

HENRY PELHAM

CHANCELLOR OF HIS MAJESTY'S EXCHEQUER

SIR,

In addressing to you the following sheets, I only embrace an opportunity of expressing the deep sense I have of the obligations you have conferred on me. For it would be unreasonable to expect that one in your station should find sufficient leisure to weigh and consider duly the subject here treated of. While your attention is so much engaged in matters of higher moment, it would seem hard that no other should be willing to undertake this inferior province of government, or should indeed be equal to it; but that one man should be obliged to support the whole.

And yet, if ever there was a time when a minister of state might find such leisure, I think it may be the present. It is true, indeed, that when a skilful governor of a ship hath brought his vessel through rocks, quicksands, and storms, to ride safely before the wind, he hath a right to enjoy that safety which he hath procured, and to indulge his own ease; and yet even then, if he is informed that his vessel is leaky, or some of the minutest tackling in disorder, should not he give some attention to those inferior matters which others neglect, which retard the vessel in her course, and may, perhaps, however slowly, at last produce her destruction?

There is perhaps, sir, something above the style of prose in this allusion, but there is nothing in it beyond that of truth.

To return, however, to the plainest style: I here present

you with that plan which I had the honour once to mention
to you, and of which I have given a former hint, to the public.
If this be carried into execution it will in its consequence, I
am convinced, remove almost every evil from the society of
which honest men at present complain—will complete the
obligation which posterity shall owe to the present age—and
will heap praises on that name which shall be then as much
loved and honoured by mankind as it is now by,

      " Sir,

         " Your most obliged,

            " Most humble,

               " And most obedient servant,

                      " HENRY FIELDING.

" Jan. 19, 1753."

A PROPOSAL

FOR

MAKING AN EFFECTUAL PROVISION

FOR

THE POOR, ETC.

INTRODUCTION

THAT the strength and riches of a society consist in the numbers of the people is an assertion which hath obtained the force of an axiom in politics. This, however, supposes the society to be so constituted that those numbers may contribute to the good of the whole: for, could the contrary be imagined—could we figure to ourselves a state in which a great part of the people, instead of contributing to the good of the public, should lie as a useless and heavy burden on the rest of their countrymen—the very reverse of the above maxim would be true; and the numbers of such a people would be so far from giving any strength to the society, that they would weaken and oppress it; so that it would, in a merely civil sense, be the interest of such a society to lessen its numbers, and by some means or other to shake or lop off the useless and burdensome part.

"Numbers of men," says Mr. Locke, "are to be preferred to largeness of dominions;" and the reason, as he well observes, is, for that labour "puts the difference of value on every thing." "Let anyone consider," says he, "what the difference is between an acre of land, planted with tobacco, or sugar, sown with wheat or barley, and an acre of the same land lying in common, without any husbandry upon it; and he will find that the improvement of labour makes the far greatest part of the value. I think it will be but a very modest computation to say that of the products of the earth, useful to the life of man, nine-tenths are the effects of labour; nay, if we will rightly estimate things, as they come to our use, and cast up the several expenses about them—what in them is purely owing to nature, and what to labour—we shall find that in most of them ninety-nine hundredths are wholly to be put on the account of labour." In this alone, as he demonstrates, lies the difference between us and the Americans, who are furnished by nature as liberally as ourselves with all the materials of plenty, yet " have not one-hundredth part of the conveniences we enjoy; and " among whom " a king of a large and fruitful territory .   .   .   feeds, lodges, and is clad worse than a day-labourer in England." [1]

It is not barely therefore in the numbers of people, but in numbers of people well and properly disposed, that we can truly place the strength and riches of a society.

From the universality of the maxim which I have mentioned—qualified, I mean, as above—it seems to follow that a state is capable of this perfection, and that some states have actually been so constituted. Of this kind particularly seems to me the Egyptian policy of old, and that of Holland in modern times. I do not mean to say that any human society is so absolutely capable of this perfection, that every individual shall contribute some share to the strength of the whole. Nature hath denied us this by laying certain individuals in every society under a natural incapacity not only of administering to the good of others, but even of providing for and protecting themselves. Such are the incapacities of infancy and of old age, and of impotency either of mind or body, natural or accidental.

Of all these policy, perhaps, would dictate to us only to

[1] Essay of Civil Government, chap. v. secs. 40-42.   Works, vol. ii., pp. 184-5 [edit. 1740].

preserve the first, and accordingly we read of nations among whom those members who were either by age, or any incurable infirmity, rendered useless and burdensome to the public, were without mercy cut off by their laws. But this neither religion nor humanity will allow; and therefore to this burden, which is imposed on us by God and nature, we must submit; nor will the evil, while confined to such absolute incapacity, be very grievous or much to be lamented.

From what I have here advanced it seems, I think, apparent that, among a civilized people, that polity is the best established in which all the members, except such only as labour under any utter incapacity, are obliged to contribute a share to the strength and wealth of the public. Secondly, That a state is capable of this degree of perfection; and, consequently, that to effect this is the business of every wise and good legislature.

And this seems to have been the great aim of the first founders of the English constitution; by the laws of which no man whatsoever is exempted from performing such duties to the public as befit his rank; according to the observation of that most wonderful young prince, *Quem tantum terris fata ostenderunt.* As " there is no part," says he, " admitted in the body that doth not work and take pains, so ought there no part of the commonwealth to be, but labour some in his vocation. The gentleman ought to labour in service in his country; the servingman ought to wait diligently on his master; the artificer ought to labour in his work; the husbandman in tilling the ground; the merchant in passing the tempests; but the vagabonds ought clearly to be banished, as is the superfluous humours of the body, that is to say, the spittle and filth; which, because it is for no use, it is put out by the strength of nature." [1] Thus far this incomparable young prince, as the excellent historian of the Reformation calls him; who was, says the bishop, the wonder of his time, and indeed will be so of all succeeding ages.

[1] King Edward's Remains, preserved at the end of the 2nd vol. of Bishop Burnet's " History of the Reformation," page 70. [Vol. v., p. 98, in the Oxford edition of 1865.]

To divide the same kind of labours equally among all the members of society is so far from being necessary that it is not even convenient; nor could it indeed be possible in any state without such a perfect equality in all its branches as is inconsistent with all government, and which befits only that which is sometimes called the state of nature, but may more properly be called a state of barbarism and wildness.

Those duties, however, which fall to the higher ranks of men, even in this commonwealth, are by no means of the highest or easiest kind. The watchings and fatigues, the anxieties and cares which attend the highest stations, render their possessors in real truth no proper objects of envy to those in the lowest, whose labours are much less likely to impair the health of their bodies, or to destroy the peace of their minds; are not less consistent with their happiness, and much more consistent with their safety.

It is true, indeed, that in every society where prosperity is established and secured by law there will be some among the rich whose indolence is superior to the love of wealth and honour, and who will therefore avoid these public duties for which avarice and ambition will always furnish out a sufficient number of candidates; yet, however idle the lives of such may be, it must be observed, first, that they are by no means burdensome to the public; but do support themselves on what the law calls their own; a property acquired by the labour of their ancestors, and often the rewards, or fruits at least, of public services. Secondly, that whilst they dispose what is their own for the purposes of idleness (and more especially perhaps, if for the purposes of luxury) they may be well called useful members of trading commonwealths, and truly said to contribute to the good of the public.

But with the poor (and such must be in any nation where property is—that is to say, where there are any rich) this is not the case. For having nothing but their labour to bestow on the society, if they withhold this from it they become useless members; and having nothing but their labour to procure a support for themselves they must of necessity become burdensome.

On this labour the public hath a right to insist; since this is the only service which the poor can do that society, which in some way or other hath a right to the service of all its members; and as this is the only means by which they can avoid laying that burden on the public which in case of absolute incapacity alone it is obliged to support.

Here then seems to arise a twofold duty to the legislature; first, to procure to such the means of labour, and, secondly, to compel them to undertake it. The former, indeed, naturally precedes the latter, and is presupposed by it: for if the means of employing them be not to be found the ablest hands will be in the same condition with the weakest, and will alike become a necessary burden on the community; which is so far from being at liberty to punish a man for involuntary idleness, that it is obliged to support him under it.

Both these, therefore, are the proper business of every legislature, and both for above a hundred years together have been very much the business of ours. If they have succeeded I am sure I shall egregiously throw away my time in composing the following sheets; in which, however, I shall have the consolation of much good company to keep me in countenance. To say truth, if the errors in our present provisions are not very great and fatal, or if the remedies proposed do not seem perfectly adequate to the removal of them, I would by no means advise any great alteration: for, as the Greek historian [1] observes of laws in general, " that city which is governed by the worst laws, but those firm and stable, is in a safer condition than the city where the laws are better and more eligible in their original institutions, but where they are administered in a loose and fluctuating manner."

Which fluctuation in our own laws hath been, I find, an old complaint in this kingdom. Holinshed tells us long ago, that our great number of laws was said to " breed a general negligence and contempt of all good order; because we have so many," says he, " that no subject can live without the transgression of some of them, and that the often alteration of our ordinances doeth much harm in this respect." [2]

[1] Thucydides.   [2] " Description of Britain," chap. 18.

But if there was any occasion of this complaint in his time, I am sure there is much more now; for as to our statutes they are increased much more than tenfold since the reign of Henry the Eighth; with such variety of alterations, explanations, and amendments, that in many cases no good lawyer will pretend readily to say what the law at present is. Even in Queen Anne's time there was a cause determined in the Queen's Bench expressly against the letter of an Act of Parliament; which, as Carthew, who reports it, tells us, was not once mentioned either at the bar or on the bench; the reason of which must have been because it was unknown.

Nor is there any walk in all this wilderness of laws more intersected or more perplexed with mazes and confusion, than this which leads to the provision for the poor; and hence it is that through no other way a more plentiful harvest hath of late years been brought into Westminster Hall.

Sensible as I am of this mischief I should not venture to propose any further experiments, if I was not also sensible that the disease is become absolutely intolerable; and had not at the same time very sanguine hopes that the remedy which I shall propose will prove in the highest degree effectual.

That the poor are a very great burden, and even a nuisance to this kingdom; that the laws for relieving their distresses, and restraining their vices, have not answered those purposes; and that they are at present very ill provided for, and much worse governed, are truths which every man, I believe, will acknowledge. Such have been the unanimous complaints of all the writers who have considered this matter down from the days of Queen Elizabeth; such is apparently the sense of our present legislature; and such is the universal voice of the nation.

The facts must be very glaring that can produce this unanimous concurrence in opinion, and so in truth they are. Every man who hath any property must feel the weight of that tax which is levied for the use of the poor; and every man who hath any understanding must see how absurdly it is applied. So very useless indeed is this heavy tax, and so wretched its disposition, that it is a question whether the poor or the rich are actually more dissatisfied, or have indeed greater reason to be dissatisfied, since the plunder of the one serves so little to the real advantage of the other: for while a million yearly is raised among the former many of the latter are starved; many more languish in want and misery; of the rest numbers are found begging or pilfering in the streets to-day, and to-morrow are locked up in gaols and bridewells.

Of all these deplorable evils we have constant evidence before our eyes. The sufferings of the poor are, indeed, less observed than their misdeeds; not from any want of compassion, but because they are less known; and this is the true reason why we so often hear them mentioned with abhorrence, and so seldom with pity. But if we were to make a progress through the outskirts of this town, and look into the habitations of the poor, we should there behold such pictures of human misery as must move the compassion of every heart that deserves the name of human. What, indeed, must be his composition who could see whole families in want of every necessary of life, oppressed with hunger, cold, nakedness, and filth; and with diseases, the certain consequences of all these —what, I say, must be his composition who could look into such a scene as this, and be affected only in his nostrils? [1]

That such wretchedness as this is so little lamented, arises therefore from its being so little known; but, if this be the case with the sufferings of the poor, it is not so with their misdeeds. They starve, and freeze, and rot among themselves; but they beg, and steal, and rob among their betters. There is not a parish in the Liberty of Westminster which doth not raise thousands annually for the poor, and there is not a street in that Liberty which doth not swarm all day with beggars, and all night with thieves. Stop your coach at what shop you will, however expeditious the tradesman is to attend you, a beggar is commonly beforehand with him; and if you should not directly face his door the tradesman must

[1] Some Members of Parliament actually made this progress in company with Mr. Welch, and owned the truth exceeded their imagination.

often turn his head while you are talking to him, or the same beggar, or some other thief at hand, will pay a visit to his shop! I omit to speak of the more open and violent insults which are every day committed on His Majesty's subjects in the streets and highways. They are enough known and enough spoken of. The depredations on property are less noticed, particularly those in the parishes within ten miles of London. To these every man is not obnoxious, and therefore it is not every man's business to suppress them. These are, however, grown to the most deplorable height; insomuch that the gentleman is daily, or rather nightly, plundered of his pleasure, and the farmer of his livelihood.

But though some of these articles are more universally notorious than others, they are in general enough known to raise an universal indignation at a very heavy tax levied for the use of those who are no less a nuisance than a burden to the public; and by which, as woeful experience hath taught us, neither the poor themselves nor the public are relieved.

With regard to the evil men will agree almost unanimously, but with regard to the remedy I shall expect no such general concurrence: nay the more deplorable and desperate the case is, the more backward may we presume men will be to allow the possibility of any cure, or the efficacy of any remedy for that purpose.

It may very reasonably be presumed that so national and atrocious a grievance, and which it is the interest of all men of great property to redress, would not have subsisted so long had it been capable of being redressed. And this presumption may very fairly be confirmed by the many endeavours which our Parliament have used, and the indefatigable pains they have taken in this matter.

If, after all these endeavours, the evil should not be removed or even abated—on the contrary, if it should be even increased—surely no man can be blamed who shall conclude it to be irremediable, and shall compare it to some inveterate defect in our animal constitution; to which, however grievous, an honest physician will advise us to submit, there being no cure for it in the art of physic.

This is indeed so rational, and at the same time so decent a conclusion, that, far from blaming it, I am almost overborne with it. I am almost deterred from prosecuting the attempt any farther, and in some degree conscious of the immodesty of my undertaking. For though some few, of tempers perhaps equally sanguine with those who still hope to see the longitude discovered, may not despair of seeing this great evil one day redressed; how little can a man as I am, without authority, hope to gain even their attention on this subject!

Let it be remembered however in my favour, that some of the noblest and most useful discoveries have been made by men of little note or authority in the world; for which perhaps a handsomer reason than the bare intervention of chance might be assigned. Men of the greatest abilities are not always the forwardest to push themselves into the public notice. If eminent fortune, or eminent friends, do not throw open to us the first gates which lead to fame and greatness; a thousand mean tricks and arts must be submitted to to procure us an admittance. These are easily known, and as easily practised, by persons of small parts and much cunning; while they are overlooked and despised by real genius, which is generally attended by a sullen pride that, disdaining to seek after the world, expects to be sought out by it. Such are the men who, as Horace expresses it, deceive mankind, and pass through the world without being known by it. A temper of mind which may be as happy for the possessor as Horace and Epicurus seem to think it, but which, very unhappily for the public, is bestowed by nature on the wrong persons.

But there is a second reason less refined, and consequently more obvious; this is the force of a long and constant application to any one subject. Very moderate parts, with this assistance, will carry us a great way—indeed may in time perform wonders; and to this I can, with great truth, and, I hope, with equal modesty, assert the strongest pretensions; having read over and considered all the laws, in any wise relating to the poor, with the utmost care and attention; and having been many years very particularly concerned in the execution of them. To these I have likewise added a careful perusal of everything which I could find that hath been written on this subject, from the original institution in the 43rd of Elizabeth to this day; and upon the whole it appears to me that there are great defects in these laws, and they are capable of being amended.

Whether I have discovered what these defects are, and have been yet farther so fortunate as to find out the method of removing them, I now submit to the public, after this preface and this short apology for an undertaking which I allow to be of very great difficulty; and to which I shall, of consequence, neither be surprised nor offended if I am thought unequal. The attempt, indeed, is such that the want of success can scarce be called a disappointment, though I shall have lost much time and misemployed much pains; and, what is above all, shall miss the pleasure of thinking that, in the decline of my health and life, I have conferred a great and lasting benefit on my country.

PROPOSALS FOR ERECTING A COUNTY WORK-HOUSE, ETC.

PAR. I. That there shall be erected, for the county of Middlesex, at some convenient place within the said county, a large building, consisting of three several courts, according to the annexed plan. The two outermost of the said courts to be called the county-house, and the innermost court to be called the county house of correction; with a chapel and offices, according to the said plan. *County-house, and County-house of Correction to be erected.*

II. That the said county-house shall be large enough to contain five thousand persons and upwards; and the said county house of correction large enough to contain six hundred persons and upwards. *What poor they shall contain.*

III. That both the said houses shall be so contrived, that the men and women may be kept entirely separate from each other. *Men and women to be kept separate.*

IV. That the said county-house shall contain, 1. Of lodgings for the officers. 2. Of lodging-rooms for the labourers. 3. Of working-rooms for the same. 4. Of an infirmary. 5. Of a chapel. 6. Of several large storerooms, with cellarage. *Of what buildings the County-house is to consist.*

V. That the said county house of correction shall consist, 1. Of lodgings for the officers. 2. Of lodging-rooms for the prisoners. 3. Of working-rooms for the same. 4. Of an infirmary. 5. Of a fasting-room. 6. Of several cells or dungeons. 7. Of a large room with iron grates which shall be contiguous to and look into the end of the chapel. *Of what the County-house of Correction*

VI. There shall be likewise built one house for the Governor, one for the Deputy-governors, one for the Chaplains, one for the Treasurer, and one other for the Receiver-general of the said house. There shall be likewise built on each side of the said county-house nine houses for the providing the labourers and prisoners with the necessaries of life. *Additional buildings.* *Suttling Houses.*

Note, the arguments in support of these proposals are printed at the end of them, to which the reader is desired to refer as he proceeds.

LEGAL WRITINGS—10

How to be leased.

VII. That the said eighteen houses shall be leased to proper persons, by the governor for the time being, for the term of seven years; subject to a condition of forfeiture and re-entry on the breach of certain rules and statutes of the said house, hereinafter particularly mentioned.

County-house,how furnished.

VIII. That the lodging-rooms of the county-house shall be furnished with beds, allowing one bed to two persons; one large joint-stool, and two small ones, for each bed. And that the working-rooms of the said house shall be provided with all kind of implements and tools, for carrying on such manufactures as shall from time to time be introduced into the said house.

How County-house of Correction.

IX. That the lodging-rooms of the county house of correction shall be furnished with a coverlet and blankets for the prisoners, and matting to lie on; and the working-rooms shall be provided with implements for beating hemp, chopping rags, and for other of the hardest and vilest labour.

X. That A, B, etc., shall be commissioners for carrying this Act into execution. That the said commissioners, or three of them, shall meet once a week, at such places within the said county as they shall think most proper, from Lady Day 1753 to Michaelmas 1753, and once a fortnight from Michaelmas 1753 to Lady Day 1755; then to make up their accounts before a committee of the House of Commons, if then sitting; if not, at the next sessions; after which the said commission to cease and be determined.

Sum to be raised.

XI. That in order to defray the expense of the aforesaid building, and provide the same with all necessary furniture, as well as to provide implements and materials for setting the poor to work, and for other expenses during the first year, a sum not exceeding   shall be immediately raised.

XII. That the following officers shall be appointed for the government and care of the said houses; and these officers shall be allowed the following salaries:

County-house.

One Governor   Two Chaplains
Two Clerks   Six Keepers

Two Deputies	Six Assistants
One Clerk each	One Superintendent to every
Treasurer	Room
Receiver	Four Watchmen
Three Clerks	Clerk
Store Keeper	Sexton
Three Clerks	

House of Correction.

One Keeper	Superintendent to every
Three Under-keepers	Room
Six Assistants	Two Watchmen

Infirmary.

| Surgeon | Matron |
| Apothecary | Nurses |

XIII. That the Governor shall sue and be sued by the name of the Governor of the County-house of Middlesex. And that, besides all other powers to be given him, he shall have power, as Governor of the said house, to make contracts with all persons whatever, and to draw on the Treasurer for any sums of money so contracted for in payment for any implements or materials of any kind of manufacture, trade, or mystery. He shall likewise have full power to exercise and carry on, in either of the said houses, any such manufacture, trade or mystery as may be lawfully exercised and carried on within this kingdom; and may once every month hold a grand market at the county-house, or in some convenient place near adjoining thereto, for the disposal of such wares and manufactures as shall be wrought by the labourers in the said houses. And that every particular article of such sale, with the price for which it was sold, shall be entered in two books; one of which shall be kept in the receiver's, the other in the store-keeper's office, as hereafter is more particularly expressed.

Who shall
be com-
mitted to
the
County-
house, etc.
1. Persons
within the
Vagrant
Act.
2. Or those
liable to
be sent to
the House
of Correc-
tion.
XIV. That when any person shall be brought before a Justice of Peace, for the County of Middlesex, and shall be convicted before him, on the oath of one credible witness, of any offence by which he is made a disorderly person, or a rogue and vagabond, by a certain Act passed in the 17th of his present Majesty, called the Vagrant Act; or shall be so convicted of any other crime for which he is liable to be committed to the House of Correction for any fixed time, or at the discretion of one or more Justices, by any law now in being, it shall be lawful for the said Justice to commit such person to the County-house, or the County House of Correction, at his discretion; which commitment shall be in the following form:

> Receive into your custody the body of J. S. herewith sent you, convicted before me, on the oath of J. N. a credible witness, of an offence within the Statute of commonly called   and him safely keep in your said custody until the next general or quarter-sessions—(or for any shorter time, to be specified in the commitment). Given, etc.

And this mittimus, if to the County-house, shall be directed to the Governor of the County-house, his Deputy, etc.; if to the County House of Correction, to the Keeper of, &c. And whereas it will happen that such prisoners will be frequently conveyed to the said house from distant parts of the county, the Justice shall endorse on the back of his commitment the sum to be paid by the Receiver of the County-house as an allowance for the charges of conveying the said prisoner or prisoners, such allowance not to exceed 6d. by the mile; and if need be 6d. more for the necessary refreshment of such prisoner.

3. Or per-
sons ap-
pointed to
be com-
mitted to
the County
Gaol in ex-
ecution.
XV. That it shall be likewise lawful for the Justices to commit to either of the said houses, all persons convicted before them of any crimes of which, by the laws now in being, any one or more Justices of Peace have cognizance in a summary way, out of their sessions, and when the offenders,

being so convicted, are appointed to be committed to the
county gaol by way of punishment for their said offences.

XVI. That where any person shall be accused on oath of 4. Or per-
petty larceny before any Justice of Peace, and it shall appear cused of
to him that it was the party's first offence, and that the theft thefts.
was not exaggerated by any heinous circumstances, the Justice may at his discretion commit the offender to either of the
aforesaid houses till the next sessions, or for a less time; or
if he sees proper may proceed to commit the person to the
county gaol, and bind over all the necessary parties to prosecute, as he may lawfully do at this time.

XVII. That it shall be lawful for any of his Majesty's sub- 5. Or wan-
jects to seize all suspicious persons who shall be found wan- without a
dering on foot, about the fields, lanes, or highways, or in the pass.
streets of any of the towns or parishes of the said county, or
within the Liberty of Westminster; and all labourers or
servants, or persons of low degree, who, after the hour of ten
in the evening shall be found harbouring in any alehouse or
victualling house; and if such persons shall not give reasonable satisfaction to him or them by whom he or she is apprehended that he or she belongs to the said county, and is going
on some lawful errand or business, or if he or she belongs to
any other county, or is then six miles distant from his own
habitation, and shall not produce a pass or certificate, signed
by some magistrate, minister, or churchwarden, expressing
whither or on what account he or she is then travelling, it
shall be lawful for the party apprehending to confine such
person till he or she can be delivered to the constable, or other
peace officer, or shall be carried by the party himself so apprehending such person before some Justice of the Peace;
who shall examine the said person; and if he or she shall
appear to be a wanderer or idle person, and shall have no legal
pass as aforesaid, such Justice may commit him or her to the
county-house, or county house of correction, as he shall think
proper, there to remain till the next general or quarter-sessions, or for any less time, at his discretion. And all constables, head-boroughs, &c. are hereby ordered to apprehend
all such persons of whom they shall have notice, and to re-

ceive all such persons into their custody as shall be delivered to them, and to convey them before some Justice, under the penalty of five pounds to be levied by warrant from the said Justices, one half to the use of the person complaining, the other half to the use of the said county-house. Provided, nevertheless, that whoever shall presume maliciously to detain any person, contrary to the plain intent of this law, shall forfeit to the person so aggrieved the sum of ten pounds, to be recovered by action, &c.

Pass, when and how to be obtained by the party.

XVIII. And whereas it may often happen that poor persons have lawful occasions to travel above six miles from home, and into a foreign county, on errands of business for themselves or others, or to procure work, or sometimes to visit their near relatives, who live at a distance from them— That any magistrate of the county or place, or minister, or churchwarden of the parish, being applied to, and properly informed of the truth of such lawful occasion, shall deliver to such persons a pass in the following words, *mutatis mutandis:*

PARISH OF MIDDLESEX

Permit A. B., the bearer hereof, to pass to the town of Shaftesbury in the County of Dorset, and there to remain during the time limited in this pass, he behaving himself orderly and according to law.

Given under my hand this 10th of Nov., 1752.

C. D., Minister of the said parish.

This pass to continue in force one month from the date hereof inclusive, and no longer.

—or by any other.

XIX. That it shall be lawful for any gentleman, farmer, artificer, or tradesman, to employ any journeyman, servant, or labourer, of any other parish or county besides his own, he having first obtained from such magistrate, minister, or churchwarden as aforesaid, such pass as aforesaid, which the said magistrate, &c., are hereby required to grant, at the desire of such gentleman, farmer, &c. Such pass to be appointed to continue in force for so long time as such gentleman, &c.,

shall require, during the continuance of which pass it shall not be lawful for any person whatever to molest or remove the said journeyman or labourer from his said service, unless for some crime cognizable before a magistrate, any law to the contrary notwithstanding.

XX. And whereas many able and industrious persons, who are willing to get a livelihood by honest labour, are often, for want of such labour, reduced to great distress, and forced against their will to become chargeable to the parishes to which they belong: that when any poor person shall apply to the minister, or churchwarden of any parish, and shew to either of them such their inability to procure a livelihood in their own parish, or in any other parish in the neighbourhood, the said minister or churchwarden shall deliver to such poor person a certificate in the words following: <sub-note>Who may go voluntarily to the County-house and how.</sub-note>

PARISH OF
MIDDLESEX

To the Governor of the County-house of the said county. I recommend to your care C. D., the bearer hereof, to be provided for in your county-house, he being an honest, industrious person, but incapable at present of procuring work in this neighbourhood.

Given under my hand this 10th Nov., 1752.

A. B., Churchwarden of the said parish.

Which said pass being produced and sworn to before any Justice of Peace of the said county, shall be countersigned by him. Provided that it shall appear to the Justice that such pass was obtained at the desire of the party obtaining it, and that from absolute want of labour in the said parish.

XXI. That whoever shall presume to counterfeit any such pass or certificate as aforesaid, or to personate him or her to whom such pass or certificate was originally granted, is hereby declared to be guilty of a very high misdemeanour, of which being convicted upon the oath of one witness, or by his own confession, before one justice of the county where he shall be apprehended, he shall be committed by the said Justice <sub-note>Penalty on counterfeit passes.</sub-note>

to the county house of correction, if within the county of Middlesex, or to the house of correction in any other county, there to be severely whipt and put to hard labour for any time not exceeding twelve, or less than six, calendar months.

—or on not returning at the expiration of the passes. XXII.   That if any person shall be absent from his parish with a pass either obtained by himself or at the request of any other, and shall not return to his said parish at the expiration thereof, (sickness or other inability excepted,) such person being lawfully convicted thereof by confession or oath of one witness, shall be sent to the county house of correction, if found in Middlesex, or, being apprehended in any other county, to the house of correction there, by any justice of the said county, there to be whipt and to remain to hard labour till the next sessions; and then to be continued or discharged at the discretion of the Justices.

Manner of admission of volunteers into the County-house. XXIII.   That when any person shall come to the county-house with a certificate as above, the Governor or his deputy shall examine the said person as to his age, ability, and skill in any work or manufacture, and shall then order the receiver to enter in a book, to be kept for that purpose, the name and age of the said person, the parish to which he belongs, and the day of his admission into the county-house, together with the kind of labour to which he is appointed; and a duplicate thereof shall likewise be entered in another book, to be kept by the storekeeper, after which the said person shall be set to work according to his abilities, &c.   In the said book shall likewise be entered an account of the monies advanced to him by the receiver, and of the repayments to be made by him as hereafter is ordered and appointed.

How volunteers to be detained. XXIV.   And if any such person shall depart from the said house more than the space of one mile, or shall absent himself above one hour from the said house, without the leave of the Governor or Deputy Governor, such person being thereof convicted upon the oath of one witness, or on his own confession, before the Governor, his deputy, or any one Justice of the Peace, shall be committed to the county house of correction, there to remain till the next sessions, or for any less time: Provided, nevertheless, that the Governor, or his deputy, are hereby required to grant a licence of departure to all such persons, whenever the same shall be demanded; unless such person shall not then have finished the particular piece of work in which he shall be employed, or unless he shall then remain indebted to the receiver of the said house; such licence of departure to be in the following words:

COUNTY-HOUSE A. B., the bearer hereof, who came volun-
OF MIDDLESEX   tarily to the county-house aforesaid, is
at his own request discharged from the
same, and at liberty to return to his
lawful habitation in the parish of
in the said county.   C. D., Governor.

To which the Governor may, at his discretion, add a clause signifying the industry or good behaviour of the said party.

XXV. That every person who shall be brought by mitti-mus to the county-house shall be examined, entered, and set to work as above; a badge with these words, " County House," in large letters, shall likewise be sewed on the left shoulder of the said person, who shall be confined within the said house till he is discharged in manner as hereafter is expressed; and whoever shall presume to tear off, or otherwise destroy the said badge, either from himself or any other person, being thereof convicted by the oath of one witness, or on his own confession, before the Governor or deputy, shall be by him committed to the county house of correction, there to remain till discharged by due course of law. *Manner of admission of those committed to the County house*

XXVI. That when any person shall be brought to the county house of correction, by a mittimus to the said house, he shall be immediately confined within the fasting-room, there to remain with no other maintenance than bread and water during the space of twenty-four hours; after which he shall be put to hard labour with the other prisoners, unless he shall give any marks, by his words or behaviour, of any outrageous degree of reprobacy; in which case the keeper of the said county house of correction shall inform the Governor *Manner of admitting into the County-house of Correction.*

or his deputy thereof, who shall convene the party before him, and may at his discretion remand the said person to the aforesaid fasting-room, or may confine him alone in a cell, to be supported with bread and water only till such time as he shall behave in a more orderly manner; or, in default thereof, till the next sessions. And all persons committed to the county house of correction shall there remain and be put to hard labour till they be discharged at the sessions, in such manner as in this Act is directed, unless in cases where a shorter confinement is appointed by the Act itself.

Rules and orders of the house —Hour of prayer.

XXVII. That the bell of the county-house shall be rung every morning at four throughout the year, and prayers shall begin in the chapel precisely at five; at the conclusion of which, on every Wednesday and Friday, some short lecture or exhortation of morality shall be read to the people; and if any person, unless on account of sickness, or for some other reasonable cause to be allowed by the Governor or his deputy, shall be absent, he shall be guilty of a misdemeanour, to be punished as hereafter.

—of work.

XXVIII. That the hours of work in the county house of correction shall be every day from six in the morning to seven in the evening, allowing half an hour for breakfast, and an hour for dinner; and in the county house the said hours of work shall be daily from six in the morning till nine, from ten to one, and from two till six in the evening, except on Thursdays, when two hours in the afternoon are to be otherwise employed, as hereafter is appointed, such holy-days likewise excepted as hereafter are mentioned; that prayers shall again be read in the chapel every evening at seven.

—of rest.

XXIX. That the bell of the county-house shall be rung every evening at nine, and that all fires and lights shall be then put out, except in the infirmary and in the apartments of the officers; that all the gates and doors of both houses, except as aforesaid, shall then be shut and fastened, the keys delivered to the Governor or deputy, and the watch shall be set.

XXX. That the keepers or under-keepers of both houses shall by turns constantly attend and supervise the labourers, and shall take an account of any neglect of work, or other misbehaviour; the keepers of the county-house shall likewise take an account of any extraordinary dilligence in any of the said labourers, and shall faithfully report the same twice in every week to the Governor or his deputy, at their court, which is hereafter appointed to be holden, and that one of the labourers of the best morals and demeanours shall in every room be appointed to supervise the conduct of the other labourers, and to report the same.

XXXI. That as often as may be, the labourers in the county-house shall be permitted to refresh themselves in the inclosed ground, contiguous to the said house, in the presence of two at least of the keepers and under-keepers, particularly on Sundays, and on every Thursday in the year, when two hours labour in the afternoon shall be remitted for that purpose; the same liberty shall be granted to any one or more of the prisoners in the house of correction, provided that the surgeon or apothecary shall certify to the Governor or his deputy that such refreshment is necessary for the health of the said prisoners, who shall on such occasions be sufficiently guarded, and none of the labourers to be present at the same time; provided that Christmas Day and the three subsequent days, Twelfth Day, Ash Wednesday, Good Friday, Monday in Easter week, Monday in Whitsun week, Michaelmas Day, Gunpowder Treason Day, and His Majesty's birthday, shall be holy-days in the county-house, and the labourers may recreate themselves on those days; which shall likewise be days of rest in the county house of correction.

—of recreation.

XXXII. That no person shall be removed from either of the said houses to the infirmary, unless by an order signed by the Governor or his deputy, to be obtained by the certificate of the surgeon or apothecary that such person is in a sick and languishing condition; and that notice of such removal shall be immediately given to the receiver and store-keeper, who shall minute the day of such removal, as they shall likewise the recovery or death of the party, (of which they shall also have notice,) in the same page where the person's name shall have afore been entered.

Order for the sick.

—and
dead.

XXXIII. And as often as any of the labourers or prisoners, in either of the said houses, shall happen to die, the Governor shall take order for their burial in the cheapest manner consistent with decency, in the burying-ground belonging to the said house; unless any of the relations of the deceased shall be desirous of removing the body to be buried elsewhere at their own expense—After which an account shall be taken of any clothes, money, or other things, of which the deceased shall die possessed, as well as an account taken of what was due from the receiver to him, or from him to the receiver; and if on the balance anything shall appear to have been due to the deceased such balance, together with his clothes, &c., shall carefully and faithfully be delivered to his lawful representative; all which shall be entered in the book of the receiver and storekeeper, in the same page where the said party's name was above ordered to be entered.

Advancement to
the labourers in
the
County-
house.

XXXIV. That as often as any person shall be committed or admitted to the county-house the receiver shall immediately advance to him or her, if desired, the sum of two shillings, and so weekly the same sum, until the first sale of the manufacture wrought by such person; after which it shall not be lawful for the said receiver to make any farther advancement, without a special order from the Governor or deputy, specifying the sum to be advanced, opposite to which shall be entered the letter O; and such order shall likewise be filed as a voucher for that purpose. All these advancements to be afterwards deducted by the receiver, after the rate of fourpence in the shilling, out of the monies due to the said labourer from the sale of his manufacture, till the whole shall be repaid.

—to the
prisoners
in the
County-
house of
Correc-
tion.

XXXV. That to all persons committed to the county-house of correction at their commitment thither shall be advanced, by the said receiver, the sum of one shilling, and so weekly the said sum during their continuance there.

Deductions from
the labourers.

XXXVI. That from all those who are committed to the county-house the sum of twopence in every shilling shall be deducted out of the net profits arising from their labour; but from those who voluntarily come thither no more than one penny in every shilling.

XXXVII. That immediately after every sale the receiver shall make up the accounts thereof with the Governor or deputy, which accounts shall be examined with and checked by those kept by the storekeeper; after which the receiver shall presently distribute to the several labourers in the county-house all such sums as shall by him be received for their several manufactures, having first made such deductions as are herein before appointed; all which deductions shall be forthwith paid into the hands of the treasurer of the said house. *Accounts to be kept.*

XXXVIII. That the receiver and storekeeper shall keep an exact account of all implements, materials, &c., from time to time brought to the said house, of those which are delivered to the labourers, and those which remain in the hands of the said store-keeper. The same exact account to be likewise kept of all the manufactures which shall be wrought in the said house, by whom; with the prices for which the said manufactures were sold, the monies paid to the labourers, and the deductions: all which shall be entered in two books by the receiver and store-keeper, allowing a separate page to every man.

XXXIX. That all such accounts shall be examined by the Governor, and shall be afterwards laid before every quarter-sessions; at which time the receiver and store-keeper shall swear to the truth thereof; to which said sessions the treasurer shall likewise transmit an account of the monies then in his hands; and if there shall at any time appear to be less than the sum of one thousand pounds remaining with the treasurer and deficiency shall be made up by a county rate, together with so much more as by the best computation shall be thought necessary for mean expenditures, so that there may still remain the said sum of one thousand pounds capital stock in the hands of the said treasurer at the ensuing quarter-sessions. And if any considerable excess of the said capital stock, over and above what shall be necessary for paying the salaries of *Governor to inspect accounts, and sessions. How deficiencies made up. How redundancies employed.*

the officers and other expenses concerning the said houses, shall be in the treasurer's hands, such redundancy shall then be applied in aid of the parochial rates in the several parishes of the said county.

Teachers of manufactures to be hired.

XL. That for the better instruction of the labourers in the manufactures and mysteries now exercised in this kingdom, as well as for the introduction of foreign manufactures and mysteries into the said kingdom, it shall be lawful for the Governor to expend annually, during the first three years, the sum of   , and every subsequent year annually the sum of   , for the pay and encouragement of persons to teach our own and foreign manufactures to the said labourers.   All such disbursements to be entered in a book to be kept for that purpose, attested by the party receiving the same, and by the Governor and one deputy at least, as well as by the receiver; and such book to be constantly inspected and examined into by the justices as they shall think fit.

Labourers may be let out to service.

XLI. Upon application made by any nobleman, gentleman, merchant, tradesman, farmer, or substantial householder, dwelling within the County of Middlesex, or within twenty miles of the said county-house, to the Governor or deputy, signifying that such nobleman, &c., is desirous to take into his service any labourer or labourers then confined in the said county-house, it shall be lawful for the Governor or deputy and he is hereby required to deliver over the said labourer or labourers to such person so applying, and to deliver to each of the said labourers a certificate in the words following:

> County-house Middlesex,
>   A. B. is delivered to C. D. as his servant,
> to serve him until   and then to
> return to the said house.
>   Dated the 5th of August, 1753.
>   E. F., Deputy-governor.

Provided, nevertheless, that where such servant shall be hired for a year certain the clause relating to his return shall be omitted; and when any labourer shall be so hired as aforesaid for any less time than one year the person so hiring such labourer shall deposit in the hands of the receiver of the said house one half of the labourer's wages for the time he shall be so hired; and if he shall be hired for any longer time than two months, then one month's wages to be deposited; which money so deposited shall be paid by the receiver to every such labourer immediately upon his return to the said house, deducting one penny in every shilling. And if such labourer shall depart, or be lawfully discharged from his said service before the wages so deposited shall become due, the receiver shall return the whole to the person depositing the same, deducting only as above; but if the said labourer shall abide with his said master during the limited time, and shall not return within two days after the expiration thereof, (sickness, or other lawful impediment, excepted,) then shall the money deposited be forfeited to the use of the said house; of all which retainers, deposits, repayments, and forfeitures, a double entry shall be made by the receiver and store-keeper.

And if any person so hiring any labourer as aforesaid shall discharge the same before the expiration of the term for which he was so hired, he shall forfeit the whole money deposited by him as above; which money shall be paid to such labourer at his return to the said house.

Provided that it shall be lawful on reasonable cause shown to the satisfaction of any one Justice of the Peace, either by the master or labourer, for such Justice to discharge such labourer and to send him back to the county-house, or order him to the county house of correction, at his pleasure; and if such labourer shall have been hired into any foreign county the Justice of such county may, if he pleases, commit him to the house of correction there: provided, likewise, that if such labourer shall by sickness or any accident be rendered incapable of working, it shall be lawful for his master, at his expense, to return him to the county-house to be provided for in the infirmary of the said house; in which case the money deposited shall be paid to him to whom it shall appear to be due.

And if any labourer so hired as aforesaid for less time than one year shall not, at the end of his term, return to the said house; or if any labourer whatsoever, so being hired, shall run away or depart from his master's service before the expiration of his term, unless for some default in his master or mistress, or shall refuse to work at the command of his said master or his agent, or be guilty of any misdemeanor in his said service, it shall be lawful for any Justice of the Peace, if such masters shall reside in the County of Middlesex, to commit the said labourer to the county house of correction, there to be first severely whipt, and to remain to hard labour till the next session, when he may be farther dealt with by the Justices at their discretion: or if the said master shall reside in any other county, then to be sent by a Justice of that county to the house of correction there, to be severely whipt, and to remain for any time not exceeding three, nor less than one calendar month. Provided that no person who comes voluntarily to the said house shall be forced into such service contrary to his own consent and option.

Crimes cognizable before the higher courts of justice. 1. Conspiracies to break the prison.

XLII. That if any persons, to the number of three or more, shall conspire together to break the said county-house, or county house of correction, and shall have provided themselves with any kind of arms or weapons for that purpose, and shall all or any of them do any act whatsoever in pursuance of such conspiracy, and with a manifest design of executing the same, in consequence of which act any officer belonging to either of the said houses shall be killed, maimed, or wounded, this shall be felony without clergy in all the conspirators.

2. To beat, wound, &c., the officers.

XLIII. That if any persons, to the number of three or more, whereof all or any part shall be confined within either of the said houses, shall maliciously beat and bruise or wound any officer belonging to either of those houses, in such manner that the surgeon or apothecary appointed to attend to the said houses shall on oath declare that the life or limb of such officer was brought into danger thereby, such persons being lawfully convicted of such offence shall suffer death as felons without clergy.

3. Assaults on the Governor, &c.

XLIV. That every person confined within either of the aforesaid houses, who shall assault the Governor, deputy governor, or chaplains, though not then in the execution of their

office; or who shall assault, beat, and bruise, or wound any
of the officers belonging to either house, anywise, on account
of or in the execution of their several officers; or who shall
actually break either of the said houses, and escape there-
from; being lawfully convicted of any of the said offences
shall be transported for fourteen years.

XLV. That all persons who shall convey any fire-arms, or
any mischievous weapon or tool, to any of the labourers or
prisoners within either of the said houses, without the privity
of the Governor or deputy-governor, shall be guilty of felony;
and being lawfully convicted thereof shall be transported
for seven years. *4. Convey-
ing arms,
&c., into
the houses.*

XLVI. That all persons committed to the county house of
correction who shall absolutely refuse or neglect to labour;
after a fortnight's confinement in the said house; and having
during that time received the discipline of the same, being
lawfully convicted of such absolute refusal or neglect, before
Justices of oyer and terminer, or gaol-delivery, shall be transported for   years; provided that it may be lawful for
any officer of the army to receive the body of such offender,
and to convey him to serve his Majesty in any of his forces in
the East or West Indies. *5. Refusal
to work.*

XLVII. That any receiver, storekeeper, clerk, or other person who shall knowingly and with a fraudulent design make
any false entry in any of the books by this Act ordered to be
kept, and in which entries are here ordered to be made, such
offender, being lawfully convicted thereof, shall be deemed
guilty of felony, and transported for seven years. *6. Frauds
in the offi-
cers.*

XLVIII. That all persons lawfully accused, by the oath of
one credible witness, of any of the aforesaid crimes before the
Governor or his deputy, shall by him be committed to the
county gaol, there to remain till discharged by due course of
law. In the same manner shall be committed all persons
accused of felony in either of the said houses, or of giving
any maim, dangerous wound, bruise, or hurt, to any person
within the said houses. *Accused
persons to
be com-
mitted.
to the
County
Gaol.*

XLIX. That if any of the officers, or any person having
liberty to sell their wares within the said houses, shall sell or *Lesser
crimes.*

1. Introducing spirituous liquors into the houses.

give, to any of the labourers in either of the said houses, any quantity, how small soever, of spirituous liquors, without the order or direction of the surgeon or apothecary, such persons, being lawfully convicted thereof before the Justices at their sessions, shall be deemed guilty of a misdemeanor, punishable by the Justices with fine and imprisonment: and all such persons being so convicted shall be incapable of bearing any office, or selling any of their wares within either of the said houses, for the future: and all those who shall be charged on oath before the Governor with the said crime shall be bound with sufficient sureties to appear and answer the same at the next sessions.

2. Destroying work, &c.

L. That all persons wilfully and maliciously destroying, spoiling, or injuring any of the furniture belonging to either of the said houses, or any of the implements, tools, materials, manufacture, or stock being therein, shall, when lawfully convicted thereof before the Justices at their sessions, be deemed guilty of an infamous crime, and may, besides fine and imprisonment, receive any corporal punishment, not extending to life or limb, at the discretion of the said Justice.

3. Escape from the County-house of Correction.

LI. That every person escaping from the county house of correction shall, on his being apprehended, be brought before the Governor or deputy, and, being thereof convicted before him, shall be by him recommitted to the said house; there to be severely whipt, and then confined during the space of ten days in one of the cells belonging to the said house, and to have only bread and water for his support: after which he shall remain in the house of correction subject to the rules of the house as before, with this likewise, that he shall on no account be liable to be discharged from the same until the next sessions which shall be held after the expiration of six calendar months.

—from the County-house.

LII. That every person escaping from the county-house shall be committed to the county house of correction, and shall be whipt at his entrance into the same.

Jurisdiction of the Governor.

LIII. That twice in every week, that is to say on every Monday and every Thursday, in the forenoon, the Governor or his deputy shall hold court within the said county-house;

in which the said Governor or his deputy shall have power to hear and determine any of the following offences.

1. Quarrels amongst the labourers where no maim, wound, violent bruise, or other dangerous hurt is given or done; but where the injury consists in some slight blow or kick, or of contumelious and provoking language. *Petty offences.*

2. Profane swearing or cursing, or other profane discourse, and all kind of indecency in word or act.

3. Drunkenness.

4. Absence from chapel without cause, or irreverent behaviour there.

5. Absence from work, idleness at it, or negligently spoiling the same.

6. Obstinate disobedience to any of the rules of the house.

All which are hereby declared to be offences against the true intent and meaning of this Act, and to be punishable by the said Governor or deputy, by rebuke, small fine, or confinement for any short time, not exceeding three days; allowing only such sustenance as shall be thought proper for the first offence; for a second offence the confinement may be enlarged to a week; and for a third the offender may be committed to the house of correction, there to remain till the next sessions or for any less time; and may likewise be ordered to be whipt. And in case of a third offence committed by any of the prisoners in the house of correction the Governor or deputy may, besides the punishment of whipping, confine such person in one of the cells, there to remain till the next sessions; or, if such offence be an absolute refusal or neglect of work, may commit him to the county gaol, there to remain till he be discharged by due course of law: provided that the second and third offence above mentioned is here intended to be an offence of the same kind with the first. All convictions to be on the view of the Governor or deputy, confession of the party, or on the oath of one credible witness

Secondly, The Governor or deputy shall at such his court enquire of all persons who have behaved themselves so as to merit a reward, and shall minute their names in a book to *Of what the Governor, &c., to enquire.*

be kept for that purpose, which shall be produced to the Justices at the next sessions.

Thirdly, They shall enquire of the conduct of all the officers under them, and if they find any of them deficient in their duty, or guilty of any cruelty, corruption, or other atrocious fault, such officer shall be suspended from his office till the next sessions, when the same shall be presented before the Justices.

Fourthly, They shall enquire of all offences within this Act, and of all other offences of which the persons lawfully accused are to be committed to the county gaol; and such as are so accused they shall commit thither.

Fifthly, They shall from time to time enquire into the prices of provisions brought into the said house, and regulate the same, subject to the supervisal of the sessions. And if any exactions shall have been made on the labourers or prisoners, or any unwholesome provisions introduced into the said houses, or other default be in the victuallers, they shall report the same to the sessions.

Jurisdiction of the sessions. LIV. That on one of the days on every sessions to be holden at Hick's Hall the said sessions shall be adjourned to the county-house, there to be holden within five days next after such adjournment; at which sessions at the county-house the Justices shall have power to enquire.

First, Of all neglects, corruptions, or other misdemeanors, in any of the officers of the said houses, and to punish the same, [unless in the Governor or deputies or chaplains of the said house], by reproof, fine, or dismission, as they shall think meet; and if by dismission, then to place some other fit person in the room of the officers so dismissed.

Secondly, They shall enquire into the general conduct of the said house; and if they shall find any default in the Governor, deputy governors, or chaplains of the same, they shall report such default before their brethren at the next ensuing sessions at Hicks's Hall, where the Governor, &c., shall have notice to appear and make his defence; and if such default shall seem to the majority of the Justices of the said sessions to be well proved, and to be of such a nature as to merit any severe censure, they may, if they please, report the same to the Lord High Chancellor of Great Britain, who shall have full cognizance of the matter, and may remove the Governor, &c., from his office, or fine him at his pleasure.

Thirdly, The Justices shall enquire of the prices of provisions, &c., which shall be brought into the said houses, and shall regulate the same at their discretion, altering, if they see fit, the orders taken by the Governor herein; and may hear the report of the Governor touching any default in the victuallers, and may punish the same by fine or by turning out such victualler at their pleasure.

Fourthly, They shall enquire of the behaviour of all persons confined within the house of correction, and such as they shall find, by the report of the keeper on his oath, or by other evidence, to have behaved themselves orderly, and to have applied closely to their labour, the Justices may enlarge from that confinement, and commit them to the county-house to be there kept till the ensuing sessions; and such as they shall find to have behaved in a less orderly manner, or to be lazy or negligent in their work, they may order to remain till the next sessions in the house of correction, where they then are; but such as they shall find to be utterly reprobate and ungovernable and to refuse all kinds of labour, the Justices are hereby required to commit to the county gaol, there to remain till discharged by due course of law.

Fifthly, The Justices shall likewise enquire by the recommendation of the Governor, deputy governor, or rector, or by the oath of other evidence, of the behaviour of the several labourers then confined within the county-house; and such as shall appear to have behaved themselves decently and orderly, and to have been diligent in their work, the Justices may, at the desire of the party, enlarge from their confinement: provided that such party shall make out, to their satisfaction, that there is any reasonable cause to hope or expect that such labourer will be able to maintain himself in an honest manner at his own home; in which case the

Justices shall give the party a pass to enable him to travel thither without molestation: provided that no person shall be discharged from the county-house while he shall remain indebted to the receiver of the said house.

And such persons as shall have behaved themselves in a less becoming manner, or who shall have been idle and negligent in their work, or who shall not be able to make it appear to the satisfaction of the Justices that they would be capable of procuring an honest livelihood at their own homes, or shall remain indebted to the said receiver, the said Justices shall order to continue in the said county-house till the next sessions. And if it shall appear to the said Justices by any of the means aforesaid that any of the said persons have behaved themselves in a notorious and outrageous manner, or have totally neglected or refused to work, then it shall be lawful for the said Justices to commit such persons to the county house of correction, there to remain till the next sessions, with hard labour, and with other such correction and punishment as they shall think proper.

Sixthly, The Justices shall inspect all the accounts relating to the said house, and shall have power to examine on oath the treasurer, receiver, store-keeper, with their several clerks, or any other person touching the same; and if the said accounts shall appear to them to be fair and just, they shall then sign the same: which accounts having been first examined and signed by the Governor or deputy, and so passed and countersigned by the said Justices, shall be good and effectual to all manner of purposes: but if there shall appear to the Justices upon their said examination to have been any gross mistakes, or any kind of false entry, fraud, or collusion, shall appear upon the face of the said accounts, the said Justices may, if they please, examine into and finally determine the same; as likewise may suspend or dismiss any officer who shall to them appear to have been guilty of any such false entry, fraud, or collusion; or may, if they shall see more convenient, adjourn over the further hearing and determination of the same to the next sessions; to which they may bind over all parties, and in the mean time may, if they shall think fit, suspend the suspected person from the exercise of his office, and may appoint another to officiate in his room.

Lastly, They shall have power to enquire into the behaviour of any of the labourers, who shall have so behaved themselves as to merit rewards, and may proceed to order them severally such reward as to them shall seem proper: all which shall be publicly paid to the said labourers in open court by the Governor, who shall draw on the treasurer for the same; such reward to be paid in the presence of all who are to receive any punishment at that time.

LV. Whereas the punishment of whipping is inflicted in some cases in this law, which whipping is always intended to be severe and exemplary, the Governor or his deputy is always to be present at the inflicting the same. Governor, &c., to inspect punishment.

LVI. That the Governor, or deputy governors, chaplains, treasurer, receiver, keeper of the house of correction, and all the other officers and ministers attending the same, shall be chose at the sessions at Hicks's Hall, by the majority of the Justices there present, by ballot; and before any of the said Justices shall be admitted to ballot he shall take the following oath: How the officers to be chose.

> You do swear that you will give your suffrage in the ballot, now to be made, impartially, not out of favour or affection, nor on account of any promise made by you or to you, nor by the force of any recommendation whatsoever; but as you are persuaded, to the best of your knowledge or belief, that the person for whom you shall give your suffrage is better qualified than any other of his competitors (if there be any——otherwise say only "is qualified") for the discharge of the trust for which he now appears a candidate. So help you God.

In like manner shall all vacancies be supplied from time to time.

Fines, &c., how disposed. LVII. That all fines and forfeitures to be imposed or to accrue by virtue of this Act, not otherwise disposed of, shall be paid to the treasurer of the county-house, and be applied to the use of the said house.

By-laws. LVIII. The Governor may make by-laws with the consent of the Justices, the same to be approved by the Lord Chancellor.

LIX. Persons tried, &c., shall plead this Act, &c.

ARGUMENTS IN EXPLANATION AND SUPPORT OF
THE FOREGOING PROPOSALS

PARAGRAPH I., &c., to XIII. The appointment of a
County-house and County-house of Correction, with the Regulation thereof.

PAR I. *In Middlesex, &c.*] It is proposed to make the
trial first in the county of Middlesex, as I am best acquainted
with the state of the poor in that county, and as the well
regulating them there is of the greatest moment to the public;
but if the plan should be approved by experience it will be
very easy to extend it over the kingdom.

Ibid. In some convenient place.] This should be at some
little distance from London; nor will it be difficult among
the many wastes which lie within a few miles to fix on some
convenient place for the purpose. I do not know myself
any so proper as a common near Acton Wells, the purchase
of which, though of three hundred acres extent, would be very
reasonable; it being at present allotted to the use of the poor
of Fulham, who derive very little benefit from it. I may
add that this is a very healthy spot, and most commodiously
situated; being at no great distance from any part of Middlesex, and not five miles from Hyde Park Corner.

II. *The County-house to be large enough, &c.*] As whatever is perfectly new is apt to affect us with surprise, and as
this surprise is increased and attended with doubt and in-
credulity in proportion to the greatness of the object, I am
well aware of the impression with which the largeness of this
building will strike many minds: the idea of a body of men
united under one government in a large city must have been
amazing when it was first propounded to men who lived a
wandering life, scattered in single families or collected in
very small numbers together; though indeed our astonishment is not quite so excusable, as we see not only the possibility of such union but the advantages arising from it.

In the present case, however, I think to make it appear
from reason, authority, and experience that, to answer the

ends proposed, *to make the poor useful members of society,* we must bring them as much as possible together; at least so as to collect the poor of a single county.

First, It is a great work, and requires many great qualifications in the person who is principally to direct it: such men are not to be found in every parish in a county; nor, if they were found, could they be induced to employ their time this way by any reward which the parish could bestow on them: for not much less time and trouble will be requisite to the directing and supervising a small body of men than a body twenty times as large, when once this is brought into regularity and order. The same abilities and the same troubles which can well order and govern a small state will suffice for the government of a large kingdom. To manage the poor so as to produce the ends proposed in this undertaking is a task to which very few are equal; and those who are equal to it will scarce undertake it unless they are well paid for their pains.

Secondly, The expense and difficulty of carrying this purpose into execution will always increase in proportion to the smallness of the body of people by whose hands it is to be executed. And this is the reason why work-houses (more properly called idle-houses) have by experience been found to produce no better effect: for if the masters of these houses had a real disposition to set the poor to work, and if they had all adequate capacities for that purpose, they would by no means be able to effect it. One or two or three manufactures will not suffice to employ the various talents, skill, and strength of a small body of men, especially when this body is eternally changing. Many inconveniences will necessarily attend such houses: the manufacturer will sometimes stand still for want of work, and at others the materials will be spoiled for want of hands; whereas in such a number of persons, as are here proposed to be collected together, some will be found capable of every manufacture, and of every branch of it; and as from a certainty of finding such hands all kind of materials and all kind of tools will be provided, both the mischiefs above complained of will, of course, be avoided. I have here supposed the existence of parish work-houses at least, (whereas in reality there are but few of those where any number of poor are lodged, and much fewer where they are in any manner employed,) for as to those parishes where the poor are left at large it is utterly impossible that they should be made in any degree useful, or indeed any other than a heavy burden on their neighbours; some of whom (by the way) are often little richer than themselves. In a large body alone the materials can be sufficiently supplied, the hands properly adapted, new manufactures taught, and the work well disposed of, to the emolument of the public and the proper encouragement of the labourer.

Thirdly, As the industrious cannot so well be employed, so neither can the lazy be so efficaciously compelled to work, in parish work-houses; the care of which must be intrusted to persons of mean consideration, where there can be no proper authority to inflict punishment, nor any adequate force to execute it on those who are most reprobate and desperate.

Fourthly, The poor cannot be so well nor so cheaply provided for in many bodies as they may be when collected into one.

Fifthly, They will not be so commodiously confined. In small and crowded work-houses, where there are no courts nor outlets to admit the air, the poor are often so distempered that their keepers are obliged by common humanity to let them frequently out; in which case the certain and immediate use which these wretches make of their liberty is to increase the number of beggars.

Sixthly, The proposal for amendments of their morals, by instilling into them notions of religion or morality, (a matter, as it appears to me, of the highest consequence), is only consistent with the scheme of bringing them together; to which scheme indeed all the rules and orders of this plan are directed, and with which alone they will, on examination, be found compatible. Everything, therefore, which I shall say on the present occasion, may be applied as an additional reason on this head.

And in this case authority will be found to be on the same side with reason. My Lord Chief Justice Hale, perceiving that the poor of a single parish could not be well provided for by themselves, advises a coalition of several parishes for this purpose. This was clearly seeing the defect in the Statute of Elizabeth, though it was not carrying the remedy far enough.

The author of an essay on the Bills of Mortality (said to be the famous Sir William Petty, under the borrowed name of Graunt,) having discoursed on the evil of beggars, of reforming their morals, curing their impotencies, and teaching them to work according to the condition and capacity of every individual, concludes in these words, but I say none of these can be effected without bringing them together; or, if it could be effected at all, neither so well nor so cheaply.[1]

The great Sir Josiah Child (for great, in his province, he certainly was) proposes, " that the city of London and West-minster, borough of Southwark, and all other places within the usual lines of communication, described in the weekly bills of mortality, may, by Act of Parliament, be associated into one province, or line of communication, for relief of the poor."

He proceeds, among other powers to be given to his cor-poration, that they, " and such as they shall authorize, may have power to purchase lands, erect and endow work-houses, hospitals, and houses of correction," &c.

Here is almost as populous, if not as large a district, as the county of Middlesex itself. It is true he doth not ex-pressly mention the bringing these workhouses, hospitals, and houses of correction, together into one place; but this will appear, I think, to have been his intention, or he would not have concluded in the following manner:—

" If it be here objected to the whole purpose of this treatise that this work may as well be done in distinct parishes, if

[1] " Natural and Political Observations . . . upon the Bills of Mortality," by John Graunt, chap. iii. [These words quoted do not appear in the place referred to, either in the original edition, 1662, or the 5th edition, 1676.—ED.]

all parishes were obliged to build work-houses and employ their poor therein; as Dorchester and some others have done with good success.

"I answer that such attempts have been made in many places to my knowledge, with very good intents and strenuous endeavours; but all that ever I heard of proved vain and ineffectual, . . . except that single instance of the town of Dorchester, which yet signifies nothing in relation to the kingdom in general, . . . nor doth the town of Dorchester entertain any but their own poor only, and whip away all others; whereas that which I design is to propose such a foundation as shall be large, wise, honest, and rich enough to maintain and employ all poor that come within the pale of their communication, without enquiring where they were born," &c.[1]

These are great authorities and will, I doubt not, much more than counterbalance any opinions which can be produced on the other side, if indeed there are any such.

Lastly, experience, the instructor of those who can learn of no other master, might, of itself alone, convince us of the truth for which I am contending. I will not here repeat what I have said in the introduction, relating to the wretched state of the poor under the present establishment, all which may be urged as an argument on this head, since it will, I think, appear that the scattered state in which the poor were left by the Statute of Elizabeth is the principal reason why this law hath produced no better effect. It is true, indeed, the management of the poor was, by that Statute, intrusted to very improper hands; but this will not universally account for the evil, since many worthy and good men have, in divers places, taken upon themselves the charge of the poor, and have employed much time and trouble therein to very little or no purpose. The true reason therefore that the poor have not yet been well provided for, and well employed, is that they have not yet been drawn together. Of this opinion were the great writers whom I have cited, and both reason

[1] " A New Discourse of Trade," by Sir Josiah Child, chap. 11. [2nd Edit. 1694.]

and experience may convince us that the matter can be accomplished no other way.

But perhaps an objection may suggest itself of the contrary kind, to which it may at first sight appear more difficult to give an answer. It will perhaps be said that I have computed the poor at too small a number, and have not proposed a method of providing for one half of them. Indeed if we are to estimate the poor by the overseer's books in the several parishes as they now stand, and add to these the inhabitants of Bridewell, with all those who ought to be inhabitants of that place, I readily grant I have not provided for half, nor perhaps for half a quarter of the poor of this county. But the objector will be pleased to observe that a great number of the latter part do not properly belong to this county, but are vagabonds from all parts of the kingdom—— witness the great expense to which this county is put by passing one in a hundred, perhaps, back to their own homes. Some of these are at present drawn hither, from those counties where their labour is often wanted, by the great encouragement which this town affords to beggars and thieves. Others come up with honester views at first; in which, being commonly disappointed, they betake themselves to the same means of procuring the bread of idleness: but when, instead of such alluring prospects, a work-house or a Bridewell shall present itself to their eyes, this swarm, it may easily be supposed, will soon cease, and the two houses will be little filled with such vagabonds. And as to the proper poor of the county when we deduct the aged, the infant, and the accidentally impotent, who are not the objects of my plan, the building proposed will perhaps be found capable of receiving the rest. But let us allow the objection its full force, and what doth it assert? Why, that there are more able poor in the county of Middlesex who are at present idle, though capable of being employed, than I have provided an accommodation for. The result of this would certainly be that the means of accommodation should be enlarged; and this I apprehend, if it should appear to be necessary, may very easily be effected.

III. *Men and women to be kept separate.*] The utility of this provision needs no comment: our present houses of correction, for want of this regulation, are places of the most infamous and profligate debauchery.

IV. &c. to the IX. inclusive.] These are only loose sketches of what it may perhaps be unnecessary to insert in this bill, and which may be left to the discretion of those to whom the legislature shall think proper to intrust the care of the building. The nomination of the commissioners I likewise submit to the legislature.

XI. *A sum to be raised.*] I have not ventured to particularize any sum, but it must undoubtedly be a large one. And yet, large as it will be, when we consider the great utility proposed of effectually providing for the poor, and of relieving the public from beggars and thieves, it must appear moderate or even trifling.

But farther: It is not only the redress of an evil, by the relieving the poor from their misery, and the public from the poor, which is the object of this plan; much of positive good is designed by it to the society. If six thousand hands, which now sit idle, can be employed, the advantages resulting hence to the public need not be explained to any who have the least notion of trade, or of the benefits arising from it.

An excellent writer on our constitution observes, that of the three main supports of the riches of a people, two of them consist in improving their natural commodities, and in setting the poor to work. The former, indeed, is only the consequence of the latter; nay, as he himself says, " the improvement of the natural commodity " can never " enrich the kingdom, so long as many mouths are fed upon the main stock, and waste the same by idleness and prodigality." [1]

The great Mr. Law, in his little treatise called " Money and Trade Considered," explains this more fully. His words are these: " An addition to the money adds to the value of the county. So long as money gives interest it is employed; and money employed brings profit, though the em-

---

[1] N. Bacon's " Discourse of the Laws and Government of England," part II., p. 40. [1682.]

ployer loses. *Ex.* If fifty men are set to work, to whom
25*s.* is paid per day, and the improvement made by their
labour be only equal to, or worth, 15*s.*, yet by so much the
value of the country is increased; but as it is reasonable to
suppose their labour equal to 40*s.* so much is added to the
value of the country; of which the employer gains 15*s.*, 15*s.*
may be supposed to equal the consumption of the labourers,
who before lived on charity, and 10*s.* remains to them over
their consumption." [1]

Nor will it bear, I think, any rational doubt, whether employments may be found for this, or indeed a much larger
number of hands.   Sir William Petty, in that excellent work
called his " Political Arithmetic," affirms, and proves too,
that there were in his days spare hands among the king's
subjects to earn two millions more than was actually earned.
He farther affirms that there was two millions' worth of work
to be done, which the king's subjects did neglect to do; [2] for
without this latter could be proved the former, as he himself
admits, would serve to little consequence.

Now the number of hands here to be provided for may
surely be computed at a very low rate (for so I would make
the computation) to do, one with another, work to the value
of ten pounds *per annum;* this will amount to £60,000, the
advantage of which to the public will be readily acknowl-
edged.   Here then the evil of the poor will not only be removed, but it will be converted into a very great emolument.

But there is yet another light in which this sum may perhaps appear more palatable; and that is by comparing it
with the sum now paid to the poor rate, which in this county
of Middlesex amounts annually to upwards of £70,000, as I
am informed: of which five parts in six are, I believe, applied to the use of those poor who are the objects of the law
proposed in this plan.

They are the able poor, either such as cannot procure work

----

[1] " Money and Trade Considered," by John Law, pp. 11, 12.   [2nd
Edit. 1720.]

[2] " Political Arithmetic," chap. viii.

or such as will not do it, who are the great burdens of the society. Of those who are absolutely impotent the number is truly inconsiderable. Sir William Petty, whom I shall beg leave to cite once more, in his "Political Anatomy of Ireland," [1] computes that "there is in nature but one in five hundred at most who are blind, lame, and under incurable impotence," as old age, &c. To every individual of these he allows six pounds *per annum;* which, he says, would maintain them without scandal: a very large allowance, when we consider the place of which he speaks and the time in which he wrote. A less sum would, I believe, answer the purpose among us.

According to this computation, if the people in Middlesex amount to 1,200,000, the impotent poor will be 2,400; the expense of maintaining which number will be £13,600. The above excellent author estimates the children under seven years of age at the rate of one fourth of the people: these then, according to my estimate in Middlesex, will be 300,000. Of these, I presume, not above one in 150 [2] will be a burden on the public. This number, then, will be 3,000; for whom three pounds each, one with another, will be sufficient, and which will make the sum of £9,000. The whole expense, therefore of the impotent poor in Middlesex will be £22,600; about the fourth part of what it now is. And if the number of hospitals, infirmaries, and various donative charities within this county of Middlesex do not reduce this sum, so as to bring the whole expense to one sixth part of what it now is, I am greatly deceived, or those must be grossly misapplied.

I have endeavoured in a former essay [3] to show that such objects as these, so cheaply to be provided for, might with great safety be left to voluntary contributions: nor shall I add anything more to the arguments I have there used,

---

[1] "Political Survey of Ireland," p. 11. [2nd Edit. 1719.]

[2] There is a slip in his calculation; probably he meant to say one in a hundred.—ED.

[3] "An Enquiry into the Causes of the late Increase of Robbers, &c.," 1751.

especially as this part of our poor have since fallen under the consideration of two very honourable and learned persons, for whom I have a very high respect and esteem.

If either of these bills, with that proposed in this plan, should pass into a law the poor rate would then entirely cease of course; and the Statute of Elizabeth, with all laws for providing for the poor as to this county, might be utterly repealed. The same indeed would be the case if the impotent poor were trusted to voluntary contributions, as they possibly might; though with less advantage to the public, especially as to the education of the infants, which is a valuable part in the schemes of those honourable persons.

I conclude the head therefore with asserting (for so I surely may) that whoever considers my plan only in this last respect, and compares the expense proposed in it with that which is at present annually incurred, must view the sum of £100,000 (beyond which the whole expense of building, furnishing, and providing all kind of implements, will not rise) as a trifling sum, well laid out in a cheap and valuable purchase. Private interest, from this respect alone, will to every wise man recommend a scheme, by which he may propose to be so great a gainer, to his fullest consideration; and this motive, in proportion as he is a good man, will be greatly enhanced by those arguments which relate to the public. There are none so stupid as not to prefer the payment of twenty pounds once to the yearly payment of that sum; and few so entirely void of all public spirit, as to be totally indifferent whether that money which is levied on them be applied to the good of the community, or squandered away, as it now is, to no manner of purpose.

If there be any enemies therefore to my plan, they must be such only as doubt its efficacy. To these I answer, that absolute certainty, with regard to a future event, is not in the nature of human affairs: but let them examine the plan with fairness, impartiality, and candour; let them well and duly weigh every part of it, and I am greatly deceived if the result will not be a strong opinion of the probability of its success; though indeed a very small degree of this probability would, in our present situation, be almost a sufficient encouragement to the undertaking.

I have hitherto supposed that this sum was to be immediately raised, among the present inhabitants of Middlesex, by an additional poor rate: but this is not necessary; for as the benefit of this plan is to extend to posterity, it is equitable that they should contribute towards the expense. If the money therefore was granted by a vote of credit, at three and a half *per cent.*, and only a twentieth or thirtieth part of the principal paid off yearly with the interest, the annual charge on the county would be so small that it would scarce be felt; nay, perhaps, if this was done by way of lottery, it might be so contrived as to reduce the whole expense to little or nothing.

XII. *The appointment of officers.*] Any alteration may be made with regard to these, if it shall appear proper. The number, I think, which I have here mentioned will not be found extravagant, any more than the salaries allotted to each, when we consider the trust which they are severally to undertake.

XIII. *The power of the Governor.*] Perhaps some further powers may be found necessary: as to that of holding a market, &c., such open sale of the commodities will give great encouragement to the labourers, and may be moreover one means of preventing frauds, which, in all public institutions, can never be too well guarded against——too often, or too strictly, enquired into——or too severely punished.

PAR. XIV. &c. to XXII. Who to be sent or admitted in the county-house, &c., with the manner of sending them.

XVI. *Persons accused of petty larceny to be committed to the said houses, &c.*] By the common law petty larceny is felony, and it is now within the power of the magistrate to compound the offence, though it be ever so trifling, or the party should appear to be in the highest degree an object of mercy. The prisoner is therefore to be committed to gaol, where he must often lie in Middlesex many weeks, in other counties many months, before he is brought to his trial. During this time his morals, however bad, are farther corrupted; his necessities, however pressing before, are increased; his family, if he hath any, made more wretched; and the means of providing for himself and them rendered more difficult, if not impossible, for the future, by the total loss of his character. If he be acquitted on his trial——as he often is by the mercy of the jury——against clear and positive evidence, he is again turned loose among the community with all the disadvantages I have mentioned above; to which, if he be convicted and whipt, I may add the circumstance of infamy; the marks of which he will be sure to carry on his forehead, though the hangman very seldom, I believe, leaves any on his back. What must be the situation of this wretch I need not mention; such in truth it is that his second theft is in reality less criminal than the first. This was perhaps choice; but that will be necessity. A late Act of Parliament hath indeed put it in the power of the court to transport these pilferers; but this, though probably it may be real mercy, hath such an appearance of extreme severity that few judges are willing to inflict such a punishment on such an offence. But if it should be the interest of a wretch in these circumstances to be banished from a country, where he must steal or starve, it is scarce the interest of the public to lose every year a great number of such able hands. By the means I have proposed it seems to me, that the offender will receive a punishment proportionable to his offence; he and his family may be preserved from utter ruin, and an able member, instead of being entirely lost to the public, will be rendered more useful to it than he was before.

XVII. *That it shall be lawful to seize all suspicious persons, &c.*] I have observed in another place [1] that though we have had several laws against vagrants, by which many misdemeanors have been called and constituted acts of vagrancy; yet vagrancy itself, or wandering about from place to place, is not of itself alone punishable. This is an egregious defect in this part of our constitution, and hath been one great cause of the increase of beggars and thieves. To prevent the wandering of the poor was the great purpose,

[1] "Enquiry into . . . . Increase of Robbers, &c."

as I have shewn, of the laws of Alfred. It was this which gave that strength and energy to those institutions which have been praised by so many pens, both of lawyers and historians. Hence it was that travellers, as we are told, might pass through the whole kingdom with safety; nay, that bracelets of gold might be hung up in the public roads, and found at a distant time by the owner in the place where they were left. Upon these principles I have formed this clause; and without it, I will venture to say, no laws whatever for the suppression of thieves and beggars will be found effectual.

I should scarce apprehend, though I am told I may, that some persons should represent the restraint here laid on the lower people as derogatory from their liberty. Such notions are indeed of the enthusiastical kind, and are inconsistent with all order and all government. They are the natural parents of that licentiousness which it is one main intent of this whole plan to cure——which is necessarily productive of most of the evils of which the public complains; of that licentiousness, in a word, which among the many mischiefs introduced by it into every society where it prevails, is sure at last to end in the destruction of liberty itself.

As the clause now stands I have drawn it with much caution, and have qualified it with such restrictions that I own I cannot see any inconvenience which can possibly attend it; if any such should appear it may be qualified yet farther. But if we must on no account deprive even the lowest people of the liberty of doing what they will, and going where they will, of wandering and drunkenness, why should we deny them that liberty which is but the consequence of this? I mean that of begging and stealing, of robbing or cutting throats at their good pleasure: for, if these be evils, they cannot be effectually abolished but by some such law as this; a law which hath not only the sanction of such an authority as Alfred, but of an Act of Parliament in the reign of Queen Elizabeth.

XVIII. *The poor to travel with a pass.*] This method of permitting the poor to go abroad to work, &c., under a pass, is taken from an Act of Parliament of Elizabeth. **I** have through this plan proposed short precedents of orders, &c., a method which it would be well if the legislature would pursue in all Acts relating to the office of a Justice of Peace.

XX. *Poor to be passed to the county-house.*] Though every commitment by the magistrate may carry with it some notion of delinquency, yet I would not have the county-house supposed to be a place of infamy, or a confinement there to be so much intended for punishment as preservation. It is true indeed that I have, to avoid confusion, left it in the breast of the magistrate to which house he will commit; but surely he will never extend this discretionary power so far as to send persons to the county-house who are convicted of any higher crimes than barely wandering and idleness, which are not infamous in themselves, and therefore should not, nay, cannot be rendered so by any punishment. The county-house is indeed a place contrived for the promotion of industry only, and is therefore a proper asylum for the industrious of their own accord to fly to for protection.

XXIII. to XLI. inclusive. The method of receiving the poor, putting them to work, and ordering them in these houses.

XXIII. *Double entry to be made.*] Through this whole plan I have endeavoured as much as possible to guard against fraud, to which human nature without proper checks is but too liable.

XXIV. *None to depart, &c.*] As it would be hard absolutely to confine volunteers like prisoners, so on the other hand it would be altogether inconvenient to give such persons full right of rambling where they please. This might fill the highways with thieves and beggars, and one great evil which the plan intends to abolish might be increased by it.

XXV. *A badge to be worn.*] As persons sent hither by the Justices must be supposed guilty of some crime——idleness at least——it may be proper to distinguish them from those labourers who are entirely guiltless. And this distinction is moreover necessary, to inform the officers whom they are to let out at their pleasure.

XXVI. *Prisoners to be confined on bread and water, during twenty-four hours.*] Scarce any person will be committed hither who would not by the law as it now stands have been committed to Bridewell, where the allowance is no more than a penny loaf a day, with water. To be confined, therefore, with such sustenance for twenty-four hours cannot be well thought a severe punishment. The particular reason why I have inserted it here is that the party, before he be let loose among the other prisoners, should be perfectly cool; which is seldom the case when profligate persons are brought before the Justice, and by him committed to the house of correction. And if, at the expiration of that term, the prisoner should still retain any signs of outrageous reprobacy it will be much more proper to confine him by himself, than to suffer him to reinfect those who may possibly have made some advancement in their cure. And indeed there can be no more effectual means of bringing most abandoned profligates to reason and order, than those of solitude and fasting; which latter especially is often as useful to a diseased mind as to a distempered body. To say truth this is a very wholesome punishment, and is not liable to those ill consequences which are produced by punishments attended with shame: for by once inflicting shame on a criminal we forever remove that fear of it, which is one very strong preservative against doing evil. Indeed, however this may have been admitted into the punishments of all countries, it appears to me to contain in it no less absurdity than that of taking away from the party all sense of honour, in order to make him a good man.

XXVII. *Prayers every morning, &c.*] Nothing can, I think, appear more strange than the policy of appointing a chaplain to Newgate, and none to Bridewell. On a religious account it is surely very fit to have a proper person for preparing men for death; but in a political view it must seem most extremely absurd to provide for the regulation of those morals in which the society are no longer concerned, and entirely to neglect the correction and amendment of persons who are shortly to be let loose again among the public, and who are even confined for the purpose of correction. The correction of the body only was doubtless not the whole end of the institution of such houses; and yet it must be allowed a great defect in that institution to leave the correction of the mind to the same hands. In real truth religion is alone capable of effectually executing this work. This Solomon asserted long ago; and the excellent Archbishop Tillotson, in a sermon on his words, which Solomon might have himself preached, hath very nobly expatiated on the subject:—

"Religion," says he, "hath a good influence upon the people; to make them obedient to government, and peaceable one towards another:

"To make them obedient to government, and conformable to laws: and that not only for wrath, and out of fear of the magistrate's power—which is but a weak and loose principle of obedience, and will cease whenever men can rebel with safety and to advantage—but out of conscience, which is a firm, and constant, and lasting principle, and will hold a man fast when all other obligations will break. He that hath entertained the true principles of Christianity is not to be tempted from his obedience and subjection by any worldly considerations; because he believes that 'whosoever resisteth authority resisteth the ordinance of God,' and that 'they who resist shall receive to themselves damnation.'

"Religion tends to make men peaceable one towards another; for it endeavours to plant all those qualities and dispositions in men which tend to peace and unity, and to fill men with a spirit of universal love and good will. It endeavours likewise to secure every man's interest, by commanding the observation of that great Rule of Equity: 'Whatsoever ye would that men should do unto you, do ye even so to them'—by enjoining that truth and fidelity be inviolably observed in all our words, promises, and contracts; and, in order hereunto, it requires the extirpation of all those passions and vices which render men unsociable and troublesome to one another; as pride, covetousness, and injustice, hatred, and revenge, and cruelty; and those likewise which are not so commonly reputed vices, as self-conceit and per-emptoriness in a man's own opinion, and all peevishness and incompliance of humour in things lawful and indifferent."

"And that these are the proper effects of true piety, the doctrine of our Saviour and His apostles everywhere teacheth us. Now if this be the design of religion to bring us to this temper—thus to heal the natures of men and to sweeten their spirits, to correct their passions, and to mortify all those lusts which are the causes of enmity and division—then it is evident that in its own nature it tends to the peace and happiness of human society; and that, if men would but live as religion requires they should do, the world would be a quiet habitation, a most lovely and desirable place, in com-parison of what now it is. And indeed the true reason why the societies of men are so full of tumult and disorder, so troublesome and tempestuous, is because there is so little of true religion among men; so that were it not for some small remainders of piety and virtue which are yet left scattered among mankind, human society would in a short space dis-band and run into confusion, the earth would grow wild and become a great forest, and mankind would become beasts of prey one towards another, &c.[1]

So far this great preacher, the truth of whose doctrine I might confirm by quotations from almost every good writer who hath treated of the rules and laws of society, as well as by the example of all those legislators by whom the several societies, which have ever been extant in the world, were first instituted; and therefore, as the learned Diodorus long since observed, all great law-givers, among whom he includes Moses, derived their commissions from Heaven, and mixed religious rites with civil institutions, well knowing how necessary the former were to strengthen and give a proper sanction to the latter. Nay the very deist and atheist him-self, if such a monster there be, must acknowledge the truth of this doctrine; since those who will not allow religion to be a divine, must at least confess that it is a political, insti-

---

[1] Sermon III. "The advantage of Religion to Society," Prov. **xiv. 34.** [Tillotson's Works, vol. i. pp. 100-102, 8vo edit., 1757.]

tution, and designed by the magistrate for the purpose of guarding his authority and of reducing the people to obedience; "therefore," says the learned archbishop, "magistrates have always thought themselves concerned to cherish religion, and to maintain in the minds of men the belief of a God and another life. Nay, that common suggestion of atheistical persons, that religion was at first a politic device, and is still kept up in the world as a state-engine to awe men into obedience, is a clear acknowledgment of the usefulness of it to the ends of government," &c.[1]

Indeed if this solemn truth wanted any further proof, it might be easy to make a melancholy experiment of it on the present occasion; since whoever should attempt, without the assistance of what I here contend for, to preserve any order or decency among such a body of people as is proposed to assemble together, would, I am convinced, find himself very egregiously and perhaps very unfortunately mistaken. If indeed such a body of men could be kept together at all, and restrained from the most violent and inordinate outrages, this could be only effected by a strong and constant military force; in short by the same degree of coercion as would restrain the fury of wild beasts, which are possibly as easy to be governed as wild men.

That religion is a very cold and unavailing motive to action in the world is, I am afraid, neither easy to be denied nor difficult to account for. Some there are who are too wise (I mean in their own opinions) to believe any of the truths of it; many more are too far immersed in the pursuits of business or pleasure; and many, almost all indeed who are the objects of this plan, very seldom or never hear the word religion mentioned; but heaven and hell when well rung in the ears of those who have not yet learnt that there are no such places, and who will give some attention to what they hear, are by no means words of little or no signification. Hope and fear, two very strong and active passions, will hardly find a fuller or more adequate object to amuse and employ them; this more especially in a place where there

[1] Ibid. [p. 103.]

will be so little of temptation to rouse or to gratify the evil
inclinations of human nature; where men will find so few
of those good things of this world, for which the other is
every day bartered; and where they will have no encouragement, from the example of their betters, to make so prudent
an exchange. In such a place, and among such a people, religion will, I am satisfied, have a very strong influence in
correcting the morals of men; and I am no less persuaded
that it is religion alone which can effectually accomplish so
great and so desirable a work.

XXVIII., XXIX. Need no explanation, but may be altered as the legislature pleases.

XXX. *The keepers, &c., to report the evil or good behaviour of the labourers.*] Though it be the duty of every
man to obey the laws of his country, and no man is entitled
to any reward for the performance of his duty: and therefore legislators are not to be accused of severity in annexing
punishment to the breach of their laws, while they have assigned no reward to the obedient: however I am inclined to
think they have not omitted the latter so much from this
persuasion, as from foreseeing the great difficulties in which
it would have involved them; for though it be impossible in
large and extended societies to preserve a general course as
well of rewarding as punishing, yet the wisest governments
have endeavoured as far as in them lies to avail themselves
of the force of allurement as well as of terror. Hence that
indulgence in all nations to the wealth and luxury of their
great men, which Gallus Asinius in Tacitus calls *delenimenta
curarum et periculorum.* Hence all those titles and honours
with which politicians have baited for the ambition of mankind, and hence, when the public stock could afford no more
of real value, those gew-gaw trifling distinctions which, in
spite of all the ridicule of the witty and scorn of the wise,
the greedy appetite of vanity will be always ready to
swallow.

In large societies, however, all these can reach but a little
way, and can be shared by very few. Of great armies scarce
the hundredth part can partake of any reward for the most

notable exploits and most complete victories. The rest must content themselves with the consciousness of having done their duty, and of having escaped that punishment to which cowardice would have subjected them, and of which they fail not of seeing sufficient examples.

I much question whether the outrageous indecency of the lowest part of mankind among us can be derived from a truer cause than this. As they have no hopes of reward, be they as good as they will, why should we wonder that they are as bad as they can be, when they have no fear of incurring punishment? And very bad indeed they may often be, without any such danger. For their idleness, at least, this will very sufficiently account. From this there is neither hope of public reward to allure, nor fear of public punishment to deter. What wonder, then, if those who are inclined to idleness should indulge their inclination, and betake themselves to begging? A better trade, perhaps, than any to which industry can tempt them to turn their heads.

Now, in the society here proposed, there will be no less opportunity of rewarding industry than of punishing idleness; nor need these rewards be very expensive to the public chest, since they will be so extremely honourable to those who receive them. By a very moderate and judicious distribution of such rewards for industry, and a very gentle infliction of punishment for idleness, I make no doubt but that in the county-house the former might be rendered as honourable, and the latter as infamous, as any virtue and vice have ever been held in any nation upon earth.

XXXI. The utility and, I think, necessity of this paragraph may be suffered to speak for itself; and so shall the two next.

XXXIV. *Money to be advanced, &c.*] As many of the persons to be committed hither, or who may voluntarily come hither, will possibly be penniless, some advancement to them will be necessary for their support. The *quantum* is submitted to the legislature, as well as the method which I have proposed for the repayment.

XXXV. *Prisoners to be allowed one shilling weekly.*]
This is somewhat less than twopence *per diem,* which is
much larger than the present Bridewell allowance; but as
the intent is that they shall be really kept to hard labour,
it will be necessary to support them somewhat better than
when they were suffered to remain in idleness.

XXXVI. *Deductions to be made, &c.*] As the society
have a right to the labour of delinquents by way of punishment, allowing them only a necessary support; and as they
here exercise this right in the case of those who are committed to the house of correction; so the defalcation from
persons committed to the county-house will, I believe, appear very reasonable; as these are in some degree offenders,
and the objects at least of some small punishment. As to
the deduction of one penny from the volunteers it should be
considered as a reasonable price for lodging, fire, candles,
&c., which are here provided for them.

XXXVII. *The receiver to make up his accounts after
every sale.*] I have endeavoured to shut out fraud as much
as possible through this whole plan; if any stronger bars can
be added I hope they will.

XXXVIII. *An account to be kept in separate pages.*] In
order to have these accounts well and often inspected they
must be rendered easy. The method I have chalked out was
the best I could invent for this purpose; but perhaps a
much better may be found by some who are more versed in
these matters.

XXXIX. The several branches of this paragraph need no
comment.

XL. *The labourers to be instructed in all kinds of manufacture.*] Upon the right management of the power given
in this paragraph depends, in a great measure, the utility of
the whole plan, and the improvement of those advantages
which I propose from bringing the poor together. It is this
principally which will require great capacity in the Governor; and that he should be always a man of much knowledge and experience. Which qualifications if he should
possess, and will do his duty in applying them, I doubt not

but most of the advantageous manufacturers of Europe may be by these means introduced into the nation.

XLII, to XLVI, inclusive. Crimes with their punishment.

XLII., XLIII. As the crimes mentioned in these two paragraphs must be guarded against with the utmost precaution, the punishment of them cannot possibly be less than that *ultimum supplicium* which is here allotted to them. This, I think, no man can have any doubt of who considers the numbers and nature of the people here to be assembled. The same consideration will remove all appearance of severity from the punishments inflicted in the 44th and 45th paragraphs.

XLVI. The persons who are here to be transported seem of all others the most proper objects of that punishment. This, however, some of them may possibly avoid by the alternative proposed, which is perhaps the only method of converting a fellow to some use who would be otherwise good for nothing. It is to be hoped that the military gentlemen will, on this occasion, depart a little from their usual nicety with regard to the morals of their recruits; since a man may have great military qualifications, and may yet be very properly turned out of civil society.

XLIX. This is taken from the last Gin Act, with little variation, and is of the utmost consequence to all the purposes of this plan.

L., LI., LII. Are submitted without any comment.

LIII. *Judicial power of the Governor, &c.*] Nothing conduces more to the good order of any society than the moderate punishment of small offences; this is properly called correction, since by it the manners of the party are often corrected and he is prevented from the commission of greater crimes. Such punishments should be always attended with reproof, and an endeavour to persuade the offender that he is corrected only for his own good. It must be remembered, however, that they are the better and milder dispositions which are to be much amended this way; and therefore shame should as little as possible be mixed with such correction. The articles here submitted to the Governor's jurisdiction are for the most part peccadilloes, and therefore he can scarce be too mild or moderate in his correction for the first offence, especially if attended with contrition. Indeed his power of punishing here is but small, and savours more of a master than a magistrate. On a second offence he may be a little more severe, and it may commonly be proper to go to the extent of his power. But a third offence of the same kind, and within the time limited, argues an incorrigible temper, and savours of the spirit of resistance to government: here he punishes as a magistrate, and the punishment is of the exemplary kind; tending rather to raise terror in others than to work the reformation of the party himself.

Among other powers the Governor hath that of regulating the price of provisions. The method of supplying the labourers with these is a problematical question; and it may admit of much debate whether it would be better to provide for them, or to suffer them to provide for themselves. In behalf of the former method it may be urged, that many persons joining together in a mess may be provided for at a much cheaper rate than the same number separately.

2. That possibly they may not of themselves choose to join; and it may therefore be proper to compel them by a coercive power.

3. That if they should for the most part agree to mess together, the savings on that account should be preserved to the use of the house.

4. That some of them, when they are masters of their own money will choose to stint themselves of food, in order to be more plentifully supplied with drink; which, besides causing disorders, will tend to weaken their bodies, to incapacitate them for labour, and render them sickly, &c.

On the other side it may be answered: 1. That allowing the expediency of their messing together, it can hardly be supposed but that in such a body sufficient numbers will always be found for that purpose.

2. That when this is voluntary it will be much more eli-

gible than when it is by coercion; which, where the spirits
of men are so fired with freedom as in this nation, is never
submitted to in small and unaccustomed matters without
uneasiness and heart-burning.

3. That by the power of constantly regulating the prices
of provisions, condescending to particularize every minute
article, there will be little difference between employing servants or employing suttlers in the manner as is here appointed; and the latter will be attended with much the less
confusion.

4. That the liberty of providing for themselves at their
own discretion, and of laying out their own money, is but a
reasonable liberty; and the refusal of it savours too much of
the treatment of children.   Nor is it without some tincture
of injustice, for those who eat less will by such means be
obliged to pay equally with those who eat more.

5. That as to the restraint from laying out too much of
their money in drink, this restraint seems needless while they
receive the allowance of the house; and when, by their own
industry, they become possessed of money it will be altogether as ineffectual.   Besides, proper care is taken on this
head, by absolutely prohibiting the introduction of spirituous liquors, and by punishing any kind of drunkenness.

Upon the whole, the method here proposed seems to me
the better; but perhaps it will be most proper to leave
this matter open to the discretion of the Governor and
sessions, who may act therein as they shall find most
convenient.

LIV. *The jurisdiction of the sessions.*]   I submit this
whole paragraph, with any alterations in it which may be
thought proper, without a comment: nor doth the residue of
the plan seem to want any explanation.

Thus have I laid my plan before the public, with all that I
have to say in its support or recommendation.   They will,
as they please, receive it in the whole or in part; will alter,
amend, or entirely reject it, at their discretion.   Whatever
shall be the fate of my labour it will not find me quite un-

prepared; and though my plan should be treated by some as an impossible, by others as an absurd or ridiculous scheme, it will neither spoil my stomach nor break my rest. I do not affect an absolute or stoical indifference on this occasion; I mean no more than to be as little solicitous as it is possible about events, whatever trouble I have taken in using the means—a temper of mind for which I am not a little obliged to my great master's advice:

Quem sors dierum cumque dabit, lucro appone.[1]

And again:

Grata superveniet, quæ non sperabitur, hora.[2]

The forming which into a general precept, and then reducing that precept into a habit, hath cost me more pains than I have employed in composing the foregoing pages; nor is the former labour thrown away, whatever may become of the latter.

Besides the fair opponents mentioned in the introduction, and those whom the imperfections of my plan may raise, I am to apprehend, I am well convinced, many who will be interested in the opposition. Some are enemies to all schemes whatever, and some to all schemes but their own; others there are who find an advantage in the present wretched state of the poor, and in the numerous laws concerning them. Lastly, I sometimes flatter myself that I have some few enemies; men who do me the honour of thinking better either of my parts, or of my fortune, than I do myself; and who consequently hate me from the only motive which can prompt a man to hate those who have done him no injury. These will, I presume, not only deny all merit to the execution of my design, but to the design itself; and will discover that, instead of intending a provision for the poor, I have been carving out one for myself, and have very cunningly projected to build myself a fine house at the expense of the public. This would be to act in direct opposition to

---

[1] Horace, Odes, I. 9.   [2] Ibid., Epistles, I. 4.

the advice of my above master; it would be indeed *struere domos immemor sepulchri.* Those who do not know me may believe this; but those who do will hardly be so deceived by that cheerfulness which was always natural to me, and which, I thank God, my conscience doth not reprove me for, to imagine that I am not sensible of my declining constitution. In real truth, if my plan be embraced, I shall be very easily recompensed for my trouble without any concern in the execution. Ambition or avarice can no longer raise a hope, or dictate any scheme to me, who have no farther design than to pass my short remainder of life in some degree of ease, and barely to preserve my family from being the objects of any such laws as I have here proposed.

NOTE. There are several little mistakes in the foregoing proposals, such as *his* or *her* for *their*, and *vice versâ;* which escaped correction in the hurry in which this pamphlet was printed: they will, it is hoped, be excused in a rough sketch, where the author intends only to convey his meaning to be amended and improved, and not to form the regular draft of a law.

A
CHARGE
DELIVERED TO THE
GRAND JURY,
AT THE

SESSIONS of the PEACE

HELD FOR THE

City and Liberty of *Westminster*, &c.

On THURSDAY the 29th of JUNE, 1749.

By *HENRY FIELDING*, Esq;
CHAIRMAN of the said SESSIONS.

PUBLISHED

By Order of the COURT, and at the unanimous
Request of the Gentlemen of the GRAND JURY.

LONDON:
Printed for A. MILLAR, opposite *Catherine-Street*, in
the *Strand*. 1749.

A CHARGE

TO

THE GRAND JURY

GENTLEMEN OF THE GRAND JURY,—There is no part in all the excellent frame of our constitution which an Englishman can, I think, contemplate with such delight and admiration; nothing which must fill him with such gratitude to our earliest ancestors, as that branch of British liberty from which, gentlemen, you derive your authority of assembling here on this day.

The institution of juries, gentlemen, is a privilege which distinguishes the liberty of Englishmen from those of all other nations; for as we find no traces of this in the antiquities of the Jews, or Greeks, or Romans, so it is an advantage which is at present solely confined to this country; not so much, I apprehend, from the reasons assigned by Fortescue, in his book *De Laudibus, cap.* 29, namely, "because there are more husbandmen and fewer freeholders in other countries," as because other countries have less of freedom than this; and, being for the most part subjected to the absolute wills of their governors, hold their lives, liberties, and properties, at the discretion of those governors, and not under the protection of certain laws. In such countries it would be absurd to look for any share of power in the hands of the people.

And, if juries in general be so very signal a blessing to this nation, as Fortescue, in the book I have just cited, thinks it: " A method," says he, " much more available and effectual

197

for the trial of truth than is the form of any other laws of the world, as it is farther from the danger of corruption and subornation," what, gentlemen, shall we say of the institution of grand juries, by which an Englishman, so far from being convicted, cannot even be tried, not even put on his trial in any capital case, at the suit of the crown; unless, perhaps, in one or two very special instances, till twelve men, at the least, have said on their oaths that there is a probable cause for his accusation! Surely we may, in a kind of rapture, cry out with Fortescue, speaking of the second jury, " Who then can unjustly die in England for any criminal offence, seeing he may have so many helps for the favour of his life, and that none may condemn him but his neighbours, good and lawful men, against whom he hath no manner of exception? "

To trace the original of this great and singular privilege, or to say when and how it began, is not an easy task; so obscure indeed are the footsteps of it through the first ages of our history, that my Lord Hale, and even my Lord Coke, seem to have declined it. Nay, this latter, in his account of his second or petty jury is very succinct; and contents himself with saying, *Co. Lit.* 155, *b,* that it is very ancient, and before the Conquest.

Spelman, in his Life of Alfred, lib. ii. page 71, will have that prince to have been the first founder of juries, but in truth they are much older; and very probably had some existence even among the Britons. The Normans likewise had anciently the benefit of juries, as appears in the Custumier de Normandy; and something like grand juries too we find in that book under the title Suit de Murdyr.

Bracton, who wrote in the reign of Henry III., in his book *De Corona, cap.* 1, gives a plain account of this matter; and by him it appears, that the grand juries before the justices in eyre differed very little at that time from what they now are before justices assigned to keep the peace, oyer, and terminer, and gaol-delivery, unless in the manner of choosing them, and unless in one other respect; there being then a grand jury sworn for every hundred; whereas, at present, one serves for the whole county, liberty, &c.

But before this time our ancestors were sensible of the great importance of this privilege, and extremely jealous of it, as appears by the twenty-ninth chapter of the great charter, granted by King John, and confirmed by Henry III. For thus my Lord Coke, 2 Instit. 46, expounds that chapter. *Nullus liber homo capiatur,* &c. " No man shall be taken, that is," says he, " restrained of liberty, by petition or suggestion to the king and his council; unless it be by indictment or presentment of good and lawful men, where such deeds be done."

And so just a value have our ancestors always set on this great branch of our liberties, and so jealous have they been of any attempt to diminish it, that when a commission to punish rioters in a summary way was awarded, in the second year of Richard II., " it was," says Mr. Lambard in his Eirenarcha, fol. 305, " even in the self-same year of the same king, resumed, as a thing over hard," says that writer, " to be borne, that a freeman should be imprisoned without an indictment, or other trial, by his peers, as Magna Charta speaketh; until that the experience of greater evils had prepared and made the stomach of the commonwealth able and fit to digest it."

And a hard morsel surely it must have been, when the commonwealth could not digest it in that turbulent reign, which, of all others in our history, seems to have afforded the most proper ingredients to make it palatable; in a reign, moreover, when the commonwealth seemed to have been capable of swallowing and digesting almost any thing; when judges were so prostituted as to acknowledge the king to be above the law; and when a parliament, which even Echard censures, and for which Mr. Rapin, with a juster indignation, tells us, he knows no name odious enough, made no scruple to sacrifice to the passions of the king, and his ministers, the lives of the most distinguished lords of the kingdom, as well as the liberties and privileges of the people. Even in that reign, gentlemen, our ancestors could not, as Mr. Lambard remarks, be brought by any necessity of the times to give up, in any single instance, this their invaluable privilege.

Another considerable attempt to deprive the subject of

the benefit of grand juries was made in the eleventh year of Henry VII. The pretence of this act of parliament was the wilful concealment of grand jurors in their inquests; and by it "power was given to the justices of assize in their sessions, and to the justices of peace in every county, upon information for the king, to hear and determine all offences and contempts (saving treason, murder, or felony) by any person against the effect of any statute."

My Lord Coke, in his 4th Institute, fol. 40, sets forth this act at large, not as a law which in his time had any force, but *in terrorem;* and, as he himself says, that the like should never be attempted in any future parliament.

"This act," says Lord Coke, "had a fair flattering preamble; but in the execution, tended diametrically contrary; viz. to the high displeasure of Almighty God, and to the great let, nay, the utter subversion of the common law; namely, by depriving the subject of that great privilege of being indicted and tried by a jury of their countrymen."

By pretext of this law, says the great writer I have just cited, Empson and Dudley did commit upon the subject insufferable pressures and oppressions. And we read in history, that soon after the act took place, Sir William Capel, alderman of London, who was made the first object of its tyranny, was fined two thousand seven hundred pounds, sixteen hundred of which he actually paid to the king, by way of composition. A vast sum, in those days, to be imposed for a crime so minute that scarce any notice is taken of it in history.

· Our ancestors, however, bore not long this invasion on their liberties; for in the very first year of King Henry VIII. this flagitious act was repealed, and the advisers of all the extortions committed by it were deservedly sacrificed to the public resentment.

Gentlemen, I shall mention but two more attacks on this most valuable of all our liberties; the first of which was indeed the greatest of all, I mean that cursed Court of Star-Chamber, which was erected under the same king.

I shall not before you, gentlemen, enter into a contest with my Lord Coke whether this court had a much older existence, or whether it first began under the statute of 3 Henry VII. For my part, I clearly think the latter.

I.   Because the statute which erects it mentions no such court as then existing, and most manifestly speaks the language of creation, not of confirmation.

II.   Because it was expressly so understood by the judges, within five years after the statute was made, as appears by the year-book of 8 Henry VII. *Pasch.* fol. 13, *Plac.* 7.

Lastly, Because all our historians and law writers before that time are silent concerning any such court; for as to the records and acts of parliament cited by my Lord Coke, they are most evidently to be applied only to the king and council, to whom, in old time, complaints were, in very extraordinary cases, preferred.

This old court, my Lord Coke himself confesses, sat very rarely; so rarely indeed, that there are no traces left of its proceedings, at least of any such as were afterwards had under the authority of the statute. Had this court had an original existence in the constitution, I do not see why the great lawyer is so severe against the before-mentioned act of the eleventh of Henry VII. or how he can, with any propriety, call the liberty of being accused and tried only by juries the birthright of an English subject.

The other instance was that of the High Commission Court, instituted by parliament in the first year of Queen Elizabeth.

This act likewise pretends to refer to an authority in being. The title of it is, " An Act restoring to the Crown the ancient jurisdiction," &c. By which, saith Lord Coke, 4 Inst. 325, the nature of the act doth appear, viz. that it is an act of restitution.

And hence the Court of Common Pleas, in the reign of James I. well argued, that the act being meant to restore to the crown the ancient ecclesiastical jurisdiction, the commissioners could drive no other power from it than before belonged to that ecclesiastical jurisdiction.

But however necessary, as my Lord Coke says, 4 Inst. 326, this act might have been at its first creation, or however the intention of the legislature might have been to restrain it, either as to time or persons, certain it is, that the commissioners extended its jurisdiction in many cases, to the great grievance of the subject, and to the depriving them of that privilege which I have just mentioned to be the birthright of an Englishman.

The uses made of these courts, and particularly under that unhappy prince Charles I., need not be mentioned. They are but too well known. Let it suffice, that the spirit of our ancestors at last prevailed over these invasions of their liberties, and these courts were for ever abolished.

And, gentlemen, if we have just reason to admire the great bravery and steadiness of those our ancestors, in defeating all the attempts of tyranny against this excellent branch of our constitution, we shall have no less reason, I apprehend, to extol that great wisdom which they have from time to time demonstrated, in well ordering and regulating their juries; so as to preserve them as clear as possible from all danger of corruption. In this light, gentlemen, we ought to consider the several laws by which the morals, the character, the substance, and good demeanour of jurors are regulated. These jurors, gentlemen, must be good and lawful men, of reputation and substance in their country, chosen at the nomination of neither party, absolutely disinterested and indifferent in the cause which they are to try. Upon the whole, the excellence of our constitution, and the great wisdom of our laws, which Fortescue, my Lord Coke, and many other great writers, have so highly extolled, is in no one instance so truly admirable as in this institution of our juries.

I hope, gentlemen, I shall not be thought impertinent in having taken up so much of your time to show you the great dignity and importance of that office which you are now assembled here to execute; the duties of which it is incumbent on me concisely to open to you; and this I shall endeavour in the best manner I am able.

The duty, gentlemen, of a grand juror, is to inquire of all crimes and misdemeanours whatsoever, which have been committed in the county or liberty for which he serves as a grand juror, and which are anywise cognizable by the court in which he is sworn to inquire.

And this inquiry is in a twofold manner, by way of indictment and by way of presentment.

Which two words Mr. Lambard, fol. 461, thus explains:

A presentment, says he, I take to be a mere determination of the jurors themselves; and an indictment is the verdict of the jurors, grounded upon the accusation of a third person; so that a presentment is but a declaration of the jurors, without any bill offered before; and an indictment is their finding a bill of accusation to be true.

The usual method of charge hath been to run over the several articles, or heads of crimes, which might possibly become subject to the inquiry of the grand jury.

This we find in Bracton, who writ so long ago as the reign of Henry III., was the practice of the justices in Eyre, 1, iii. c. 1. And my Lord Coke says, 4 Inst. 183, that the charge to be given at the sessions of the peace consisteth of two parts; laws ecclesiastical for the peace of the church, and laws civil and temporal for the peace of the land. And Mr. Lambard, in his Eirenarcha, gives the whole form of the charge at length, in which he recapitulates every article which was at that time inquirable in the sessions.

But, gentlemen, I think I may be excused at present from taking up so much of your time; for though we are assembled to exercise the jurisdiction of a very ancient and honourable liberty, yet, as there is another sessions of justices, within that county of which this liberty is a part, before whom indictments for all crimes of the deeper dye are usually preferred, it seems rather to savour of ostentation than utility, to run over those articles which in great probability will not come before you.

And indeed a perfect knowledge of the law in these matters is not necessary to a grand juror; for in all cases of indictments, whether for a greater or a lesser, a public, or private crime, the business of a grand jury is only to attend to the evidence for the king; and if on that evidence there shall appear a probable cause for the accusation, they are to find the true bill, without listening to any circumstances of defence, or to any matter of law.

And therefore my Lord Hale, vol. ii. fol. 158, puts this case: "If A be killed by B, so that the person of the slayer and slain be certain; and a bill of murder be presented to the grand jury, regularly they ought to find the bill for murder, and not for manslaughter, or *se defendendo;* because otherwise offences may be smothered without due trial; and when the party comes on his trial, the whole fact will be examined before the court and the petty jury; for if a man kills B in his own defence or *per infortunium,* or possibly in executing the process of law upon an assault made upon him, or in his own defence on the highway, or in defence of his house against those that come to rob him (in which three last cases it is neither felony nor forfeiture, but, upon not guilty pleaded, he ought to be acquitted) ; yet if the grand inquest find an *ignoramus* upon the bill, or find the special matter, whereby the prisoner is dismissed and discharged, he may nevertheless be indicted for murder seven years after; " whereas, if upon a proper finding he had been acquitted he could never afterwards be again arraigned without having the plea of *autrefoits acquit.*

This doctrine of the learned chief justice you will apply to whatever case may come before you; for wherever you shall find probable cause, upon the oaths of the king's witnesses, you will not discharge your office without finding the bill to be true, showing no regard to the nature of the crime, or the degree of the guilt; which are matters proper for the cognizance and determination of the court only.

I must not, however, omit, on the authority of the last-mentioned judge, H. P. C. ii. 157, " that if, upon the hearing the king's evidence, or upon your own knowledge of the incredibility of the witnesses, you shall be dissatisfied, you may then return the bill *ignoramus."*

It is true my Lord Hale confines this to indictments for capital offences; but I see no reason why it may not be extended to any indictment whatever.

One caution more occurs on this head of indictment; and

it is the duty of secrecy. To have revealed the king's counsel disclosed to the grand jurors was formerly taken to be felony; nay, Justice Shard, in the 27th year of the book of assizes, Placit. 63, doubted whether it was not treason; and though at this day the law be not so severe, yet is this still a very great misdemeanour, and fineable as such, and is moreover a manifest breach of your oath.

I come now, gentlemen, to the second branch of your duty, namely, that of presenting all offences which shall come to your knowledge.

And this is much more painful, and of greater difficulty than the former; for here you are obliged, without any direct accusation, to inform yourselves as well as is possible of the truth of the fact, and in some measure likewise to be conusant of those laws which subject offences to your presentment.

Upon this head, therefore, I shall beg leave to remind you of those articles which seem to be most worthy of your inquiry at this time; for indeed it would be useless and tedious to enumerate the whole catalogue of misdemeanours that are to be found in our statutes; many of which, though still in force, are, by the changes of times and fashions, become antiquated, and of little use. *Cessante ratione legis, cessat et ipsa lex;* and there are some accidental and temporary evils which at particular seasons have, like an epidemic distemper, affected society, but have afterwards disappeared, or at least made very faint efforts to corrupt the public morals. The laws made to suppress such, though very wholesome and necessary at the time of their creation, become obsolete with the evil which occasioned them, and which they were intended to cure. But, gentlemen, there are evils of a more durable kind, which rather resemble chronical than epidemic diseases; and which have so inveterated themselves in the blood of the body politic, that they are perhaps never to be totally eradicated. These it will be always the duty of a magistrate to palliate and keep down as much as possible. And these, gentlemen, are the misdemeanours of which you are to present as many as come to your knowledge.

And first, gentlemen, I will remind you of presenting all

offences committed immediately against the Divine Being; for though all crimes do include in them some degree of sin, and may therefore be considered as offences against the Almighty; yet there are some more directly levelled at His honour, and which the temporal laws do punish as such.

And, 1. All blasphemous expressions against any one of the Sacred Persons in the Trinity are severely punishable by the common law; for, as my Lord Hale says, in Taylor's case, 1 Vent. 293, 3 Keb. 607, 621, S. C., " Such kind of wicked blasphemous words are not only an offence against God and religion, but a crime against the laws, state, and government;" and in that case the defendant for blasphemy, too horrible indeed to be repeated, was sentenced to stand three times in the pillory, to pay a great fine, and to find security for his good behaviour during life.

In like manner, all scandalous and contemptuous words spoken against our holy religion are by the wisdom of the common law made liable to an indictment; for " Christianity " (says that excellent chief justice, in the case I have just cited) " is parcel of the laws of England; therefore to reproach the Christian religion is to speak in subversion of the law." And to the same purpose is Atwood's case, in Cro. Jac. 421, where one was indicted before the justices of peace for saying, that the religion now professed was a new religion within fifty years, &c. For as to the doubt concerning the high commissioners started in that case, and then, as it appears, over-ruled, that is now vanished.

Nor are our statutes silent concerning this dreadful offence; particularly by Eliz. c. 2, sect. 9, a severe punishment is enacted for any person who shall, in any interludes, plays, songs, rhymes, or by other open words, declare or speak any thing in derogation, depraving or despising the Book of Common Prayer, &c.

Mr. Lambard, I find, mentions this act in his charge, though the execution of it be in the counties confined to the justices of Oyer and Terminer, and of assize; but the 22nd sect. of the statute seems to give a clear jurisdiction to this court, at two of our quarter-sessions.

The last offence of this kind which the wicked tongue of man can commit is by profane cursing and swearing. This is a sin expressly against the law delivered by God Himself to the Jews, and which is as expressly prohibited by our blessed Saviour in His sermon on the mount.

Many statutes have been made against this offence; and by the last of these, which was enacted in the nineteenth year of the present king, every day-labourer, common soldier, common sailor, and common seaman, forfeits one shilling; every other person under the degree of a gentleman, two shillings; and every person of or above that degree five shillings.

And in case any person shall after such conviction offend again he forfeits double; and for every offence after a second conviction treble.

Though the execution of this act be entrusted to one single magistrate, and no jurisdiction, unless by appeal, given to the sessions; yet I could not forbear mentioning it here, when I am speaking in the presence of many peace-officers, who are to forfeit forty shillings for neglecting to put the act in execution. And I mention it the rather to inform them, that whenever the offender is unknown to any constable, petty constable, tithingman, or other peace officer, such constable, &c. is empowered by the act, without any warrant, to seize and detain any such persons, and forthwith to carry him before the next magistrate.

And if these officers would faithfully discharge the duty thus enjoined them, and which religion, as well as the law, requires of them, our streets would soon cease to resound with this detestabe crime, so injurious to the honour of God, so directly repugnant to His positive commands, so highly offensive to the ears of all good men, and so very scandalous to the nation in the ears of foreigners.

Having despatched those misdemeanours (the principal ones at least) which are immediately committed against God, I come now to speak of those which are committed against the person of the king, which person the law wisely holds to be sacred.

Besides those heinous offences against this sacred person

which are punished *ultimo supplicio,* there are many articles, some of which involve the criminal in the guilt of præmunire, and others are considered in law as misprisions or contempts. The former of these is by Mr. Serjeant Hawkins, in his Pleas of the Crown, divided into two general heads: viz.—

Into offences against the crown.

And offences against the authority of the king and parliament.

Under the former head he enumerates nine several articles; but as these chiefly relate to such invasions of the royal prerogative as were either made in Popish ages in favour of the Bishops of Rome, or in those times which bordered on the reformation in favour of the Church of Rome, and are not practised, at least not openly practised, in these days, I shall have no need to repeat them here.

Under the latter head he mentions only one, which was enacted in the reign of Queen Anne, 6 Ann. c. 7. If any person shall maliciously and directly, by preaching, teaching, or advised speaking, declare, maintain, and affirm, that the pretended Prince of Wales hath any right or title to the crown of these realms, or that any other person or persons hath or have any right or title to the same, otherwise than according to the acts of settlement; or that the kings or queens of this realm, with the authority of parliament, are not able to make laws to limit the crown and the descent, &c., thereof, shall incur a præmunire.

A most wholesome and necessary law. And yet so mild hath been our government, that I remember no one instance of putting it in execution.

Misprisions or contempts are against the king's prerogative, against his title, or against his sacred person or government.

Under these heads will fall any act of public and avowed disobedience; any denying his most just and lawful title to the crown; any overt act which directly tends to encourage or promote rebellion or sedition; all false rumours against his majesty, or his councils; all contemptuous language concerning his sacred person, by cursing, reviling him, &c., or by uttering any thing which manifests an intention of lessening that esteem, awe, and reverence, which subjects ought to bear to the best of princes.

These are offences, gentlemen, which I must earnestly recommend to your inquiry. This, gentlemen, is your duty as grand jurors; and it must be a most pleasing task to you as you are Englishmen; for in proportion as you love and esteem your liberties, you will be fired with love and reverence toward a prince under whose administration you enjoy them in the fullest and amplest manner.

Believe me, gentlemen, notwithstanding all which the malice of the disappointed, the madness of republicans, or the folly of Jacobites, may insinuate, there is but one method to maintain the liberties of this country, and that is, to maintain the crown on the heads of that family which now happily enjoys it.

If ever subjects had reason to admire the justice of that sentiment of the poet Claudian, " That liberty never flourishes so happily as under a good king," we have reason at present for that admiration.

I am afraid, gentlemen, this word liberty, though so much talked of, is but little understood. What other idea can we have of liberty than that it is the enjoyment of our lives, our persons, and our properties in security; to be free masters of ourselves and our possessions, as far as the known laws of our country will admit; to be liable to no punishment, no confinement, no loss, but what those laws subject us to! Is there any man ignorant enough to deny that this is a description of a free people? or base enough to accuse me of panegyric, when I say this is our present happy condition?

But if the blessing of liberty, like that of health, be not to be perceived by those who enjoy it, or at least must be illustrated by its opposite, let us compare our own condition with that of other countries; of those whose polity some among us pretend to so much admire, and whose government they seem so ardently to affect. *Lettres de Cachet,* Bastiles, and Inquisitions, may, perhaps, give us a livelier sense of a just and mild administration, than any of the blessings we enjoy under it.

Again, gentlemen, let us compare the present times with the past. And here I need not resort back to those distant ages when our unhappy forefathers petitioned their conqueror, " that he would not make them so miserable, nor be so severe to them, as to judge them by a law they understood not." These are the very words, as we find them preserved in Daniel; in return to which, the historian informs us, nothing was obtained but fair promises. I shall not dwell here on the tyranny of his immediate successor, of whom the same historian records, that, " seeking to establish absolute power by force, he made both himself and his people miserable."

I need not, gentlemen, here remind you of the oppressions under which our ancestors have groaned in many other reigns, to shake off which the sword of civil war was first drawn in the reign of King John, which was not entirely sheathed during many successive generations.

I might, perhaps, have a fairer title to your patience in laying open the tyrannical proceedings of latter times, while the crown was possessed by four successive princes of the House of Stuart. But this, gentlemen, would be to trespass on your patience indeed; for to mention all their acts of absolute power, all their attempts to subvert the liberties of this nation, would be to relate to you the history of their reigns.

In a word, gentlemen, all the struggles which our ancestors have so bravely maintained with ambitious princes, and particularly with the last mentioned family, was to maintain and preserve to themselves and their posterity that very liberty which we now enjoy, under a prince to whom I may truly apply what the philosopher long ago said of virtue, *That all who truly know him, must love him.*

The third general head of misdemeanours, gentlemen, is of those which are committed against the subject; and these may be divided into two branches:—

Into such as are committed against individuals only:
And into such as affect the public in general.

The former of these will probably come before you by way of indictment; for men are apt enough to revenge their own quarrels; but offences *in commune nocumentum* do not so certainly find an avenger; and thus those crimes, which it is the duty of every man to punish, do often escape with impunity.

Of these, gentlemen, it may be therefore proper to awaken your inquiry, and particularly of such as do in a more especial manner infest the public at this time.

The first of this kind is the offence of profligate lewdness; a crime of a very pernicious nature to society, as it tends to corrupt the morals of our youth, and is expressly prohibited by the law of God, under the denunciation of the severest judgment, in the New Testament. Nay, we read in the 25th chapter of Numbers the exceeding wrath of God against the children of Israel for their fornication with the daughters of Moab. Nor did the plague, which on that occasion was sent among them, and which destroyed four and twenty thousand, cease, till Phineas, the son of Eleazer, and grandson of Aaron, had slain the Israelite together with his harlot.

And this, gentlemen, though a spiritual offence, and of a very high nature too, as appears from what I have mentioned, is likewise a temporal crime, and as Mr. Lambard (122) says, against the peace.

My Lord Coke, in his third Institute, 206, tells us, that, in ancient times, adultery and fornication were punished by fine and imprisonment, and were inquirable in turns and leets. And in the year-book of Hen. VII. 1 H. vii. fol. 6. plac. 3, we find the custom of London pleaded for a constable to seize a woman taken in the act of adultery, and to carry her to prison.

And though later times have given up this matter in general to ecclesiastical jurisdiction, yet there are two species which remain at this day cognizable by the common law.

The first is, any open act of lewdness and indecency in public, to the scandal of good manners.

And therefore, in Michaelmas term, 15 Car. II B. R. Sir Charles Sedley was indicted for having exposed himself naked in a balcony in Covent Garden, to a great multitude of people, with many indecent words and actions; and this was laid to be contrary to the king's peace, and to the great scandal of Christianity. He confessed the indictment; and Siderfin, 1 Sid. 168, who reports the case, tells us, that the court, in consideration of his embarrassed fortune, fined him only two thousand marks, with a short imprisonment, and to be bound three years to his good behaviour. An infamous punishment for a gentleman, but far less infamous than the offence. If any facts of this nature shall come to your knowledge, you will, I make no doubt, present them, without any respect to persons. Sex or quality may render the crime more atrocious, and the example more pernicious; but can give no sanction to such infamous offences, nor will, I hope, ever give impunity.

The second species which falls under this head, is the crime of keeping a brothel or bawdy-house. This is a kind of common nuisance, and is punishable by the common law.

It is true, that certain houses of this kind, under the name of public stews, have been sometimes tolerated in Christian countries, to the great scandal of our religion, and in direct contradiction to its positive precepts; but in the thirty-seventh year of Henry VIII. they were all suppressed by proclamation. And those infamous women who inhabited them were not, says Lord Coke, either buried in Christian burial when they were dead, nor permitted to receive the rites of the church while they lived.

And, gentlemen, notwithstanding the favour which the law in many cases extends to married women, yet in this case the wife is equally indictable, and may be found guilty with her husband.

Nor is it necessary that the person be master or mistress of the whole house; for if he or she have only a single room, and will therewith accommodate lewd people to perpetrate acts of uncleanness, they may be indicted for keeping a bawdy-house. And this was the resolution of the whole court, in the Queen and Pierson. Salk. 332.

Nor is the guilt confined to those who keep such houses;

those who frequent them are no less liable to the censure of the law. Accordingly we find in the select cases printed at the end of Lord, Ch. J. Popham's reports, that a man was indicted in the beginning of the reign of Charles I., at the sessions of peace for the town of Northampton for frequenting a suspected bawdy-house. And the indictment being removed into the King's Bench, several objections were taken to it, which were all over-ruled, judgment was given upon it, and the defendant fined.

If you shall know, therefore, gentlemen, of any such crimes, it will be your duty to present them to the court.

For however lightly this offence may be thought or spoken of by idle and dissolute persons, it is a matter of serious and weighty consideration. It is the cause, says my Lord Coke, of many mischiefs, the fairest end whereof is beggary; and tends directly to the overthrow of men's bodies, to the wasting of their livelihood, and to the endangering of their souls.

To eradicate this vice out of society, however it may be the wish of sober and good men, is, perhaps, an impossible attempt; but to check its progress, and to suppress the open and more profligate practice of it, is within the power of the magistrate, and it is his duty. And this is more immediately incumbent upon us, in an age when brothels are become in a manner the seminaries of education, and that especially of those youths, whose birth makes their right institution of the utmost consequence to the future well-being of the public; for whatever may be the education of these youths, however vitiated and enervated their minds and bodies may be with vices and diseases, they are born to be the governors of our posterity. If therefore, through the egregious folly of their parents, this town is to be the school of such youths, it behoves us, gentlemen, to take as much care as possible to correct the morals of that school.

And, gentlemen, there are other houses, rather less scandalous, perhaps, but equally dangerous to the society; in which houses the manners of youth are greatly tainted and corrupted. These are those places of public rendezvous, where idle persons of both sexes meet in a very disorderly manner, often at improper hours, and sometimes in disguised habits. These houses, which pretend to be the scenes of innocent diversion and amusement, are, in reality, the temples of iniquity. Such meetings are *contra bonos mores;* they are considered in law in the nature of a nuisance; and, as such, the keepers and maintainers of them may be presented and punished.

There is a great difference, gentlemen, between a morose and over sanctified spirit which excludes all kind of diversion, and a profligate disposition which hurries us into the most vicious excesses of this kind. " The common law," says Mr. Pulton, in his excellent treatise *de Pace,* fol. 25, b. " allows many recreations, which be not with intent to break or disturb the peace, or to offer violence, force, or hurt to the person of any; but either to try activity, or to increase society, amity, and neighbourly friendship." He there enumerates many sorts of innocent diversions of the rural kind, and which for the most part belong to the lower sort of people. For the upper part of mankind, and in this town, there are many lawful amusements, abundantly sufficient for the recreation of any temperate and sober mind. But, gentlemen, so immoderate are the desires of many, so hungry is their appetite for pleasure, that they may be said to have a fury after it; and diversion is no longer the recreation or amusement, but the whole business of their lives. They are not content with three theatres, they must have a fourth; where the exhibitions are not only contrary to law, but contrary to good manners, and where the stage is reduced back again to that degree of licentiousness which was too enormous for the corrupt state of Athens to tolerate; and which as the Roman poet, rather, I think, in the spirit of a censor than a satirist, tells us, those Athenians, who were not themselves abused, took care to abolish, from their concern for the public.

Gentlemen, our newspapers, from the top of the page to the bottom, the corners of our streets up to the very eaves of our houses, present us with nothing but a view of masquerades, balls, and assemblies of various kinds, fairs, wells, gardens, &c., tending to promote idleness, extravagance, and immorality, among all sorts of people.

This fury after licentious and luxurious pleasures is grown to so enormous a height, that it may be called the characteristic of the present age. And it is an evil, gentlemen, of which it is neither easy nor pleasant to foresee all the consequences. Many of them, however, are obvious; and these are so dreadful, that they will, I doubt not, induce you to use your best endeavours to check the farther increase of this growing mischief; for the rod of the law, gentlemen, must restrain those within the bounds of decency and sobriety, who are deaf to the voice of reason, and superior to the fear of shame.

Gentlemen, there are another sort of these temples of iniquity, and these are gaming-houses. This vice, gentlemen, is inseparable from a luxurious and idle age; for while luxury produces want, idleness forbids honest labour to supply it. All such houses are nuisances in the eye of the common law; and severe punishments, as well on those who keep them, as on those who frequent and play at them, are inflicted by many statutes. Of these houses, gentlemen, you will, I doubt not, inquire with great diligence; for though possibly there may be some offenders out of your reach, yet if those within be well and strictly prosecuted, it may, perhaps, in time, have some effect on the others. Example in this case may, contrary to its general course, move upwards; and men may become ashamed of offending against those laws with impunity, by which they see their inferiors brought to punishment. But if this effect should not be produced, yet, gentlemen, there is no reason why you should not exert your duty as far as you are able, because you cannot extend it as far as you desire. And to say the truth, to prevent gaming among the lower sort of people, is principally the business of society; and for this plain reason, because they are the most useful members of the society; which, by such means, will lose the benefit of their labour. As for the rich and great, the consequence is generally no other than the exchange of property from the hands of a fool into those of a sharper, who is, perhaps, the more worthy of the two to enjoy it.

I will mention only one article more, and that of a very high nature indeed. It is, gentlemen, the offence of libelling, which is punished by the common law, as it tends immediately to quarrels and breaches of the peace, and very often to bloodshed and murder itself.

The punishment of this offence, saith my Lord Coke, is fine or imprisonment; and if the case be exorbitant, by pillory and loss of ears.

And, gentlemen, even the last of these judgments will appear extremely mild, if we consider, in the first place, the atrocious temper of mind from which this proceeds.

Mr. Pulton, in the beginning of his treatise *de Pace,* says of a libeller, " that he is a secret canker, which concealeth his name, hideth himself in a corner, and privily stingeth his neighbour in his fame, reputation, and credit; who neither knows from whom, nor from what cause he receiveth his blows, nor hath any means to defend himself : " and my Lord Coke, in his 5th Report (125), compares him to a poisoner, who is the meanest, the vilest, and most dangerous of all murderers. Nor can I help repeating to you a most beautiful passage in the great orator Demosthenes, who compares this wretch to a viper, which men ought to crush wherever they find him, without staying till he bite them.

In the second place, if we consider the injury done by these libellers, it must raise the indignation of every honest and good man; for what is this but, as Mr. Pulton says, " a note of infamy, intended to defame the person at whom it is levelled, to tread his honour and estimation in the dust, to extirpate and root out his reputation from the face of the earth, to make him a scorn to his enemies, and to be derided and despised by his neighbours? "

If praise, and honour, and reputation, be so highly esteemed by the greatest and best of men, that they are often the only rewards they propose to themselves from the noblest actions; if there be nothing too difficult, too dangerous, or too disagreeable for men to encounter, in order to acquire and preserve these rewards; what a degree of wickedness and barbarity must it be, unjustly and wantonly to strip men of that on which they place so high a value?

Nor is reputation to be considered as a chimerical good, or as merely the food of vanity and ambition. Our worldly interest is closely connected with our fame; by losing this, we are deprived of the chief comforts of society, particularly of that which is most dear to us, the friendship and love of all good and virtuous men. Nay, the common law indulged so great a privilege to men of good reputation in their neigh-bourhood, that in many actions the defendant's word was taken in his own cause, if he could bring a certain number of his neighbours to vouch that they believed him.

On the contrary, whoever robs us of our good name, doth not only expose us to public contempt and avoidance, but even to punishment; for by the statute 34 Edw. III. c. 1, the justices of the peace are empowered and directed to bind all such as be not of good fame to their good behaviour, and, if they cannot find sufficient sureties, they may be committed to prison.

Seeing, therefore, the execrable mischiefs perpetrated by this secret canker, this viper, this poisoner, in society, we shall not wonder to hear him so severely condemned in Scrip-ture; nor that Aristotle in his Politics should mention slan-der as one of those great evils which it is difficult for a legis-lator to guard against; that the Athenians punished it with a very severe and heavy fine, and the Romans with death.

But though the libeller of private persons be so detestable a vermin, yet is the offence still capable of aggravation, when the poison is scattered upon public persons and magistrates. All such reflections are, as my Lord Coke observes, a scandal on the government itself; and such scandal tends not only to the breach of the peace, but to raise seditions and insurrec-tions among the whole body of the people.

And, gentlemen, the higher and greater the magistrates be against whom such slanders are propagated, the greater is the danger to the society; and such we find to have been the sense of the legislature in the second year of Richard II. For in the statute of that year, chap. 5, it is said, "that by such means discords may arise between the lords and commons, whereof great peril and mischief might come to all the realm, and quick subversion and destruction of the said realm." And of such consequence was this apprehended to be, that we find no less than four statutes to prohibit and punish it; viz. Westm. 1 c. 33. 2 R. II. c. 5. 12 R. II. 11. and 2 and 3 P. & M. c. 12. By this last statute a jurisdiction was given to the justices of peace to inquire of all such offences; and if it was by book, ballad, letter, or writing, the offender's right hand was to be stricken off for the first offence, and for the second he was to incur a præmunire.

This last statute was afterwards prolonged in the last year of Queen Mary, and in the first of Elizabeth, during the life of that princess, and of the heirs of her body.

I have mentioned these laws to you, gentlemen, to show you the sense of our ancestors of a crime, which, I believe, they never saw carried to so flagitious a height as it is at present; when, to the shame of the age be it spoken, there are men who make a livelihood of scandal. Most of these are persons of the lowest rank and education, men, who lazily declining the labour to which they were born and bred, save the sweat of their brows at the expense of their consciences; and in order to get a little better livelihood, are content to get it, perhaps, in a less painful, but in a baser way than the meanest mechanic.

Of these, gentlemen, it is your business to inquire; of the devisers, of the writers, of the printers, and of the publishers of all such libels; and I do heartily recommend this inquiry to your care.

To conclude, gentlemen, you will consider yourselves as now summoned to the execution of an office of the utmost importance to the well-being of this community; nor will you, I am confident, suffer that establishment, so wisely and carefully regulated, and so stoutly and zealously maintained by your wise and brave ancestors, to degenerate into mere form and shadow. Grand juries, gentlemen, are, in reality, the only censors of this nation. As such, the manners of the people are in your hands, and in yours only. You, therefore, are the only correctors of them. If you neglect your duty, the certain consequences to the public are too apparent; for, as in a garden, however well cultivated at first, if the weeder's care be omitted, the whole must in time be over-run with weeds, and will resemble the wildness and rudeness of a desert; so if those immoralities of the people, which will sprout up in the best constitution, be not from time to time corrected by the hand of justice, they will at length grow up to the most enormous vices, will overspread the whole nation, and, in the end, must produce a downright state of wild and savage barbarism.

To this censorial office, gentlemen, you are called by our excellent constitution. To execute this duty with vigilance, you are obliged by the duty you owe both to God and to your country. You are invested with full power for the purpose. This you have promised to do, under the sacred sanction of an oath; and you are all met, I doubt not, with disposition and resolution to perform it, with that zeal which I have endeavoured to recommend, and which the peculiar licentiousness of the age so strongly requires.

A

CLEAR STATE

OF THE

CASE

OF

ELIZABETH CANNING,

Who hath fworn that fhe was robbed and almoſt ſtarved
to Death by a Gang of Gipſies and other Villains in
January laſt, for which one MARY SQUIRES now
lies under Sentence of Death.

---

*Quæ, quia ſunt admirabilia, contraque Opinionem
omnium ; tentare volui poſſentne proferri in Lucem, &
ita dici ut probarentur.*

CICERO. Parad.

By HENRY FIELDING, Eſq;

LONDON:

Printed for A. MILLAR in the *Strand.*
M.DCC.LIII.

(Price One Shilling.)

THE CASE

OF

ELIZABETH CANNING

THERE is nothing more admirable, nor, indeed, more amiable, in the Law of England, than the extreme tenderness with which it proceeds against persons accused of capital crimes. In this respect it justly claims a preference to the institutions of all other countries; in some of which a criminal is hurried to execution, with rather less ceremony than is required by our law to carry him to a prison; in many, the trials (if they may be called such) have little of form, and are so extremely precipitate, that the unhappy wretch hath no time to make his defence, but is often condemned without well knowing his accuser, and sometimes without well understanding his accusation. In this happy kingdom, on the contrary, so tender is the law of the life of a subject, so cautious of unjustly or erroneously condemning him, that, according to its own maxim, *De Morte Hominis nulla est Cunctatio longa*, it proceeds by slow and regular gradations, and requires so many antecedent ceremonies to the ultimate discussion of a court of justice, that so far from being in danger of a condemnation without a fair and open trial, every man must be tried more than once, before he can receive a capital sentence. By the law of England, no man can be apprehended for felony without a strong and just suspicion of his guilt; nor can he be committed to prison, without a charge on oath before a lawful magistrate. This charge must be again proved on oath, to the satisfaction of a large number (twelve at least) of the better sort of his countrymen (except in the case of an Appeal of Felony, which is now obsolete, and where the proceedings are still more ceremonial and tedious) ; before the accused can be required to answer to it, or be put on his defence; and after all these preparatives, the truth of his charge is to be tried in an open court of justice, before one at least and often many judges, by twelve indifferent and unexceptionable men: I may truly say unexceptionable, since it is in the prisoner's power to except against twenty-four without showing any cause, and as many more as he can show a reasonable cause of exception against. These, after a patient hearing of the witnesses against him, and after attending to his defence (in the making which, the law prescribes that every indulgence shall be shown him, and that even his judge shall be his counsel and assist him) must all concur in declaring on their oaths, that he is guilty of the crime alleged against him, or he is to be discharged, and can never more be called in question for the same offence, save only in the case of murder.

It seems, I think, that the wit of man could invent no stronger bulwark against all injustice and false accusation than this institution, under which not only innocence may rejoice in its own security, but even guilt can scarce be so immodest as to require a fairer chance of escaping the punishment it deserves.

And yet, if after all this precaution it should manifestly appear that a person hath been unjustly condemned, either by bringing to light some latent circumstance, or by discovering that the witnesses against him are certainly perjured, or by any other means of displaying the party's innocence, the gates of mercy are still left open, and upon a proper and decent application, either to the Judge before whom the trial was had, or to the Privy Council, the condemned person will be sure of obtaining a pardon, of preserving his life, and of regaining both his liberty and reputation.

To make, therefore, such an application on the behalf of injured innocence is not only laudable in every man, but it is a duty, the neglect of which he can by no means answer to his own conscience; but this, as I have said, is to be done in a proper and decent manner, by a private application to those with whom the law hath lodged a power of correcting its errors and remitting its severity; whereas to resort immediately to the public by inflammatory libels against the justice of the nation, to establish a kind of Court of Appeal from this justice in the bookseller's shop, to re-examine in newspapers and pamphlets the merits of causes which, after a fair and legal trial, have already received the solemn determination of a Court of Judicature, to arraign the conduct of magistrates, of juries, and even judges, and this even with the most profligate indecency, are the effects of a licentiousness to which no government, jealous of its own honour, or indeed provident of its own safety, will ever indulge or submit to.

Sensible as I am of this, I should by no means become an aggressor of this kind; but surely when such methods have been used to mislead the public, and to censure the justice of the nation in its sagacity at least, and grossly to misrepresent their proceedings, it can require little apology to make use of the same means to refute so iniquitous an attempt. However unlawful a weapon may be in the hands of an assailant, it becomes strictly justifiable in those of the defendant: and as the judges will certainly excuse an undertaking in defence of themselves, so may I expect that the public (that part of it, I mean, whose esteem alone I have ever coveted or desired) should show some favour to a design which hath in view not a bare satisfaction of their curiosity only, but to prevent them from forming a very rash, and, possibly, a very unjust judgment. Lastly, there is something within myself which rouses me to the protection of injured innocence, and which prompts me with the hopes of an applause much more valuable than that of the whole world.

Without this last motive, indeed, it may be imagined I should scarce have taken up my pen in the defence of a poor little girl, whom the many have already condemned. I well know the extreme difficulty which will always be found in obtaining a reversal of such a judgment. Men who have applauded themselves, and have been applauded by others, for their great penetration and discernment, will struggle very hard before they will give up their title to such commendation. Though they, perhaps, heard the cause at first with the impartiality of upright judges, when they have once given their opinion, they are too apt to become warm advocates, and even interested parties in defence of that opinion. Deplorable, indeed, and desperate is the case of a poor wretch against whom such a sentence is passed! No writ of error lies against this sentence, but before that tremendous court of the public where it was first pronounced, and no court whatever is, for the reasons already assigned, so tenacious of the judgments which it hath once given.

In defiance, nevertheless, of this difficulty, I am determined to proceed to disclose, as far as I am able, the true state of an affair, which, however inconsiderable the parties may be in their station of life (though injured innocence will never appear an inconsiderable object to a good mind), is now become a matter of real concern and great importance to the public; against whom a most horrible imposture, supported by the most impudent as well as impious perjury is dressed up, either on the one side or on the other. To discover most manifestly on which side it lies seems to be within the power of the government, and it is highly incumbent on them to exert themselves on this occasion, in order that by the most exemplary punishment they may deter men from that dreadful crime of perjury, which, in this case, either threatens to make the sword of justice a terror to the innocent, or to take off all its edge from the guilty; which of these it is likeliest to do in the present instance, I will endeavour to assist the reader, at least, in forming a probable conjecture.

Elizabeth Canning, a young girl of eighteen years of age, who lived at Aldermanbury Postern, in the City of London, declares, That on Monday, the 1st of January last, she went to see her uncle and aunt, who are people of a very good character, and who live at Saltpetre Bank, near Rosemary Lane; that having continued with them till towards nine in the evening, her uncle and aunt, it being late, walked a great part of the way home with her; that soon after she parted with them, and came opposite to Bethlehem Gate in Moorfields, she was seized by two men who, after robbing her of half a guinea in gold, and three shillings in silver, of her hat, gown, and apron, violently dragged her into a gravel-walk that leads down to the gate of Bethlehem Hospital, about the middle of which one of the men, after threatening to do for her, gave her a violent blow with his fist on the right temple, that threw her into a fit, and entirely deprived her of her senses. These fits she says she hath been accustomed to; that they were first occasioned by the fall of a ceiling on her head; that they are apt to return upon her whenever she is frightened, and that they sometimes continue for six or seven hours; that when she came to herself she perceived that two men were hurrying her along in a large roadway, and that in a little time after she was recovered, she was able to walk alone; however they still continued to pull and drag her along; that she was so intimidated by their usage that she durst not call out, nor even speak to them; that in about half an hour after the recovery of her senses, they carried her into an house where she saw in the kitchen an old gipsy woman and two young women; that the old gipsy woman took hold of her by the hand, and promised to give her fine clothes if she would go their way, which expression she understanding to mean the becoming a prostitute, she utterly refused to comply with; upon which the old gipsy woman took a knife out of a drawer and cut the stays off this Elizabeth Canning, and took them away from her, at which time one of the men likewise took off her cap, and then both the men went away; that soon after they were gone, and about an hour after she had been in the house, the old gipsy woman forced her up an old pair of stairs, and pushed her into a back room like a hay-loft, without any furniture whatsoever in the same, and there locked her up, threatening that if she made the least noise or disturbance, the old gipsy woman would come up and cut her throat, and then fastened the door on the outside and went away. She says, that when it was daylight, upon her looking round to see in what dismal place she was confined, she discovered a small black jug, with the neck much broken, filled with water, and several pieces of bread, amounting to about the quantity of a quartern loaf, scattered on the floor, where was likewise a large parcel of hay. In this room, she says, she continued from that time till about half an hour after four of the clock in the afternoon of Monday, the 29th day of the same month of January, being in all twenty-seven days and upwards, without any other sustenance than the aforesaid bread and water, except one small mince-pie which she had in her pocket, which she was carrying home as a present to her little brother. She likewise says, that she had some part of this provision remaining on the Friday before she made her escape, which she did by breaking out at a window of the room or loft in which she was confined, and whence having escaped, she got back to her friends in London in about six hours, in a most weak and miserable condition, being almost starved to death, and without ever once stopping at any house or place by the way. She likewise says, that during her whole confinement no person ever came near her to ask her any question whatever, nor did she see any belonging to the house more than once, when one of the women peeped through a hole in the door, and that she herself was afraid to call or speak to any one. All this she hath solemnly sworn before a magistrate and in a court of justice.

Such is the narrative of Elizabeth Canning, and a very extraordinary narrative it is, consisting of many strange particulars resembling rather a wild dream than a real fact. First, it doth not well appear with what motive these men carried this poor girl such a length of way, or indeed that they had any motive at all for so doing. Secondly, that they should be able to do it is not easy to believe; I do not mean that it is not within the strength of two men to carry a little girl (for so she is) ten miles, but that they could do this without being met, opposed, or examined by any persons in the much frequented roads near this town, is extremely strange and surprising. Thirdly, the gipsy woman doth not seem to have had any sufficient motive to her proceedings. If her design was to make a prostitute, or a gipsy, or both, of this poor girl, she would, in all probability, have applied to her during her confinement, to try what effect that confinement had produced. If her design was murder, she had many easier and better ways than by starving, or if she had chosen this method of destroying the girl, it seems impossible to account for the conveying to her that bread and water, which would serve for no other purpose but to lengthen out the misery of a wretch against whom the gipsy woman had, as appears, no foundation whatever of anger or revenge, and might have increased the danger of discovering the whole villainy. Fourthly, that Elizabeth Canning herself should have survived this usage, and all the terrors it must have occasioned, and should have been kept alive with no other sustenance than she declares she had, are facts very astonishing and almost incredible. Fifthly, that she should so well have husbanded her small pittance as to retain some of it till within two days of her escape, is another surprising circumstance. Sixthly, that she should undergo all this hardship and fasting without attempting sooner to make her escape, or without perceiving the possibility of making it in the manner in which she at last says she did effect it, seems to be no less shocking to reason and common sense. Lastly, that, at the time when she dates this escape, she should have strength sufficient left, not only to break her prison in the manner she declares, but to walk eleven or twelve miles to her own home, is another fact which may very well stagger our belief, and is a proper close to this strange, unaccountable, and scarce credible story.

Thus have I set the several particulars of this narrative in as strong a light against the relator, and in one as disadvantageous to the credibility of her relation, as I think they can fairly be placed. Certain it is, that the facts seem at first to amount to the very highest degree of improbability, but I think that they do not amount to an impossibility; for, as to those objections which arise from the want of a sufficient motive in the transactors of this cruel scene, no great stress I think can be laid on these. I might ask what possible motive could induce two ruffians, who were executed last winter for murder, after they had robbed a poor wretch who made no resistance, to return and batter his skull with their clubs, till they fractured it in almost twenty different places. How many cruelties, indeed, do we daily hear of, to which it seems not easy to assign any other motive than barbarity itself? In serious and sorrowful truth, doth not history, as well as our own experience, afford us too great reasons to suspect, that there is in some minds a sensation directly opposite to that of benevolence, and which delights and feeds itself with acts of cruelty and inhumanity? And if such a passion can be allowed any existence, where can we imagine it more likely to exist than among such people as these?

Besides, though to a humane and truly sensible mind such actions appear to want an adequate motive, yet to wretches very little removed, either in their sensations or understandings, from wild beasts, there may possibly appear a very sufficient motive to all that they did; such might be a desire of increasing the train of gipsies, or of whores in the family of the Mother Wells. One of these appears to have been the design of the gipsy woman from the declaration of Elizabeth Canning, who, if she had said nothing more improbable, would certainly have been entitled to our belief in this, though this design seems afterwards not to have been pursued. In short, she might very possibly have left the alternative, with some indifference, to the girl's own option; if she was starved out of her virtue, the family might easily apprehend she would give them notice; if out of her life, it would be then time enough to convey her dead body to some ditch or dunghill, where, when it was found it would tell no tales: possibly, however, the indifference of the gipsy woman was not so absolute, but that she might prefer the girl's *going her way,* and this will account for her conveying to her that bread and water, which might give the poor girl a longer time to deliberate, and consequently the love of life might have a better chance to prevail over the love of virtue.

So much for the first and third objection arising from the want of motive, from which, as I observed above, no very powerful arguments can be drawn in the case of such wretches: as to the second objection, though I mentioned it as I would omit none, the reader, I presume, will lay so little weight upon it, that it would be wasting time to give it much answer. In reality, the darkness of the night at that season of the year, and when it was within two days of the new moon, with the indifference of most people to what doth not concern themselves, and the terror with which all honest persons pass by night through the roads near this town, will very sufficiently account for the want of all interruption to these men in their conveyance of the poor girl.

With regard to the fourth objection—how she could survive this usage, &c? I leave the degree of probability to be ascertained by the physicians. Possible, I think it is, and I contend for no more. I shall only observe here, that she barely did survive it, and that she, who left her mother in a plump condition, returned so like a spectre, that her mother fainted away when she saw her; her limbs were all emaciated, and the colour of her skin turned black, so as to resemble a state of mortification; her recovery from which state since, is a proof of that firm and sound constitution which supported her, if she says true, under all her misery.

As to the fifth objection, she answers, that the cruel usage she had met with, and the condition she saw herself in, so affected both her mind and body, that she ate scarce anything during the first days of her confinement, and afterwards had so little appetite, that she could scarce swallow the hard morsels which were allotted her.

The sixth objection hath, in my opinion, so little in it that had I not heard it insisted on by others, I should not myself have advanced it; common experience every day teaches us, that we endure many inconveniences of life, while we overlook those ways of extricating ourselves, which, when they are discovered, appear to have been, from the first, extremely easy and obvious. The inference, which may be drawn from this observation, a modern degree of candour will oblige us to extend very far in the case of a poor simple child, under all the circumstances of weakness of body and depression and confusion of spirits, till despair, which is a quality that is ever increasing as its object increases, grew to the highest pitch, and forced her to an attempt which she had not before had the courage to undertake.

As to her accomplishing this, and being able to escape to her friends, the probability of this likewise I leave to the discussion of physicians: possible it surely is, and I question very much whether the degree of despair, which I have just mentioned, will not even make it probable; since this is known to add no less strength to the body than it doth to the mind, a truth which every man almost may confirm by many instances.

But if, notwithstanding all I have here said, the narrative should still appear ever so improbable, it may yet become a proper object of our belief, from the weight of the evidence; for there is a degree of evidence by which every fact that is not impossible to have happened at all, or to have happened in the manner in which it is related, may be supported and ought to be believed. In all cases, indeed, the weight of evidence ought to be strictly conformable to the weight of improbability; and when it is so, the wiser a man is the sooner and easier he will believe. To say truth, to judge well of this conformity is what we truly call sagacity, and requires the greatest strength and force of understanding. He who gives a hasty belief to what is strange and improbable, is guilty of rashness; but he is much more absurd who declares that he will believe no such fact on any evidence whatever. The world are too much inclined to think that the credulous is the only fool; whereas, in truth, there is *another fool* of a quite opposite character, who is much more difficult to deal with, less liable to the dominion of reason, and possessed of a frailty more prejudicial to himself and often more detrimental to mankind in general.

To apply this reasoning to the present case, as we have, it is hoped, with great fairness and impartiality, stated all the improbabilities which compose this girl's narrative, we will now consider the evidence that supports them. And when we have done this, it will possibly appear, that the credulous person is he who believes that Elizabeth Canning is a liar.

First, then, there is one part of this story which is incon-

testably true, as it is a matter of public notoriety, and known
by almost every inhabitant in the parish where her mother
dwells. This is, that the girl, after the absence of a month,
returned on the 29th of January, in the dreadful condition
above described. This being an established fact, a very fair
presumption follows that she was confined somewhere, and
by some person; that this confinement was of equal duration
with her absence; that she was almost starved to death; that
she was confined in a place whence it was difficult to make her
escape; that, however, this escape was possible, and that at
length she actually made it. All these are circumstances
which arise from the nature of the fact itself. They are what
Tully calls *Evidentia Rei,* and are stronger than the positive
testimony of any witnesses; they do, indeed, carry conviction
with them to every man who hath capacity enough to draw
a conclusion from the most self-evident premises.

These facts being established, I shall oppose improbability
to improbability, and first I begin by asking, Why did this girl
conceal the person who thus cruelly used her? It could not
be a lover; for among all the cruelties by which men have
become infamous in their commerce with women, none of this
kind can, I believe, be produced. What reason, therefore,
can be assigned for this great degree of more than Christian
forgiveness of such barbarous usage is to me, I own, a secret;
such forgiveness, therefore, is at least as great a degree of
improbability as any which can be found, or which can be
feigned in her narrative.

Again, what motive can be invented for her laying this
heavy charge on those who are innocent? That street robbers
and gipsies, who have scarce even the appearance of humanity,
should be guilty of wanton cruelty without a motive hath
greatly staggered the world, and many have denied the probability of such a fact: Will they then imagine that this girl
hath committed a more deliberate, and, therefore, a more
atrocious crime, by endeavouring to take away the lives of an
old woman, her son, and another man, as well as to ruin another woman, without any motive whatever? Will they believe this of a young girl, hardly eighteen years old, who hath

the unanimous testimony of all who ever knew her from her infancy, to support the character of a virtuous, modest, sober, well-disposed girl; and this character most enforced by those who know her best, and particularly by those with whom she hath lived in service?

As to any motive of getting money by such an attempt, nothing can be more groundless and evidently false than the suggestion; the subscription which was proposed and publicly advertised, was thought of long after the girl's return to her mother, upon which return she immediately told the story in the presence of numbers of people, with all the circumstances with which she hath since, without any variation, related it. The real truth is, that this subscription was set on foot by several well disposed neighbours and very substantial tradesmen, in order to bring a set of horrid villains to justice, which then appeared (as it hath since proved) to be a matter which would be attended with considerable expense, nor was any reward to the girl then thought of; the first proposer of which reward was a noble and generous lord, who was present at the last examination of this matter in Bow Street; so that this charge of the gipsy woman, and the rest, if a false one, was absolutely without any motive at all. A second improbability which rises as much higher than that to which it is opposed, as the crime would be higher, since it would be more deliberate in the girl, and as her character is better than that of street robbers and gipsies.

Again, as the girl can scarce be supposed wicked enough, so I am far from supposing her witty enough to invent such a story; a story full of variety of strange incidents, and worthy the invention of some writer of romances, in many of which we find such kind of strange improbabilities that are the productions of a fertile, though commonly, a distempered brain; whereas this girl is a child in years, and yet more so in understanding, with all the evident marks of simplicity that I ever discovered in a human countenance; and this I think may be admitted to be a third improbability.

A fourth seems to me to arise from the manner in which this poor simple girl hath supported this story; which, as it requires the highest degree of wickedness of heart, and some tolerable goodness of head to have invented, so doth it require no small degree of assurance to support; and that in large assemblies of persons of a much higher degree than she had ever before appeared in the presence of—before noblemen and magistrates, and judges—persons who must have inspired a girl of this kind with the highest awe. Before all these she went through her evidence without hesitation, confusion, trembling, change of countenance, or other apparent emotion. As such a behaviour could proceed only from the highest impudence, or most perfect innocence, so it seemed clearly to arise from the latter, as it was accompanied with such a show of decency, modesty, and simplicity, that if these were all affected, which those who disbelieve her must suppose, it must have required not only the highest art, but the longest practice and habit to bring it to such a degree of perfection.

A fifth improbability is, that this girl should fix on a place so far from home, and where it doth not appear she had ever been before. Had she gone to this place of her own accord, or been carried thither by any other than the person she accused, surely Mother Wells would have told this, as it must have acquitted her of the fact laid to her charge, and would indeed have destroyed the whole character of Elizabeth Canning, and of consequence have put an end to the prosecution; but Mother Wells, on the contrary, denied absolutely that Elizabeth Canning had ever been in her house, or that she had ever seen her face before she came there with the peace officers.

In this point, viz: That Elizabeth Canning was not acquainted with Mother Wells, or her house, nor ever there, in any other manner than as she herself hath informed us, her evidence stands confirmed by the best and strongest testimony imaginable, and that is by the declaration of the defendant Wells herself. It is true, indeed, that as to her being confined there, Wells utterly denies it, but she as positively affirms that this Elizabeth Canning was never there at any other time, nor in any other manner. From this point then, so established, will result an utter impossibility; for unless this poor girl had been well acquainted with the house, the hay-loft, the pitcher, &c., how was it possible that she should describe them all so very exactly as she did, at her return to her mother's, in the presence of such numbers of people? Nay, she described likewise the prospect that appeared from the hay-loft, with such exactness, as required a long time to furnish her with the particulars of. I know but two ways of her being enabled to give this description; either she must have been there herself, or must have had her information from some other. As to the former, Wells herself denies it; and as to the latter, I leave to the conjecture of my ingenious reader, whether it was Mother Wells herself, the gipsy woman, Virtue Hall, or who else that instructed Elizabeth Canning in all these particulars.

In the meantime, I shall beg leave to conclude, either that we must account for the girl's knowledge one of the ways which I have mentioned; or, secondly, we must believe an impossibility; or, thirdly, we must swallow the truth of this relation, though it be as hard a morsel as any which the poor girl fed on during her whole confinement.

And now I come to a piece of evidence which hath been the principal foundation of that credit which I have given to this extraordinary story. It appeared to me at first to be convincing and unsurmountable, in the same light it appeared to a gentleman whose understanding and sagacity are of the very first rate, and who is one of the best lawyers of his time; he owned that this evidence seemed to him to be unanswerable, so I acknowledge it yet seems to me, and till I shall receive an answer, I must continue to believe the fact which rests upon it.

In order to lay this evidence before the reader in a fair and just light, it will be necessary to give a brief relation of the order of proceedings in this case, down to the time when Virtue Hall appeared first before me.

Upon the return of Elizabeth Canning to her mother's house in the manner above set forth, and upon the account which she gave of her unprecedented sufferings, the visible marks of which then appeared on her body, all her neighbours began to fire with resentment against the several actors concerned in so cruel a scene; and presently some of the most substantial of these neighbours proposed to raise a contribution amongst themselves, in order, if possible, to bring the villains who had injured this poor girl to exemplary justice: as soon, therefore, as she was able to bear the journey, they put her into a chaise, and taking with them proper peace officers, conveyed the girl along the Hertford Road, to see if she was able to trace out the house where she had been confined; for she at that time knew not the name of the place, nor could she sufficiently describe the situation of Wells's house, though she had before so exactly described the inside of it. Possibly, indeed, she might never have been able to have discovered the house at all, had it not been for a very extraordinary incident, and this was, that through the chinks or crevices of the boards of the hay-loft, she saw at a distance the Hertford stage coach pass by, the driver of which she knew, though he passed not near enough for her to call to him with any hopes of success, and by this extraordinary circumstance she came to know that the house stood on the Hertford Road.

When they arrived at this house the poor girl was taken out of the chaise, and placed on a table in the kitchen, where all the family passed in review before her: she then fixed on the gipsy woman, whom she had very particularly described before, and who is, perhaps, the most remarkable person in the whole world; she charged likewise Virtue Hall, whose countenance likewise is very easy to be remembered by those who have once seen her.

The whole family, however, though no more were positively charged by Elizabeth Canning, being put all into a cart were conducted before Mr. Tyshemaker, who is a justice of the peace for the County of Middlesex, who, having first examined Elizabeth Canning alone, but without taking from her any information in writing, did afterwards examine all the parties, and in the end committed the gipsy woman and Wells—the former for taking away the stays from Elizabeth Canning, and the latter for keeping a disorderly house.

And here the reader will be pleased to observe these facts:

First, That Elizabeth Canning did not make any information in writing before this justice.

Secondly, That the history of the fact that she related to the justice was not in the presence of Virtue Hall.

Thirdly, That Elizabeth Canning, so cautious is she in taking her oath, declared that she could not swear to the gipsy's son, as the men's hats were flapped over their faces in the house, and as when she was first assaulted it was so very dark, she could not distinguish their countenances, nor did she charge Wells with any crime at all, except that which resulted from the tenor of her whole evidence of keeping a disorderly house.

Lastly, That Virtue Hall did, at that time, absolutely deny that she knew anything of the matter, and declared that Elizabeth Canning had never been in Wells's house, to her knowledge, till that day, nor had she ever seen her face before; the consequence of which declaration was, that the gipsy's son, whom this Virtue Hall hath since accused of the robbery, was discharged by Mr. Tyshemaker.

Elizabeth Canning, with her friends, now returned home to her mother's house, where she continued to languish in a very deplorable condition; and now Mr. Salt, the attorney, who hath been employed in this cause, advised the parties to apply to counsel, and upon this occasion, as he hath done upon many others, he fixed upon me as the counsel to be advised with.

Accordingly, upon the 6th of February, as I was sitting in my room, Counsellor Maden being then with me, my clerk delivered me a case, which was thus, as I remember, endorsed at the top, " The Case of Elizabeth Canning for Mr. Fielding's opinion," and at the bottom, " Salt, Solr." Upon the receipt of this case, with my fee, I bid my clerk give my service to Mr. Salt and tell him that I would take the case with me into the country, whither I intended to go the next day, and desired he would call for it on the Friday morning afterwards; after which, without looking into it, I delivered it to my wife, who was then drinking tea with us, and who laid it by.

The reader will pardon my being so particular in these circumstances, as they seem, however trifling they may be in themselves, to show the true nature of this whole transaction, which hath been so basely misrepresented, and as they will all be attested by a gentleman of fashion, and of as much honour as any in the nation. My clerk presently returned up stairs, and brought Mr. Salt with him, who, when he came into the room, told me that he believed the question would be of very little difficulty, and begged me earnestly to read it over then, and give him my opinion, as it was a matter of some haste, being of a criminal nature, and he feared the parties would make their escape. Upon this, I desired him to sit down, and when the tea was ended, I ordered my wife to fetch me back the case, which I then read over, and found it to contain a very full and clear state of the whole affair relating to the usage of this girl, with a *quere* what methods might be proper to take to bring the offenders to justice; which *quere* I answered in the best manner I was able. Mr. Salt then desired that Elizabeth Canning might swear to her information before me, and added, that it was the very particular desire of several gentlemen of that end of the town, that Virtue Hall might be examined by me relating to her knowledge of this affair.

This business I at first declined, partly, as it was a transaction which had happened at a distant part of the county, as it had been examined already by a gentleman, with whom I have the pleasure of some acquaintance, and of whose worth and integrity I have with all, I believe, who know him, a very high opinion; but principally, indeed, for that I had been almost fatigued to death, with several tedious examinations at that time, and had intended to refresh myself with a day or two's interval in the country, where I had not been, unless on a Sunday, for a long time.

I yielded, however, at last, to the importunities of Mr. Salt; and my only motives for so doing were, besides those importunities, some curiosity, occasioned by the extraordinary nature of the case, and a great compassion for the dreadful condition of the girl, as it was represented to me by Mr. Salt.

The next day Elizabeth Canning was brought in a chair to

my house, and being led up stairs between two, the following information, which I had never before seen, was read over to her, when she swore to the truth and set her mark to it.

MIDDLESEX.] The information of Elizabeth Canning, of Aldermanbury Postern, London, spinster, taken upon oath this 7th day of February, in the year of Our Lord 1753, before Henry Fielding, Esq., one of His Majesty's Justices of the Peace for the County of Middlesex.

This informant, upon her oath, saith, That on Monday, the 1st day of January last past, she, this informant, went to see her uncle and aunt, who live at Saltpetre Bank, near Rosemary Lane, in the County of Middlesex, and continued with them until the evening, and saith, That upon her return home about half an hour after nine, being opposite Bethlehem-gate in Moorfields, she, this informant, was seized by two men (whose names are unknown to her, this informant) who both had brown bob-wigs on, and drab-coloured great-coats, one of whom held her, this informant, whilst the other feloniously and violently, took from her one shaving hat, one stuff gown, and one linen apron, which she had on; and also, half a guinea in gold, and three shillings in silver; and then he that held her threatened to do for this informant. And this informant saith, that, immediately after, they, the same two men, violently took hold of her, and dragged her up into the gravel-walk that leads down to the said gate, and about the middle thereof, he, the said man that first held her, gave her, with his fist, a very violent blow upon the right temple, which threw her into a fit, and deprived her of her senses (which fits she, this informant, saith she is accustomed and subject to upon being frighted, and that they often continue for six or seven hours). And this informant saith, that when she came to herself, she perceived that she was carrying along by the same two men, in a large roadway: and saith, that in a little time after, she was so recovered she was able to walk alone; however they continued to pull her along, which still so intimidated and frighted her, that she durst not call out for assistance, or speak to them. And this informant saith, that, in about half an hour after she had so recovered herself, they, the said two men, carried her, this informant, into a house, (which, as she, this informant, heard from some of them, was about four o'clock in the morning, and which house, as she, this informant, hath since heard and believes, is situate at Enfield Wash in the County of Middlesex, and is reputed to be a very bad and disorderly bawdy-house, and occupied by one—Wells widow,) and there this informant saw, in the kitchen, an old gipsy woman, and two young women, whose names were unknown to this informant; but the name of one of them this informant hath since heard and believes is Virtue Hall, and saith, that the said old gipsy woman took hold of this informant's hand, and promised to give her fine clothes if she would go their way (meaning, as this informant understood, to become a prostitute); which this informant, refusing to do, she, the said old gipsy woman, took a knife out of a drawer, and cut the lace of the stays of her, this informant, and took the said stays away from her; and one of the said men took off her cap, and then the said two men went away with it, and she, this informant, hath never since seen any of her things. And this informant saith, that soon after they were gone (which she, this informant, believes was about five in the morning) she, the said old gipsy woman, forced her, this informant, up an old pair of stairs, and pushed her into a back room like a hayloft, without any furniture whatsoever in the same, and there locked her, this informant, up, threatening her, this informant, that if she made the least noise or disturbance, she, the said old gipsy woman, would cut her throat, and then she went away. And this informant saith, that when it grew light, upon her looking round to see in what a dismal place she was, she, this informant, discovered a large black jug, with the neck much broken, wherein was some water; and upon the floor, several pieces of bread, near in quantity to a quartern loaf, and a small parcel of hay: and saith, that she continued in this room or place, from the said Tuesday morning, the

LEGAL WRITINGS—16

2nd day of January, until about half an hour after four of the clock in the afternoon of Monday, the 29th day of the same month of January, without having or receiving any other sustenance or provision than the said bread and water (except a small mince-pie, which she, this informant, had in her pocket) ; or any thing to lie on other than the said hay, and without any person or persons coming to her, although she often heard the name of Mrs. and Mother Wells, called upon, whom she understood was the mistress of the house. And this informant saith, that on Friday, the 26th day of January last past, she, this informant, had consumed all the aforesaid bread and water, and continued without having any thing to eat or drink until the Monday following, when she this informant, being almost famished with hunger and starved with cold, and almost naked during the whole time of her confinement, about half an hour after four in the afternoon of the said 29th day of January, broke out at a window of the said room or place, and got to her friends in London, about a quarter after ten the same night, in a most weak, miserable condition, being very near starved to death. And this informant saith, that she ever since hath been, and now is, in a very weak and declining state and condition of health, and although all possible care and assistance is given her, yet whatever small nutriment she, this informant, is able to take, the same receives no passage through her, but what is forced by the apothecary's assistance and medicines.

The mark of
E.C.
(Elizabeth Canning.)

Sworn before me,
   this 7th of Feb. 1753.
    H. Fielding.

Upon this information, I issued a warrant against all who should be found resident in the house of the said Wells, as idle and disorderly persons, and persons of evil fame, that they might appear before me, to give security for their good behaviour; upon which warrant, Virtue Hall, and one Judith

Natus were seized and brought before me, both being found at Mother Wells's: they were in my house above an hour or more before I was at leisure to see them, during which time, and before I had ever seen Virtue Hall, I was informed that she would confess the whole matter. When she came before me she appeared in tears, and seemed all over in a trembling condition; upon which I endeavoured to soothe and comfort her: the words I first spoke to her, as well as I can remember, were these,—Child, you need not be under this fear and apprehension; if you will tell us the whole truth of this affair, I give you my word and honour, as far as it is my power to protect you; you shall come to no manner of harm. She answered, that she would tell the whole truth, but desired to have some time given her to recover from her fright; upon this, I ordered a chair to be brought her, and desired her to sit down, and then, after some minutes, began to examine her; which I continued doing, in the softest language and kindest manner I was able, for a considerable time, till she had been guilty of so many prevarications and contradictions, that I told her I would examine her no longer, but would commit her to prison, and leave her to stand or fall by the evidence against her; and at the same time advised Mr. Salt to prosecute her as a felon, together with the gipsy woman; upon this, she begged I would hear her once more, and said that she would tell the whole truth, and accounted for her unwillingness to do it, from the fears of the gipsy woman and Wells. I then asked her a few questions, which she answered with more appearance of truth than she had done before; after which, I recommended to Mr. Salt to go with her and take her information in writing; and at her parting from me, I bid her be a good girl, and to be sure to say neither more nor less than the whole truth. During this whole time there were no less than ten or a dozen persons of credit present, who will, I suppose, testify the truth of this whole transaction as it is here related. Virtue Hall then went from me, and returned in about two hours, when the following information, which was, as she said, taken from her mouth, was read over to her and signed with her mark.

The Information of Virtue Hall, late of the parish
of Enfield in the County of Middlesex, Spinster, taken upon oath this 13th day of February, 1753, before me, Henry Fielding, Esq.,
one of His Majesty's Justices of the Peace
for the County of Middlesex.

This informant, upon her oath, saith, that on Tuesday, the
2nd day of January, last past, about four of the clock in
the morning, a young woman, whose name, this informant
hath since heard, is Elizabeth Canning, was brought (without
any gown, hat, or apron on) to the house of one Susannah
Wells, of Enfield Wash, in the county aforesaid, widow, by
two men, the name of one of whom is John Squires, the
reputed son of one Mary Squires, an old gipsy woman, who
then, and some little time before, had lodged at the house
of the said Susannah Wells, but the name of the other of the
said two men this informant knows not, she, this informant,
never having seen him before or since to the best of her
knowledge. And this informant saith, that when she the
said Elizabeth Canning was brought into the kitchen of the
said Wells's house, there were present the said Mary Squires,
John Squires, the man unknown, Catherine Squires, the reputed daughter of the said Mary Squires, and this informant;
and this informant does not recollect that any one else was in
the said kitchen at that time: and saith, that immediately
upon her, the said Elizabeth Canning being brought in, the
said John Squires said, here mother take this girl, or used
words to that effect; and she, the said Mary Squires, asked
him where they had brought her from: and John said from
Moorfields; and told his said mother that they had taken her
gown, apron, hat, and half a guinea from her, to the best of
this informant's recollection and belief; whereupon she, the
said Mary Squires, took hold of the said Elizabeth Canning's
hand, and asked her if she would go their way, or words to
that effect; and upon the said Elizabeth Canning answering
no, she, the said Mary Squires, took a knife out of the drawer
of the dresser in the kitchen, and therewith cut the lace of the

said Elizabeth Canning's stays, and took the said stays away from her, and hung them on the back of a chair, and the said man unknown took the cap off the said Elizabeth Canning's head, and then he, with the said John Squires, went out of doors with it. And this informant saith, that quickly after they were gone, she, the said Mary Squires, pushed the said Elizabeth Canning along the kitchen towards and up a pair of stairs leading into a large back room like a loft, called the workshop, where there was some hay; and whilst she, the said Mary Squires, was pushing her, the said Elizabeth Canning, towards the stairs, she, the said Susannah Wells, came into the kitchen and asked the said Mary Squires what she was going to push the girl up stairs for, or words to that effect, and to the best of this informant's recollection and belief, the said Mary Squires answered—What is that to you? you have no business with it. Whereupon the said Susannah Wells directly went out of the kitchen into an opposite room called the parlour, from whence she came, as this informant believes. And this informant saith that the said Mary Squires forced the said Elizabeth Canning up stairs into the said workshop, and buttoned the door at the bottom of the stairs in the kitchen upon her, and confined her there. And this informant saith, that about two hours after, a quantity of water in an old broken-mouthed large black jug was carried up the said stairs, and put down upon the floor of the said workshop at the top of the stairs, to the best of this informant's recollection and belief. And this informant saith, that soon after the said Elizabeth Canning was so put into the said workshop, and the said Susannah Wells was returned into the parlour, the said John Squires returned again into the kitchen, and took the stays from off the chair and went away with the same, and in about an hour's time returned and went into the parlour with the said Susannah Wells; he, the said John Squires, came again into the kitchen, and then this informant went into the parlour to the said Susannah Wells, and the said Susannah Wells there said to the informant, Virtue, the gipsy man (meaning the said John Squires) has been telling me that his mother had cut the girl's (meaning the said Elizabeth Canning's) stays off her back, and that he has got them; and further said I desire you will not make a clack of it for fear it should be blown, or used words to that or the like effect. And this informant saith that from the time of the said Elizabeth Canning being so confined in the morning of the said 2nd day of January, in manner as aforesaid, she, the said Elizabeth Canning was not missed or discovered to have escaped out of the said workshop until Wednesday, the 31st day of the same month of January, as she, this informant, verily believes; for that to the best of this informant's recollection and belief, she was the person that first missed the said Elizabeth Canning thereout. And this informant saith, that the said Susannah Wells harboured and continued the said Mary Squires in her aforesaid house from the time of the said Mary Squires robbing the said Elizabeth Canning of her stays, until Thursday, the 1st day of February last past, when the said Susannah Wells, Sarah, her daughter, Mary Squires, John Squires, his two sisters, Catherine and Mary Squires, Fortune Natus, and Sarah, his wife, and this informant, were apprehended on account thereof, and carried before Justice Tyshemaker. And this informant saith, that Fortune Natus and Sarah his wife, to the best of this informant's recollection and belief, have lodged in the house of the said Susannah Wells about eleven weeks next before Monday, the 5th day of February instant, and layed on a bed of hay spread in the kitchen at night, which was in the daytime pushed up in a corner thereof, and continued lying there, when at home, until Thursday, the said 5th day of February, when, before the said Mr. Tyshemaker, all, except the said Susannah Wells and Mary Squires, were discharged, and then that evening the said Fortune Natus and Sarah, his wife, laid up in the said workshop where the said Elizabeth Canning had been confined, so that, as this informant understood, it might be pretended that they had lain in the said workshop for all the time they had lodged in the said Susannah Wells's house. And saith, that on the day on which it was discovered that the said Elizabeth Canning had made her escape out of the said workshop, by breaking down some boards slightly affixed across the window-place, the said Sarah, daughter of the said Susannah Wells, nailed up the said window-place again with boards, so that the said window-place might not appear to have been broke open. And lastly, this informant saith, that she, this informant, hath lived with the said Susannah Wells about a quarter of a year last past, and well knows that the said Susannah Wells, during that time, hath kept a very notorious, ill-governed and disorderly house, and has had the character of doing so for many years past; and that the said Susannah Wells well knew and was privy to the confinement of the said Elizabeth Canning.

	Her
Sworn before me this	VIRTUE HALL ✕ Mark,
14th February, 1753.	
H. FIELDING.	

The reader will be pleased to consider the nature of this information truly taken in the manner above set down, to compare it with the evidence given by this Virtue Hall at her trial, and lastly, to compare it with the evidence of Elizabeth Canning, and then I am much mistaken if he condemns either the judge or jury.

After I had finished the examination of Virtue Hall, one Judith Natus, the wife of Fortune Natus, whom I apprehend to belong to the gipsies, and who was found in the house with Virtue Hall, being examined upon her oath before me, declared, that she and her husband lay in the same room where Elizabeth Canning pretended to have been confined during the whole time of her pretended confinement, and declared that she had never seen nor heard of any such person as Elizabeth Canning in Wells's house. Upon this, Virtue Hall, of her own accord, affirmed, as she doth in her information in writing, these two persons were introduced into that room, to lie there, by Mother Wells, to give a colour to the defence which Wells was to make, and which these people, in the presence of Virtue Hall, had agreed to swear to.

Upon this some persons, who were present, were desirous that this Judith Natus should be committed for perjury, but I told them that such a proceeding would be contrary to law, for that I might as well commit Virtue Hall upon the evidence of Judith Natus. However, as I confess I myself thought her guilty of perjury, I gave her some little caution, and told her that she ought to be very sure of the truth of what she said, if she intended to give that evidence at the Old Bailey, and then discharged her.

The next day Virtue Hall came again before me, but nothing material passed, nor was she three minutes in my presence. I then ordered detainers for felony against the gipsy woman and Wells to be sent to the prisons where they then lay, upon the commitments of Mr. Tyshemaker, and thus ended all the trouble which I thought it was necessary for me to give myself in this affair; for, as to the gipsy woman or Wells, those who understand the law well know I had no business with them.

Some days afterwards, however, upon my return to town, my clerk informed me that several noble lords had sent to my house in my absence, desiring to be present at the examination of the gipsy woman. Of this I informed Mr. Salt, and desired him to bring Elizabeth Canning and Virtue Hall, in order to swear their several informations again in the presence of the gipsy woman and Wells, and appointed him a day for so doing, of which I sent an advice to the noble lords.

One of these, namely, Lord Montfort, together with several gentlemen of fashion, came at the appointed time. They were in my room before the prisoners or witnesses were brought up. The informations were read to the two prisoners; after which I asked the prisoners a very few questions, and in what manner I behaved to them, let all who were present testify; I can truly say, that my memory doth not charge me with having ever insulted the lowest wretch that hath been brought before me.

The prisoners and witnesses left the room while all the company remained in it; and from that time to this day I

never saw the face of Virtue Hall, unless once when she
came before me with Canning, to see a man who was taken
on suspicion of the robbery, and when I scarce spoke to her;
nor should I have seen Elizabeth Canning more, had not I
received a message from some gentlemen desiring my advice
how to dispose of some money which they had collected for
the use of Elizabeth Canning, in the best manner for her
advantage; upon which occasion I ordered her to be sent
for, to meet one of the gentlemen at my house: and had I
not likewise been informed, since the trial, that a great
number of affidavits, proving that the gipsy woman was at
Abbotsbury in Dorsetshire, at the very time when Elizabeth
Canning had sworn that she was robbed by her at Enfield
Wash, were arrived at my Lord Mayor's office. Upon this I
sent for her once more, and endeavoured by all means in
my power to sift the truth out of her, and to bring her to a
confession if she was guilty; but she persisted in the truth of
the evidence that she had given, and with such an appearance
of innocence, as persuaded all present of the justice of her
cause.

Thus have I very minutely recited the whole concern which
I had in this affair, unless that after I had discharged
my whole duty as a justice of the peace, Mr. Salt came
again to consult with me concerning the crime of which
Wells was accused, and the manner of prosecuting her, upon
a point of law, which is by no means a very easy one,
namely, that of accessories after the fact in felony, upon
which I gave him my opinion.

And now, having run through the process of the affair as
far as to the trial, which is already in print, I come to lay
before the reader that point of evidence on which, as I
have said, so great a stress ought to be laid, a point on
which indeed any cause whatever might be safely rested:
this is the agreement, in so many particular circumstances,
between the evidence of Elizabeth Canning and Virtue Hall.
That Virtue Hall had never seen nor heard the evidence of
Elizabeth Canning at the time when she made her own information, is a fact; nay, had she even heard the other repeat

it once over before a justice of peace, that she should be able, at a distance of time, to retain every particular circumstance so exactly as to make it tally in the manner her information doth with that of Elizabeth Canning, is a supposition in the highest degree absurd, and those who can believe it can believe that which is much more incredible than any thing in the narrative of Elizabeth Canning.

The only way therefore to account for this is, by supposing that the two girls laid this story together. To the probability and indeed possibility of this supposition, I object.

First, That from the whole circumstances of this case it appears manifestly that they had never seen the face of each other (unless Canning be believed as to the time when she was brought into Wells's) before the persons came to apprehend her, nay, Wells herself declared before me that Canning had never been in her house, and the other scarce ever out of it during the whole month in question.

Secondly, If we could suppose they had met together so as to form this story, the behaviour of Virtue Hall before Mr. Tyshemaker would entirely destroy any such supposition, for there this Virtue Hall was so far from being in the same story with Elizabeth Canning, that she there affirmed she knew nothing of the matter, and she had then no reason to apprehend any further examination; nor is it possible to conceive that these two girls should afterwards enter into any such agreement. From the day of the examination before Mr. Tyshemaker, till Virtue Hall came before me, the two girls never saw the face of each other, the one remained sick at her mother's in town, the other continued at Wells's house at Enfield, in company with those who yet persist in their friendship to Wells and the gipsy. In reality, I never yet heard a fact better established in a court of justice than this, that Elizabeth Canning and Virtue Hall did not lay this story together, nay, even she herself doth not, as I have heard, since her apostasy, pretend to say any such thing, but imputes her evidence to her being threatened and bullied into it, which, to my own knowledge, and that of many others, is a most impudent falsehood; and, secondly, ascribes her agreeing with Elizabeth Canning to having heard her deliver her evidence, which, besides being impossible, can be proved to be another notorious falsehood, by a great number of witnesses of indisputable credit.

So that I think I am here entitled to the following syllogistical conclusion:

Whenever two witnesses declare a fact, and agree in all the circumstances of it, either the fact is true or they have previously concerted the evidence between themselves.

But in this case it is impossible that these girls should have so previously concerted the evidence:

And, therefore, the fact is true.

The reader will be pleased to observe, that I do not here lay any weight on the evidence of Virtue Hall, as far as her own credit is necessary to support that evidence, for in truth she deserves no credit at all; the weight which I here lay on her evidence is so far only as it is supported by that evidence of fact which alone is always safely to be depended upon, as it is alone incapable of a lie.

And here, though I might very well rest the merits of the whole cause on this single point, yet I cannot conclude the case of this poor girl without one observation, which hath, I own, surprised me, and will, I doubt not, surprise the reader. It is this, Why did not the gipsy woman and Wells produce the evidence of Fortune Natus and his wife in their defence at their trial, since that evidence, as they well knew, was so very strong in their behalf, that had the jury believed it, they must have been acquitted? For my own part, I can give but one answer to this, and that is too obvious to need to be here mentioned.

Nor will I quit this case without observing the pretty incident of the mince pie, which, as it possibly saved this poor girl's life, so doth the intention of carrying it home to her little brother serve very highly to represent the goodness as well as childishness and simplicity of her character; a character so strongly imprinted in her countenance, and attested by all her neighbours.

Upon the whole, this case, whether it be considered in a

private or a public light, deserves to be scrutinised to the bottom; and that can be only done by the government's authorising some very capable and very indifferent persons to examine into it, and particularly into the *alibi* defence of Mary Squires, the gipsy woman. On the one side, here is the life of a subject at stake, who, if her defence is true, is innocent; and a young girl, guilty of the blackest, most premeditated, and most audacious perjury, levelled against the lives of several innocent persons. On the other side, if the evidence of Elizabeth Canning is true, and perjury should, nevertheless, prevail against her, an innocent young creature, who hath suffered the most cruel and unheard of injuries, is in danger of being rewarded for them by ruin and infamy; and what must extremely aggravate her case, and will distinguish her misery from that of all other wretches upon earth, is, that she will owe all this ruin and infamy to this strange circumstance, that her sufferings have been beyond what human nature is supposed capable of bearing; whilst robbery, cruelty, and the most impudent of all perjuries, will escape with impunity and triumph; and, therefore, will so escape, because the barbarity of the guilty parties hath risen to a pitch of wanton and untempted inhumanity, beyond all possibility of belief.

As to my own conduct in this affair, which I have deduced with the most minute exactness, I know it to be highly justifiable before God and before man. I frankly own I thought it entitled me to the very reverse of censure. The truth is, the same motive prevailed with me then, which principally urged me to take up my pen at this time, a desire to protect innocence and to detect guilt; and the delight in so doing was the only reward I ever expected, so help me God; and I have the satisfaction to be assured that those who know me best will most believe me.

In solemn truth, the only error I can ever be possibly charged with in this case is an error in sagacity. If Elizabeth Canning be guilty of a false accusation, I own she hath been capable of imposing on me; but I have the comfort to think the same imposition hath passed not only on two juries, but likewise on one of the best judges that ever sate on the bench of justice, and on two other very able judges who were present at the trial.

I do not, for my own part, pretend to infallibility, though I can at the same time with truth declare that I have never spared any pains in endeavouring to detect falsehood and perjury, and have had some very notable success that way.

In this case, however, one of the most simple girls I ever saw, if she be a wicked one, hath been too hard for me; supposing her to be such, she hath indeed most grossly deceived me, for I remain still in the same error; and I appeal, in the most solemn manner, to the Almighty for the truth of what I now assert. I am at this very time on this 15th day of March, 1753, as firmly persuaded as I am of any fact in this world, the truth of which depends solely on the evidence of others, that Mary Squires, the gipsy woman, IS GUILTY of the robbery and cruelty of which she stands convicted; that the *alibi* defence is not only a false one, but a falsehood very easy to be practisd on all occasions where there are gangs of people, as gipsies, &c.; that very foul and unjustifiable practices have been used in this whole affair since the trial, and that Elizabeth Canning is a poor, honest, innocent, simple girl, and the most unhappy and most injured of all human beings.

It is this persuasion alone, I repeat it again, which occasioned me to give the public this trouble; for as to myself I am, in my own opinion, as little concerned in the event of this whole matter as any other man whatever.

Whatever warmth I have at last contracted in this matter, I have contracted from those who have been much warmer on the other side; nor can any such magistrate blame me, since we must, I am persuaded, act from the same motive of doing justice to injured innocence. This is surely the duty of every man, and a very indispensable duty it is, if we believe one of the best of writers. *Qui non defendit, nec obsistit, si potest, injuriæ, tam erit in vitio quam si parentes, aut amicos, aut patriam deserat.* These are Tully's words, and they are in the most especial manner applicable to every magistrate.

To the merit of having discharged this duty, my Lord Mayor as well as myself have a just title at all events. And for my own part, as I do not expect to gain, so neither do I fear to lose any other honour on the final issue of this affair; for surely the cause is of such a nature that a man must be intolerably vain who is ashamed of being mistaken on either side. To be placed above the reach of deceit is to be placed above the rank of a human being; sure I am that I make no pretension to be of that rank; indeed I have been often deceived in my opinion of men, and have served and recommended to others those persons whom I have afterwards discovered to be totally worthless. I shall, in short, be very well contented with the character which Cicero gives of Epicurus. *Quis illum negat et bonum virum et comem et humanum fuisse!* And whoever will allow me this, which I must own I think I deserve, shall have my leave to add, *tamen, si hæc vera sunt non satis acutus fuit.*

In solemn truth so little desirous am I to be found in the right, that I shall not be in the least displeased to find myself mistaken. This indeed I ought, as a good man, to wish may be the case, since that this country should have produced one great monster of iniquity is a reflection much less shocking than to consider the nation to be arrived at such an alarming state of profligacy, and our laws and government to lie in so languishing a condition that a gang of wretches like these should dare to form such an impudent attempt to elude public justice, nay, rather to overbear it by the force of associated perjury in the face of the whole world; and that this audacious attempt should have had, at least, a very high probability of succeeding.

This is the light in which I see this case at present. I conclude, therefore, with hoping that the government will authorise some proper persons to examine to the very bottom, a matter in which the honour of our national justice is so deeply concerned.

POSTSCRIPT.

In the extreme hurry in which the foregoing case was drawn up, I forgot to observe one strange circumstance which will attend the case of Elizabeth Canning, if it should be admitted to be a forgery; this is, that she should charge the gipsy woman, when she must have known that woman could prove an *alibi,* and not Susannah Wells, who could have had no such proof. This will be very strong if applied to the evidence of Canning, but much stronger when applied to the evidence of Virtue Hall, who lived in the house the whole time.

This appears to be very simple conduct; and, as such, indeed, is consistent enough with her character. So is not the artful manner in which the charge was brought out; first, Canning accused the gipsy woman, and went no further; then Hall brought the rest upon the stage, all in such regularity, and with such appearance of truth that no Newgate solicitor ever ranged his evidence in better order. But, perhaps, I might have spared my reader these observations, as I can now inform him that I have this very afternoon (Sunday the 18th instant) read over a great number of affidavits corroborating the whole evidence of Canning, and contradicting the *alibi* defence of the gipsy woman. I shall only add, that these affidavits are by unquestionable witnesses, and sworn before three worthy justices of the County of Middlesex, who lived in the neighbourhood of Enfield Washe.

A
TRUE STATE
OF THE
CASE
OF
BOSAVERN PENLEZ,

Who fuffered on Account of the late
Riot in the *STRAND.*

IN WHICH

The Law regarding thefe Offences, and the
Statute of George the Firft, commonly
called the Riot Act, are fully confidered.

By *HENRY FIELDING,* Efq;

Barrifter at Law, and one of his Majefty's Juftices
of the Peace for the County of *Middlefex,* and
for the City and Liberty of *Weftminfter.*

LONDON:

Printed for A. Millar, oppofite *Katherine-
ftreet* in the *Strand.* 1749.

[Price One Shilling.]

THE CASE

OF

BOSAVERN PENLEZ

IT may easily be imagined that a man whose character
hath been so barbarously, even without the least regard to
truth or decency, aspersed on account of his endeavours to
defend the present government, might wish to decline any
future appearance as a political writer; and this possibly
may be thought by some a sufficient reason of that reluctance
with which I am drawn forth to do an act of justice to my
King and his administration, by disabusing the public, which
hath been, in the grossest and wickedest manner, imposed
upon, with relation to the case of Bosavern Penlez, who was
executed for the late riot in the Strand.

There is likewise another reason of this reluctance with
which those only who know me well can be certainly acquainted; and that is my own natural disposition. Sure I
am, that I greatly deceive myself, if I am not in some
little degree partaker of that milk of human kindness which
Shakespeare speaks of. I was desirous that a man who had
suffered the extremity of the law should be permitted to rest
quietly in his grave. I was willing that his punishment
should end there; nay, that he should be generally esteemed
the object of compassion, and, consequently, a more dreadful
example of one of the best of all our laws.

But when this malefactor is made an object of sedition,
when he is transformed into a hero, and the most merciful

259

prince who ever sat on any throne is arraigned of blamable severity, if not of downright cruelty, for suffering justice to take place; and the sufferer, instead of remaining an example to incite terror, is recommended to our honour and admiration; I should then think myself worthy of much censure, if having a full justification in my hands, I permitted it to sleep there, and did not lay it before the public, especially as they are appealed to on this occasion.

Before I enter, however, into the particulars of this man's case, and perform the disagreeable task of raking up the ashes of the dead, though of the meanest degree, to scatter infamy among them, I will premise something concerning the law of riots in general. This I shall do, as well for the justification of the law itself, as for the information of the people, who have been long too ignorant in this respect; and who, if they are now taught a little better to know the law, are taught at the same time to regard it as cruel and oppressive, and as an innovation on our constitution: for so the statute of George the First, commonly called the Riot Act, hath lately been represented in a public newspaper.

If this doctrine had been first broached in this paper, the ignorance of it would not have been worth remarking; but it is in truth a repetition only of what hath been formerly said by men who must have known better. Whoever remembers the political writings published twenty years ago, must remember that among the articles exhibited against a former administration, this of passing the Riot Act was one of the principal.

Surely these persons mean to insinuate that by this statute riots were erected into a greater crime than they had ever before been esteemed, and that a more severe punishment was enacted for them than had formerly been known among us.

Now the falsehood of this must be abundantly apparent to every one who hath any competent knowledge of our laws. Indeed whoever knows anything of the nature of mankind, or of the history of free countries, must entertain a very indifferent opinion of the wisdom of our ancestors, if he can imagine they had not taken the strongest precautions to guard against so dangerous a political disease, and which hath so often produced the most fatal effects.

Riots are in our law divided into those of a private and into those of a public kind. The former of these are when a number of people (three at the least) assemble themselves in a tumultuous manner, and commit some act of violence amounting to a breach of the peace, where the occasion of the meeting is to redress some grievance, or to revenge some quarrel of a private nature; such as to remove the enclosures of lands in a particular parish, or unlawfully and forcibly to gain the possession of some tenement, or to revenge some injury done to one or a few persons, or on some other such private dispute, in which the interest of the public is no ways concerned. Such riot is a very high misdemeanour, and to be punished very severely by fine and imprisonment.

Mr. Pulton, speaking of this kind of riot, writes thus: "Riots, routs, unlawful and rebellious assemblies, have been so many times pernicious and fatal enemies to this kingdom, the peace and tranquillity thereof, and have so often shaken the foundation, and put in hazard the very form and state of government of the same, that our law-makers have been enforced to devise from age to age, one law upon another, and one statute after another for the repressing and punishing of them, and have endeavoured by all their wits to snip the sprouts, and quench the very first sparks of them. As every man may easily perceive there was cause thereof, who will look back and call to his remembrance what that small riot, begun at Dartmouth, in Kent, in the reign of King Richard the Second, between the collector of a subsidy and a Tyler and his wife, about the payment of one poor groat, did come unto, which being not repressed in time, did grow to so great a rebellion, that after it put in hazard the life of the king, the burning of the City of London, the overthrow of the whole nobility, gentlemen, and all the learned of the land, and the subversion of this goodly monarchy and form of government. Or, if they will call to mind the small riot or quarrel begun in the reign of King Henry the Sixth, between a yeoman of the guard and a serving-man of Richard

Nevils, Earl of Warwick, which so far increased for want of restraint, that it was the root of many woeful tragedies, and a mean to bring to untimely death first Richard Plantagenet, Duke of York, proclaimed successor to the Crown, and the chief pillar of the House of York, and after him King Henry the Sixth, and Prince Edward his son, the heirs of the House of Lancaster, and to ruinate with the one or the other of them, most of the peers, great men, and gentlemen of the realm, besides many thousands of the common people. And therefore King Edward the First did well ordain, that no sheriffs shall suffer barritors or maintainers of quarrels in their counties. And that to all parliaments, treaties, and other assemblies, each man shall come peaceably, without any armour; and that every man shall have armour in his house, according to his ability, to keep the peace. And King Edward the Third provided, that no man shall come before the justices, nor go or ride armed. And that suspected, lewd, and riotous persons shall be arrested, and safely kept until they be delivered by the justices of gaol delivery. And that justices of peace shall restrain offenders, rioters, and all other barritors, and pursue, take, and chasten them according to their trespass and offence. King Richard the Second did prohibit riots, routs, and forcible entries into lands, that were made in divers counties and parts of the realm. And that none from thenceforth should make any riot, or rumour. And that no man shall ride armed, nor use launcegaies. And that no labourer, servant in husbandry, or artificer, or victualler, shall wear any buckler, sword, or dagger. And that all the King's officers shall suppress and imprison such as make any riots, routs, or unlawful assemblies against the peace. King Henry the Fourth enacted, That the justices of peace and the sheriff shall arrest those which commit any riot, rout, or unlawful assembly, shall enquire of them, and record their offences. King Henry the Fifth assigned commissioners to enquire of the same justices and sheriffs defaults in that behalf, and also limited what punishment offenders attainted of riot should sustain. King Henry the Seventh ordained, that such persons as were returned to enquire of riots should have sufficient freehold or copyhold land within the same shire. And that no maintenance should hinder their inquisition. And in the reign of Queen Mary there was a necessary statute established to restrain and punish unlawful and rebellious assemblies raised by a multitude of unruly persons, to commit certain violent, forcible, and riotous acts."

The second kind of riot is of a public kind; as where an indefinite [1] number of persons assembled themselves in a tumultuous manner, in manner of war, arrayed, and commit any open violence with an avowed design of redressing any public grievance; as to remove certain persons from the King, or to lay violent hands on a privy-counsellor, or to revenge themselves of a magistrate for executing his office, or to bring down the price of victuals, or to reform the law or religion, or to pull down all bawdy houses, or to remove all enclosures in general, &c.[2] This riot is high-treason within the words levying war against the king, in the statute of Edward III. " For here," says Lord Coke, " the pretence is public and general, and not private in particular.[3] And this, says he, though there be no great number of conspirators, is levying war within the purview of the above statute."

In the reign of King Henry VIII. it was resolved by all the judges of England, that an insurrection against the statute of labourers for the enhancing of salaries and wages, was a levying of war against the King, because it was generally against the King's law, and the offenders took upon them the reformation thereof, which subjects, by gathering power, ought not to do.[4]

In the 20th of Charles II. a special verdict was found at the Old Bailey, that A, B, C, &c., with divers others, to the number of an hundred, assembled themselves in manner of

---

[1] It may be gathered, perhaps, from Lord Coke, 3 Inst. 176, that the number ought to be above 7 or at most 34, for such number is, he says, called an army. And a lesser number cannot, I think, be well said to be *modo guerrino arraiati.*

[2] Hawk, lib. i. cap. 17, sect. 25.

[3] 3 Inst. 9.

[4] 3 Inst. 10.

war arrayed to pull down bawdy houses, and that they marched with a flag on a staff, and weapons, and pulled down houses in prosecution of their conspiracies; which by all the judges assembled, except one, was ruled to be high treason.[1]

My Lord Chief-Justice Kelyng, who tried the cause, tells us, in his reports,[2] " that he directed the jury, that he was well satisfied in his own judgment, that such assembling together as was proved, and the pulling down of houses upon pretence they were bawdy houses; was high treason, because they took upon them regal power to reform that which belonged to the King by his law and justices to correct and reform; and it would be a strange way and mischievous to all people to have such a rude rabble, without an indictment to proceed in that manner against all persons' houses which they would call bawdy houses, for then no man were safe; therefore as that way tore the government out of the King's hands, so it destroyed the great privilege of the people, which is not to be proceeded against, but upon an indictment first found by a grand jury, and after, upon a legal trial by another jury, where the party accused was heard to make his defence; yet, says he, because the kings of this nation had oftentimes been so merciful as when such outrages had been heretofore done, not to proceed capitally against the offenders but to proceed against the offenders in the star-chamber, being willing to reduce their people by milder ways, if it were possible, to their duty and obedience; yet that lenity of the King in some cases did not hinder the King, when he saw there was need to proceed in a severer way, to take that course which was warranted by law, and to make greater examples, that the people may know the law is not wanting so far to the safety of the King and his people, as to let such outrages go without capital punishment, which is at this time absolutely necessary, because we ourselves have seen a rebellion raised by gathering people together upon fairer pretences than this was, for no such persons use at first to declare their wickedest design, but when they see that they may

[1] Hale's History of the Pleas of the Crown, vol. i. p. 134.
[2] Kel. 71.

Hans Holbein, Pinxt.

effect their design, then they will not stick to go further, and give the law themselves, and destroy all that oppose them; but yet because there was no body of the long robe there but my brother Wylde, then Recorder of London, and myself, and that this example might have the greater authority, I did resolve that the jury should find the matter specially, and then I would procure a meeting of all the judges of England, and what was done should be by their opinion, that so this question might have such a resolution as no person afterwards should have reason to doubt the law, and all persons might be warned how they for the time to come mingle themselves with such rabble on any kind of such pretences."

And afterwards out of six against whom special verdicts were found, four were executed.

In the 13th year of Queen Elizabeth, it was made treason to compass, imagine, invent, devise, or intend to levy war against the Queen, &c.

On this statute Richard Bradshaw, a miller, Robert Burton, a mason, and others at Oxfordshire, were indicted and attainted. "This case," says Lord Coke, "was that they conspired and agreed to assemble themselves, with as many as they could procure, at Emflowe Hill, in the said county, there to rise, and from thence to go from gentleman's house to gentleman's house, and to cast down enclosures as well for enlargement of highways as of arable lands, &c." This was resolved to be a compassing to levy war against the Queen, and to be treason, and the offenders were executed at Emflowe Hill.[1]

The last mentioned case was in the 30th year of Queen Elizabeth: and two years before that several apprentices of London assembled themselves to the number of three hundred and upwards at Bunhill and Tower Hill, in order to deliver some of their fellows out of prison, and threatened to burn my Lord Mayor's house, and to break open two houses near the Tower where arms were lodged. They had with them a trumpet, and a cloak upon a pole was carried

[1] 3 Inst. 10, 2 And. 66. Poph. 122.

as their colours, and being opposed by the sheriff and sword-bearer of London, offered violence to their persons, and for the offence they were indicted of treason, attainted and executed.[1]

Now the reason of the judgment in all these cases was because the offenders had attempted by force and violence to redress grievances of a public nature; for as Anderson, in his report of the last case tells us, " When any persons intend to levy war for any matter which the King by his law and justice ought or can regulate in his government as King, this shall be intended a levying of war against the King; nor is it material whether they intend any hurt to the person of the King, if their intent be against his office and authority." This is within the statute of the 13th Elizabeth, and wherever the intent is within that statute, the real levying war is within the statute of Edward III.

I have set down these cases only to show the light in which these kinds of riots have been always considered by our ancestors, and how severely they have been punished in the most constitutional reigns.

And yet extensive as this branch of treason on the statute of Edward the Third may seem to have been, it was not held sufficient. For by the 3 and 4 of Edward VI. it was made high treason for twelve persons, or above, being assembled together, to attempt to alter any laws, &c., or to continue together above an hour after they are commanded by a justice of peace, mayor, sheriff, &c., to return. And by the same Act it was made felony for twelve persons, or above, to practise to destroy any park, pond, conduit, or dove-house, &c., or to pull down any houses, barns, or mills, or to abate the rates of any lands, or the prices of any victual, &c.

This statute was repealed in the first year of Queen Mary, and then it was enacted that " If any persons to the number of twelve, or above, being assembled together, shall intend, go about, practise, or put in use, with force and arms, unlawfully and of their own authority, to change any laws made for religion by authority of parliament standing in force, or any other laws or statutes of this realm, or any of them, the

[1] 2 And. 2.　Hale's Hist., vol. i. 125.

same number of twelve, or above, being commanded or required by the sheriff of the shire, or by any justice of peace of the same shire, or by any mayor, sheriff, justices of peace, or bailiffs of any city, borough, or town corporate, where any such assemblies shall be lawfully had or made, by proclamation in the Queen's name to retire and repair to their houses, habitations, or places from whence they came, and they or any of them, notwithstanding such proclamation, shall continue together by the space of one whole hour after such commandment or request made by proclamation; or after that shall willingly in forcible and riotous manner attempt to do or put in ure any of the things above specified, that then, as well every such abode together, as every such act or offence, shall be adjudged felony, and the offenders therein shall be adjudged felons, and shall suffer only execution of death, as in case of felony. And if any persons to the said number of twelve, or above, shall go about, &c., to overthrow, cut, cast down, or dig the pales, hedges, ditches, or other enclosure of any park, or other ground enclosed, or the banks of any fish-pond or pool, or any conduits for water, conduit-heads, or conduit-pipes having course of water, to the intent that the same, or any of them, should from thenceforth lie open, or unlawfully to have way or common in the said parks or other grounds enclosed, or to destroy the deer in any manner of park, or any warren of conies, or any dove-houses, or any fish in any fish-pond or pool, or to pull or cut down any houses, barns, mills, or bayes, or to burn any stacks of corn, or to abate or diminish the rents of any lands, or the price of any victual, corn or grain, or any other thing usual for the sustenance of man; and being required or commanded by any justice of peace, &c., by proclamation to be made, &c., to retire to their habitations, &c., and they or any of them notwithstanding shall remain together by the space of one whole hour after such commandment made by proclamation, or shall in forcible manner put in ure any of the things last before mentioned, &c. That then every of the said offenders shall be judged a felon, &c. And if any person or persons unlawfully, and without authority, by ringing of any bell or bells, sounding of any trumpet, drum, horn, or other instrument, or by firing of any beacon, or by malicious speaking of any words, or making any outcry, or by setting up or casting of any bill or writing, or by any other deed or act, shall raise, or cause to be raised, any persons to the number of twelve, or above, to the intent that the same persons should do or put in ure any of the acts above mentioned, and that the persons so raised and assembled, after commandment given in form aforesaid, shall make their abode together in form as is aforesaid, or in forcible manner put in ure any of the acts aforesaid, that then all and singular persons by whose speaking, deed, act, or other the means above specified, to the number of twelve so raised, shall be adjudged felons. And if the wife, servant, or other person shall any way relieve them that be unlawfully assembled, as is aforesaid, with victuals, armours, weapons, or any other thing, that then they shall be adjudged felons. And if any persons above the number of two, and under the number of twelve, shall practise or put in ure any of the things above mentioned, and being commanded by a justice of peace, &c., to retire, &c., and they make their abode by the space of one hour together, that then every of them shall suffer imprisonment by the space of one year without bail or mainprise, and every person damnified shall or may recover his triple damages against him; and every person able, being requested by the King's officers, shall be bound to resist them. If any persons to the number of forty or above, shall assemble together by forcible manner, unlawfully and of their own authority, to the intent to put in ure any of the things above specified, or to do other felonies or rebellious act or acts, and so shall continue together by the space of three hours after proclamation shall be made at or nigh the place where they shall be so assembled, or in some market-town thereunto next adjoining, and after notice thereof to them given, then every person so willingly assembled in forcible manner, and so continuing together by the space of three hours, shall be adjudged a felon. And if any copyholder or farmer being required by any of the King's officers having authority, to aid and assist them in repressing any of the said offenders do refuse so to do, that then he shall forfeit his copyhold or lease only for term of his life."

Some well-meaning honest Jacobite will perhaps object that this last statute was enacted in a Popish reign; but he will please to observe, that it is even less severe than that of Edward VI., to which I shall add, that by the 1st of Queen Elizabeth, chap. 16, this very Act of Queen Mary was continued during the life of Queen Elizabeth, and to the end of the parliament then next following.

Having premised thus much, we will now examine the statute of George I., commonly called the Riot Act; which hath so often been represented either by the most profound ignorance, or the most impudent malice, as unconstitutional, unprecedented, as an oppressive innovation, and dangerous to the liberty of the subject.

By this statute all persons to the number of twelve or more, being unlawfully, riotously, and tumultuously assembled together, to the disturbance of the public peace, and not dispersing themselves within an hour after the proclamation is read to them by a proper magistrate, are made guilty of felony without benefit of clergy.

Secondly. The statute gives a power to all magistrates and peace officers, and to all persons who are by such magistrates and peace officers commanded to assist them, to apprehend all such persons so continuing together as above after the proclamation read, and indemnifies the said magistrates and peace officers, and all their assistants, if in case of resistance any of the rioters should be hurt, maimed, or killed.

Thirdly. It is enacted, that if any persons unlawfully, riotously, and tumultuously assembled together, to the disturbance of the public peace, shall unlawfully and with force demolish or pull down, or begin to demolish or pull down any church or chapel, or any building for religious worship certified and registered, &c., or any dwelling-house, barn, stable, or other out-house, that then every such demolishing, or pulling down, or beginning to demolish or pull down, shall be adjudged felony without benefit of clergy.

Fourthly. If any persons obstruct the magistrate in reading the proclamation, so that it cannot be read, such obstruction is made felony without clergy; and the continuing together, to the number of twelve, after such let or hindrance of reading the proclamation, incurs the same guilt as if the proclamation had really been read.

These are all the penal clauses in the statute.

I observe then that this law cannot be complained against as an innovation: for as to that part of the statute by which rioters, who continued together for the space of an hour, after they are commanded by the magistrate to disperse, are made guilty of felony without benefit of clergy, what does it more than follow the precedents of those laws which were enacted in the time of Edward VI., Queen Mary and Queen Elizabeth? And if the law now under our consideration be a little more severe than one of the former acts, it must be allowed to be less severe than the other.

Indeed this power of the magistrates in suppressing all kind of riots hath been found so necessary, that from the second year of Edward III. even down to these days, the legislature hath from time to time more and more increased it. Of such consequence hath this matter appeared, and so frequently hath it been under the consideration of parliament, that I think there are almost twenty statutes concerning it.

And upon the statute of 13 H. IV. cap. 7, by which the justices, sheriff, &c., are empowered and ordered to suppress all riots, it hath been holden, that not only the justices, &c., but all who attended them, may take with them, such weapons as shall be necessary to enable them effectually to do it; and that they may justify the beating, wounding, and even killing such rioters as shall resist or refuse to surrender themselves.[1]

As to that branch of the statute by which demolishing, &c., houses, &c., is made felony, the offence, instead of being aggravated, seems to be lessened, namely, from treason into felony; according to the opinion of Judge Walmsley in Pop-

[1] Paph. 121. 2 And. 67. Hawk. lib. i. cap. 65, f. 21, &c.

ham's Reports, and of Lord Chief Justice Hale in his Pleas of the Crown.[1]

It is true, as that learned judge observes,[2] the statutes of Edward or Mary did not require (nor doth that of George I. require) that the rioters should be in manner of war arrayed. But how little of this array of war was necessary upon the head of the constructive treason, must have appeared from the cases I have mentioned; in one of which the *Insignia Belli* were a few aprons carried on staves.[3] In another they had a trumpet, and a cloak carried upon a pole,[4] and in others, as appears, there were no such insignia at all.

Again. Upon the indictment of treason any overt act would be sufficient; but here the offence is restrained to such acts as most manifestly threaten, not only the public peace, but the safety of every individual.

How then can this statute be said, in the second place, to be oppressive? Is it not rather the most necessary of all our laws, for the preservation and protection of the people?

The houses of men are in law considered as the castles of their defence; and that in so ample a manner, that no officer of justice is empowered by the authority of any mesne civil process to break them open. Nay, the defence of the house is by the law so far privileged beyond that of the person, that in the former case a man is allowed to assemble a force, which is denied him in the latter; and to kill a man who attacked your house was strictly lawful, where as some degree of guilt was by the common law incurred by killing him who attacked your person. To burn your house (nay, at this day to set fire to it) is felony without benefit of clergy. To break it open by night, either committing a felony, or with intent to commit it, is burglary. To break it open by day, and steal from it the value of five shillings, or privately to steal from any dwelling-house to the value of forty shillings, is felony without benefit of clergy. Is it then an unreasonable or oppressive law, to prohibit the demolishing or pulling down your house, and that by numbers riotously and tumultuously assembled, under as severe a penalty? Is not breaking open your doors

[1] Vol. i. 134.   [2] Vol. i. 154.   [3] Kel. 70.   [4] 2 And. 2.

and demolishing your house, a more atrocious crime in those who commit it, and much more injurious to the person against whom it is committed, than the robbing it forcibly of goods to the value of five shillings, or privately to the value of forty? If the law can here be said to be cruel, how much more so is it to inflict death on a man who robs you of a single farthing on the highway, or who privately picks your pocket of thirteen pence?

But I dwell, I am afraid, too long on this head. For surely no statute had ever less the mark of oppression; nor is any more consistent with our constitution, or more agreeable to the true spirit of our law.

And where is the danger to liberty which can arise from this statute? Nothing in reality was ever more fallacious or wicked than this suggestion. The public peace and the safety of the individual are indeed much secured by this law; but the government itself, if their interest must be or can be considered as distinct from, and indeed in opposition to, that of the people, acquires not by it the least strength or security. And this, I think, must sufficiently appear to every one who considers what I have said above. For surely there is no lawyer who can doubt, even for a single moment, whether any riotous and tumultuous assembly, who shall avow any design directly levelled against the person of the King or any of his counsellors, be high treason or not, whether, as Lord Hale says, the assembly were greater or less, or armed or not armed. And as to the power of the magistrate for suppressing such kinds of riots, and for securing the bodies of the offenders, it was altogether as strong before as it is now.

It seems, therefore, very difficult to see any evil intention in the makers of this act, and I believe it will be as difficult to show any ill use that hath been made, or attempted to be made of it. In thirty-four years I remember to have heard of no more than two prosecutions upon it; in neither of which any distinct interest of the government, or rather, as I suppose is meant, of the governors, was at all concerned. And to evince how little any such evil use is to be apprehended at present, I shall here repeat the sentiments of our present excellent Lord Chief Justice, as I myself heard them delivered in the Kings Bench, viz., that the branch of the statute which empowers magistrates to read the proclamation for the dispersing rioters was made, as the preamble declares, on very important reasons, and intended to be applied only on very dangerous occasions; and that he should always regard it as a very high crime in any magistrate, wantonly or officiously to attempt to read it on any other.

So much for this law, on which I have dwelt perhaps longer than some may imagine to be necessary; but surely it is a law well worthy of the fullest justification, and is altogether as necessary to be publicly and indeed universally known, at a time when so many wicked acts are employed to infuse riotous principles into the mob, and when they themselves discover so great a forwardness to put these principles in practice.

I will now proceed to the fact of the late riot, and to the case which hath been so totally misrepresented. Both of which I shall give the public from the mouths of the witnesses themselves.

Middlesex,   The information of Nathanael Munns, one of
  to wit.   the beadles of the Dutchy-liberty of Lancas-
              ter.

This informant on his oath saith, that on Saturday, the 1st day of July last, this informant was summoned to quell a disturbance which was then in the strand, near the New Church, where a large mob was assembled about the house of one Owen, the cause of which, this informant was told, was, that a sailor had been there robbed by a woman. When this informant first came up, the populace were crying out, "Pull down the house, pull down the house!" and were so very outrageous, that all his endeavours, and those of another beadle of the same liberty, to appease them were vain. This informant, however, attempted to seize one of the ringleaders, but he was immediately rescued from him, and he himself threatened to be knocked down; upon which this informant sent for the constables, and soon after went to his own home. And this informant saith, that between eleven and twelve the same evening two of the aforesaid rioters, being seized by the constable, were delivered into the custody of this informant, who confined them in the night prison of the said liberty, which night prison is under this informant's house.

And this informant further saith, that on the succeding night, being Sunday, the 2nd day of July, about twelve at night, a great number of the mob came to this informant's house, and broke open the windows, and entered thereat, seized his servant, and demanded the keys of the prison, threatening to murder her if she did not deliver them; but not being able to procure the same, they wrenched the bars out of the windows, with which, as this informant has been told, and verily believes, they broke open the prison, and rescued the prisoners. And this informant further saith, that he was the same evening at the watch-house of the said liberty, where two other prisoners were confined for the said riot, and saith that a very great mob came to the said watch-house, broke the windows of the same all to pieces, demanding to have the prisoners delivered to them, threatening to pull the watch-house down if the said prisoners were not set at liberty immediately; after which they forced into the said watch-house, and rescued the prisoners. And this informant further saith, that he apprehends himself to have been in the most imminent danger of his life, from the stones and brick-bats thrown into the windows of the said watch-house by the said mob, before they forced the same.

NATHANAEL MUNNS.

Sworn before me,
HENRY FIELDING.

Middlesex,   The information of John Carter one of the
to wit.   constables of the Dutchy-liberty of Lancaster.

This informant upon his oath saith, that on Saturday, the 1st of July, between the hours of seven and eight in the

evening, he was present at the house of one Owen, in the
Strand, where there were a great mob at that time assembled,
which filled up the whole space of the street for near two
hundred yards; and saith, that the said house was then broke
open, and the mob within it were demolishing and stripping
the same; that the windows of the said house were all broke
to pieces, and the mob throwing out the goods, which they
soon after set fire to, and consumed them in the street; and
saith, that he believes there were near two waggon loads of
goods consumed, which caused so violent a flame, that the
beams of the houses adjoining were so heated thereby, that the
inhabitants were apprehensive of the utmost danger from the
fire, and sent for the parish engines upon that occasion, which
not being immediately to be procured, several firemen attended, by whose assistance, as this informant verily believes,
the fire was prevented from doing more mischief. Upon this,
this informant, not daring himself to oppose the rage and
violence of the mob, and not being able to find any magistrate
in town, applied to General Campbell, at Somerset House,
for the assistance of the guards there, who presently detached
a corporal and twelve men, upon the approach of whom, the
word was given by the mob to quit the house, which was immediately done by all except two, whom this informant, by
the assistance of the guards, seized upon, and presently conveyed them safe to the night prison of the liberty aforesaid.
The mob, however, without doors, rather increased than dimin-
ished, and continued in a very riotous and tumultuous manner, insomuch that it was thought necessary to apply for a
further guard, and accordingly an officer and a considerable
body of men, to the number, as this informant believes, of
forty, was detached from the tilt-yard; but the mob, far
from being intimidated by this reinforcement, began to attack
a second house, namely, the house of one Stanhope, throwing
stones, breaking the windows, and pelting, not only the sen-
tinels who were posted before the door, but the civil as well as
the military officers. And this informant further saith, that
though by the interposition of the soldiers, the mob were prevented from doing further mischief that night, yet they con-

tinued together till he was relieved by another peace officer, which was not till twelve at night; nor was the said mob, as this informant has heard, and verily believes, dispersed until between two and three in the morning.

And this informant further saith, that on Sunday, the 2nd July, being the succeeding day, he was called out of his bed on account of the reassembling of the mob before the house of Stanhope, which they had attacked the night before. That upon his arrival there, he found a vast mob got together, the house broke open and demolished, and all the goods thereof thrown into the street and set on fire; and saith, that the said fire was larger than that the preceding night. That he was then applied to by Mr. Wilson, woollen-draper, and principal burgess of the said liberty, and one Mr. Acton, another woollen-draper, both of whom expressed the greatest apprehension of danger to the whole neighbourhood, and desired this informant immediately to apply to the tilt-yard for a number of soldiers, which he accordingly did; but being sent by the officer to a magistrate, to obtain his authority for the said guard, before he could obtain the same, Mr. Welch, high-constable of Holborn division, procured the said guard, by which means the aforesaid rioters were soon after dispersed.

JOHN CARTER.

Sworn before me,
  H. FIELDING.

Middlesex, The information of James Cecil, one of the
to wit.   constables of the parish of St. George the
     Martyr, in the said county.

This informant upon oath saith, that on the 3rd of July last, he was ordered by Justice Fielding to attend the prisoners to Newgate. That though an officer, with a very large guard of soldiers, attended upon the said occasion, it was not without the utmost difficulty that the said prisoners were conveyed in coaches through the streets, the mob frequently endeavouring to break in upon the soldiers, and crowding towards the coach doors. And saith, that he seized one of the most active of the mob, and carried him before the said justice, who, after having reprimanded, dismissed him. And further this informant saith, that as he passed near the Old Bailey with the aforesaid prisoners, he saw a great mob assembled there, who, as this informant was then acquainted, had been breaking the windows of some house or houses there; and saith, that several of the said mob were in sailors' habits, but upon the approach of the soldiers they all ran away.

JAMES CECIL.

Middlesex,   The information of Saunders Welsh, gentle-
to wit.   man, high-constable of Holborn division, in
the said county.

This informant saith, that on Sunday morning, about ten of the clock, on the 2nd of July last, one Stanhope, who then kept a house in the Strand, near the New Church, came to this informant and told him, that a house had been demolished the night before in the Strand by a great mob, and that he had great reason to fear that the said mob would come and demolish his house, they having threatened that they would pull down all bawdy houses. Upon which this informant directed the said Stanhope to apply to a magistrate, telling him that he, this informant, would conduct himself upon the magistrate's directions. Upon which the said Stanhope departed, and returned no more to this informant.

And this informant saith, that as he was returning the same evening between the hours of eleven and twelve, from a friend's house in the City, as he passed through Fleet Street he perceived a great fire in the Strand, upon which he proceeded on till he came to the house of one Peter Wood, who told this informant that the mob had demolished the house of Stanhope, and were burning his goods, and that they had threatened, as soon as they had finished their business there, that they would come and demolish his house likewise, and prayed the assistance of this informant. Upon which this informant, despairing of being able to quell the mob by his own authority, and well knowing the impossibility of procuring any magistrate at that time who would act, applied to the tilt-yard for a military force, which with much difficulty

he obtained, having no order from any justice of peace for
the same. And this informant saith, that having at last
procured an officer with about forty men, he returned to the
place of the riot; but saith, that when he came to Cecil Street
end, he prevailed upon the officer to order his drum to beat,
in hopes, if possible, of dispersing the mob without any mischief ensuing. And this informant saith, that when he came
up to the house of Peter Wood, he found that the mob had in
a great part demolished the said house, and thrown a vast
quantity of his goods into the street, but had not perfected
their design, a large parcel of the goods still remaining in the
house, the said house having been very well furnished. And
this informant says, that he hath been told there was a debate
among the mob concerning burning the goods of that house
likewise, as they had served those of two other houses. And
this informant says, that had the goods of the said house been
set on fire, it must infallibly have set on fire the houses on
both sides, the street being there extremely narrow, and saith,
that the house of Messrs. Snow and Denne, the bankers, is
almost opposite to that of Peter Wood. And this informant
saith, that at his coming up, the mob had deserted the house
of the said Peter, occasioned, as he verily believes, and hath
been informed, by the terror spread among them from beating
the drum as aforesaid, so that this informant found no person
in the aforesaid house, save only Peter Wood, his wife, and
man-servant, and two or three women who appeared to
belong to it, and one Lander, who was taken by a soldier in
the upper part of the house, and who, it afterward appeared
at his trial, to the satisfaction of the jury, came along with
the guard.

And this informant further says, that the said rioters not
immediately dispersing, several of them were apprehended by
the soldiers, who being produced to Peter Wood, were by him
charged as principally concerned in the demolition of his
house, upon which they were delivered by this informant to a
constable of the Duchy-liberty, and were by that constable
conveyed, under a guard of soldiers, to New Prison. And
this informant further saith, that he remained on the spot,

together with part of the guards, till about three of the clock the next morning, before which time the mob were all dispersed, and peace again restored.

And this informant further saith, that on the Monday morning, about twelve of the clock, he attended H. Fielding, Esq., one of His Majesty's Justices of the Peace for the County of Middlesex, who had been out of town during all the preceding riot, and acquainted him with it. That immediately the said justice sent an order for a party of the guards to conduct the aforesaid prisoners to his house, the streets being at that time full of mob, assembled in a riotous and tumultuous manner, and danger of a rescue being apprehended. And saith, that the above mentioned prisoners, together with Bosavern Penlez, who was apprehended by the watch in Carey Street, were brought before the said justice, who, after hearing the evidence against them, and taking the depositions thereof, committed them to Newgate. And this informant saith, that whilst he attended before the said justice, and while the prisoners were under examination, there was a vast mob assembled, not only in Bow Street, but many of the adjacent streets, so that it was difficult either to pass or repass. And further saith, that he, this informant, received several informations that the mob had declared that, notwithstanding what had been done, they intended to carry on the same work again at night. Upon which, this informant was, by the said justice, despatched to the Secretary of War, to desire a reinforcement of the guard.

And this informant further saith, that he was present when the said justice, from his window, spoke to the mob, informed them of their danger, and exhorted them to depart to their own habitations: for which purpose, this informant likewise went among them, and entreated them to disperse, but all such exhortations were ineffectual. And this informant further saith, that he was present at the house of the said justice, when several informations were given, that a body of sailors, to the number four thousand, were assembling themselves at Tower Hill, and had declared a resolution of marching to Temple Bar, in the evening. And so riotous did the disposition of the mob appear that whole day, to wit, Monday, that numbers of persons, as this informant hath been told, removed their goods from their own houses, from apprehension of sharing the fate of Owen, Stanhope, and Wood. To obviate which danger, the aforesaid justice, the officer of the guard and this informant, sat up the whole night, while a large party of soldiers were kept ready under arms, who with the peace-officers patrolled the streets where the chief danger was apprehended; by means of all which care the public peace was again restored. SAUNDERS WELCH.

Sworn before me,

HENRY FIELDING.

Middlesex,   The information of Samuel Marsh, Edward
to wit.   Fritter, Robert Oliver, and John Hoare.

Samuel Marsh, of St. Clement Danes, in the said county, labourer, one of the watchmen of St. Dunstan's in the West, in the City of London, maketh oath, that on the 3rd of July last, as he was going his rounds, a little after one in the morning, one Mr. Philip Warwick, an engraver by trade, who then lived at Pimlico, near Buckingham House, from whence he is since removed, came to this informant in Bell-yard, opposite the Apollo-passage, and said, there was a man above who had a great bundle of linen, which he (Warwick) thought the said man had stolen, and desired this informant to take care of him. And further acquainted this informant, that the said man told him that the linen which he then had in the bundle was his wife's, which said Warwick did not believe to be true. And this informant further saith, that when he had received this account, he went directly to the place where the said man was; and saith, that the said man, before this informant came up to him, had thrust most of the above said linen into his bosom and pockets; and saith, that just as this informant came up to him, and called out to him saying, friend, here, come and take the cap you have dropped, the said man scrambled up the rest of the things, and ran away as fast as he could all up Bell-yard; upon which this informant ran after him, and called to Edward Fritter, another watchman, to stop him. And this informant further saith, that the said man, being afterwards taken by Fritter, and in custody of him and this informant, being asked by them to whom the said linen belonged, declared that they belonged to the b—— his wife, who had pawned all his clothes; and that he had taken away these that she might not pawn them likewise. To which this informant answered, that answer would not do; for that he was resolved to have a better answer before he left him. And this informant saith, that he and the said Fritter then carried the said man to the watch-house, where he sat down on a bench. And this informant saith, that whilst the said man sat there, several persons came into the watch-house unknown to this informant, one of whom said to the prisoner, " You son of a b—— pull the things out of your bosom and out of your pockets, and don't let the constable find them upon you, unless you have a mind to hang yourself." Upon which the prisoner pulled out the linen from his bosom and pockets, and laid it upon the bench, and saith that the said linen was afterwards delivered to Mr. Hoare, the constable. And further saith, that the aforesaid man, who was apprehended as above said, was the same Bosavern Penlez, who was afterwards convicted of the riot at the Old Bailey, and executed for the same. And further saith, that he believes the said Penlez was then a little in liquor, but by no means dead drunk; for that he talked and behaved very rationally all the time he was in the said watch-house. And further saith, that Penlez, when he was in the watch-house, said, that the woman to whom the linen belonged was not his wife; for that he was an unfortunate young fellow, and had kept company with bad women, and that he had been robbed by one of them of fifteen shillings, and had taken away her linen out of revenge.

Edward Fritter, of the precinct of Whitefriars, in the City of London, shoemaker, one of the watchmen of the liberty of the rolls, maketh oath, that upon the 3rd of July last, a little after one in the morning, as he was at his stand at the upper end of Bell-yard, Samuel Marsh, another watchman, called out to him, " Stop that man before you: stop that man before you." And this informant saith, that when he heard these words, the said man had just passed by him, making off as fast as he could; upon which this informant ran after him, and at about an hundred yards' distance overtook him, and pushed him up against the rails in Carey Street. And this informant then said to him, "So, brother, what is all this you have got here?" To which the man answered, "I am an unfortunate young man, and have married one of the women of the town, who hath pawned all my clothes, and I have got all her linen for it." And this informant saith, that the said man had at that time some linen under his arm. Soon after which, the said man who, as this informant saith, was Bosavern Penlez, was carried to the watch-house, where this informant was present when all passed that informant Marsh hath sworn. And this informant, hearing the information of Marsh read, declares, that all which is there related to have passed, is true.

Robert Oliver, of the liberty of the rolls, shoemaker, and beadle of that liberty, maketh oath and saith, that he was present when Bosavern Penlez was brought into the watch-house belonging to the said liberty, on the 3rd of July last, between one and two in the morning; and saith, that he was present in the said watch-house upon his duty all the time that the said Penlez staid there; and upon hearing the information of Marsh read to him, this informant, he, this informant, upon his oath confirms the same in every particular.

John Hoare, of the liberty of the rolls aforesaid, victualler, then one of the constables of the liberty of the rolls, maketh oath and saith, that at two in the morning, on the 3rd of July, he was called by one of the watchmen of that liberty, and informed that a thief was apprehended and confined in the watch-house; upon which this informant went directly thither, and found Bosavern Penlez and the linen lying on the bench, as mentioned in Marsh's information. And this informant further says, that he then examined said Penlez how he came by that linen, to which the said Penlez answered, that he had taken up the said linen in the street, to which this informant answered, that if he (Penlez) could give no better account, he must secure him till the morning. Then this informant asked him, if he could send to any one who would give him a character. Upon which Penlez, after some hesitation, mentioned the name of a barber who lived next to the Bunch of Grapes in the Strand, who was sent to, and refused to come. And this informant saith, that he then proposed to Penlez to send for some other person; but that the said Penlez mentioned no other person. Upon which this informant carried the said Penlez to New-prison, and there delivered him into custody. And this informant further saith, that he attended the next day before H. Fielding, Esq.; one of His Majesty's Justices of the Peace for the said county, when the said Penlez was examined, and the aforesaid linen was produced by this informant. To wit; ten laced caps, four laced handkerchiefs, three pair of laced ruffles, two laced clouts, five plain handkerchiefs, five plain aprons, and one laced apron, all which the wife of Peter Wood swore to be her property. And this informant saith, that Penlez being asked by the justice, how he came by the said linen, answered he had found them; and could not, or would not give any other account.

The mark of SAM. MARSH.
ED. FRITTER.
ROB. OLIVER.
JOHN HOARE.

Sworn before me,
    H. FIELDING.

Middlesex,
  to wit.

Robert Oliver aforesaid further on his oath says, that when Penlez was examined before the justice, he solemnly denied that he was in the house of Peter Wood, or near it.

ROB. OLIVER.

Sworn before me,
    H. FIELDING.

Now upon the whole of this evidence, which I have taken the pains to lay before the public, and which is the evidence of persons entirely disinterested and of undoubted credit, I think it must be granted by every impartial and sensible person:

1. That the riot here under consideration was of a very high and dangerous nature, and far from deserving those light or ludicrous colours which have been cast upon it.

2. That the outrages actually committed by this mob, by demolishing the houses of several people, by cruelly and barbarously misusing their persons, by openly and audaciously burning their goods, by breaking open prisons and rescuing offenders, and by resisting the peace-officers, and those who came to their assistance, were such as no government could justify passing over without some censure and example.

3. That had not Mr. Welch (one of the best officers who was ever concerned in the execution of justice, and to whose care, integrity and bravery the public hath, to my knowledge, the highest obligations) been greatly active in the discharge of his duty; and had he not arrived time enough to prevent the burning of that pile of goods which was heaped up before Wood's house, the most dreadful consequences must have ensued from this riot. For not to mention the mischiefs which must necessarily have happened from the fire in that narrow part of the town, what must have been the consequence of exposing a banker's shop to the greediness of the rabble? Or what might we have reasonably apprehended from a mob encouraged by such a booty, and made desperate by such atrocious guilt?

4. I think it may be very fairly inferred, that the mob, which had already carried on their riotous proceedings during two successive nights, and who, during the whole day on Monday, were in motion all over the town, had they not been alarmed and intimidated by the care of the magistrate, would have again repeated their outrage, as they had threatened on Monday night. And had such a riot continued a little longer, no man can, I think, foresee what it might have produced. The cry against bawdy houses might have been easily converted into an outcry of a very different nature, and goldsmiths

might have been considered to be as great a nuisance to the public as whores.

5. The only remaining conclusion which I shall draw, is, that nothing can be more unjust, or indeed more absurd, than the complaint of severity which hath been made on this occasion. If one could derive this silly clamour from malevolence to the government, it might be easily converted into the most delicate of compliments. For surely those must afford very little cause of complaint, whose enemies can find no better object of their censure than this. To say the truth, the government is here injudiciously attacked in its most defensible part. If it be necessary, as some seem to think, to find fault with their superiors, our administration is more liable to the very opposite censure. If I durst presume to look into the royal breast, I might with certainty affirm, that mercy is there the characteristic. So truly is this benign prince the father of his people, that he is never brought, without paternal reluctance, to suffer the extremity of justice to take place. A most amiable excess, and yet an excess by which, I am afraid, subjects may be as liable to be spoiled as children.

But I am willing to see these clamours in a less culpable light, and to derive them from a much better motive; I mean from a zeal against lewd and disorderly houses. But zeal in this case, as well as in all others, may hurry men too far, and may plunge them headlong into the greater evils, in order to redress the lesser.

And surely this appears to be the case at present, when an animosity against these houses hath made men blind to the clearest light of evidence; and impelled them to fly in the face of truth, of common sense, I might say yet more, and all in the behalf of a licentious, outrageous mob, who, in open defiance of law, justice or mercy, committed the most notorious offences against the persons and properties of their fellow-subjects, and who had undoubtedly incurred the last and highest degree of guilt, had they not been happily and timely prevented.

When I mention this zeal as some kind of excuse or mitigation, I would be understood to apply it only to those persons who had been so weak (at least) to espouse the cause of these malefactors. As to the rioters themselves, I am satisfied they had no such excuse. The clamour against bawdy houses was in them a bare pretence only. Wantonness and cruelty were the motives of most; and some, as it plainly appeared, converted the inhuman disposition of the mob to the very worst of purposes, and became thieves under the pretence of reformation.

How then is it possible for any man in his senses to express a compassion for such offenders, as for men, who, while they are doing an illegal act, may yet be supposed to act from a laudable motive? I would ask men this question. By whom are these houses frequented and supported? Is it not by the young, the idle, and the dissolute?—This is, I hope, true; no grave zealot will, I am convinced, assert the contrary. Are these then the people to redress the evil? Play-houses have been in a former age reputed a grievance; but did the players rise in a body to demolish them? Gaming-houses are still thought a nuisance; but no man, I believe, hath ever seen a body of gamesters assembled to break them open, and burn their goods. It is indeed possible, that after a bad run of luck they might be very well pleased with an opportunity of stealing them.

The nuisance which bawdy houses are to the public, and how far it is interested in suppressing them, is not our present consideration. The law clearly considers them as a nuisance, and hath appointed a remedy against them; and this remedy it is in the power of every man who desires it to apply. But surely it will not be wished by any sober man, that open illegal force and violence should be with impunity used to remove this nuisance; and that the mob should have an uncontrolled jurisdiction in this case. When, by our excellent constitution, the greatest subject, no, not even the King himself, can, without a lawful trial and conviction, divest the meanest man of his property, deprive him of his liberty, or attack him in his person; shall we suffer a licentious rabble to be accuser, judge, jury, and executioner; to inflict corporal punishment, break open men's doors, plunder their houses, and burn their goods? I am ashamed to proceed further in a case so plain, where the absurdity is so monstrous, and where the consequences are so obvious and terrible.

As to the case of the sufferer, I shall make no remarks. Whatever was the man's guilt, he hath made all the atonement which the law requires, or could be exacted of him; and though the popular clamour made it necessary to publish the above depositions, nothing shall come from me to add to, or to aggravate them.

If, after perusing the evidence which I have here produced, there should remain any private compassion in the breast of the reader, far be it from me to endeavour to remove it. I hope I have said enough to prove that this was such a riot as called for some example, and that the man who was made that example deserved his fate. Which, if he did, I think it will follow, that more hath been said [1] and done in his favour than ought to have been; and that the clamour of severity against the government hath been in the highest degree unjustifiable.

To say truth (as I have before hinted) it would be more difficult to justify the lenity used on this occasion. The first and second day of this riot, no magistrate, nor any other higher peace officer than a petty constable (save only Mr. Welch) interfered with it. On the third day, only one magistrate took upon him to act. When the prisoners were committed to Newgate, no public prosecution was for some time ordered against them; and when it was ordered, it was carried on so mildly, that one of the prisoners (Wilson) being sick in prison, was, though contrary to law, at the desire of a noble person in great power, bailed out, when a capital indictment was then found against him. At the trial, neither the attorney- nor solicitor-general, nor even one of the King's counsel, appeared against the prisoners. Lastly, when two were convicted, only one was executed: and I doubt very much whether even he would have suffered, had it not appeared that

---

[1] He was buried by a private subscription, but not at the public expense of the parish of St. Clement Danes, as hath been falsely asserted

a capital indictment [1] for burglary was likewise found by the grand jury against him, and upon such evidence as I think every impartial man must allow would have convicted him (had he been tried) of felony at least.

Thus I have finished this ungrateful task, which I thought it the more incumbent on me to undertake, as the real truth of this case, from the circumstance mentioned at the bottom of the preceding page, was known only to myself, and a very few more.   This I thought it my duty to lay before some very noble persons, in order to make some distinction between the two condemned prisoners, in favour of Wilson, whose case to me seemed to be the object of true compassion.   And I flatter myself that it might be a little owing to my representation, that the distinction between an object of mercy, and an object of justice at last prevailed, to my satisfaction, I own entirely, and I hope, now at last, to that of the public.

[1] Upon this indictment he was arraigned, but as the judge said as he was already capitally convicted for the same fact, though of a different offence, there was no occasion of trying him again; by which means the evidence, which I have above produced, and which the prosecutor reserved to give on this indictment, was never heard at the Old Bailey, nor in the least known to the public.

END OF LEGAL WRITINGS—XIII

www.ingramcontent.com/pod-product-compliance
Lightning Source LLC
Chambersburg PA
CBHW031920190326
41519CB00007B/354